BASIC THEORY OF
PSYCHOANALYSIS

BASIC THEORY OF PSYCHOANALYSIS

Robert Waelder

SCHOCKEN BOOKS · NEW YORK

CONTENTS

INTRODUCTION

Part I
THE HISTORICAL DEVELOPMENT OF
PSYCHOANALYTIC THOUGHT

Part II
SURVEY AND DISCUSSION
OF BASIC CONCEPTS

CONTENTS vii

PREFACE

These essays do not offer a comprehensive survey of psychoanalytic theory; some aspects of analytic theory, particularly the more abstract ones, are not treated at all or treated only in a cursory fashion. The following chapters will deal only with what I consider to be *basic* theory—its rationale, its implications, and the questions which it stimulates us to ask. They deal with questions such as these: Can psychoanalytic interpretations and theories be verified in a scientifically satisfactory way? How must such verification proceed? What is instinct in psychoanalysis? Why do psychoanalysts seem to insist on using this concept which biologists seem inclined to discard? What is the role of sexuality in psychoanalytic theory? Why do analysts speak of a destructive instinct? What does "ego" mean in psychoanalysis? Why was ego psychology a relatively late addition in psychoanalytic theory? What is the nature of psychoanalytic therapy? Why is consciousness supposed to have a therapeutic value? What are the indications and limits of psychoanalytic therapy? These and similar questions will be considered, though not necessarily solved, in the following pages.

I hope that these essays will serve three goals: to combat widespread misunderstandings of psychoanalysis and thereby to help conserve what we have inherited; to see psychoanalysis in its context in the history of our civilization; and

to help to discover the most promising avenues of advancement.

In science, as in most other affairs, we should first try
to keep what we already have—cultivate the land that has
been cleared and guard it against a return of the jungle
and against corrosion—and then try to improve on it or to
enlarge it.

As far as conservation is concerned, many people take it
for granted that scientific achievements can never be lost
and that change always means progress. Historical experience does not support this optimistic assumption. The
foundations of many sciences that had been laid by the
Greeks were lost to the West for a thousand years until
the ancient writings were rediscovered in the eleventh and
twelfth centuries. The idea, developed in the middle of the
nineteenth century, by Claude Bernard, on the basis of
ancient, Hippocratic, heritage, that health depended on the
ability of the organism to adjust to its external environment
while keeping its internal environment fairly constant, was
all but lost when the doctrine of a single etiology of diseases
carried everything before it and dominated the scene until
the recent past. And we must remember that we know of
achievements lost only if they had not been entirely lost,
and particularly if they have been rediscovered and re-
appreciated in the meantime; how many fruitful ideas have
been lost and have not been found again, or are no longer
correctly understood, we have no way of knowing.

Psychoanalysis is persistently misunderstood, not only
extra muros. Psychoanalysis—its intellectual substance and
the categorical imperative of ceaseless self-exploration
which provides its moral mainspring—is always in jeopardy
because it arouses strong resistances from which nobody
seems to be exempt. The causes for these resistances are

manifold; some are characteristic only of a particular time and place, others seem to be of more lasting significance. Much of them is probably due to the fact that psychoanalysis, properly understood, presents a constant challenge to complacency and mental laziness[1] and perpetually interferes with wishful thinking.

For decades, the hostility which psychoanalysis has aroused in the world and which has caused much discomfort to psychoanalysts has also, as outside pressure often does, helped to preserve psychoanalysis because it has welded us together and has given us protection against the danger of succumbing to an alliance of our resistances and our more superficial ambitions.

More recently, psychoanalysis has been facing a new situation, at least in this country; outside pressure—not resistances as such but their expression in pressure brought to bear on psychoanalysts—has diminished and opportunities for positions have correspondingly increased. Desirable though this is from one point of view, it has also laid psychoanalysis more open to inner perils.

It appears more and more likely that psychoanalysis has a good chance of recognition and integration into existing institutions if analysts are only willing to modify some of their traditional attitudes. The appeal of this combination of temptation and subtle pressure is further increased by the widespread inclination to regard things that have existed for some time as worth discarding on account of their age alone.

In this situation, it may not be useless to try to take stock of the essential ideas of psychoanalysis and to discuss their pros and cons in the light of available experience.

---

[1] Improperly understood psychoanalysis can become itself a source of complacency and an excuse for mental laziness.

The place of psychoanalysis in the history of Western thought is not made subject of a special discussion, but frequent references to other areas of human knowledge and practice should make it clear that psychoanalytic thought is not the isolated, esoteric doctrine for which it is often held. Despite the ill will which psychoanalysis has encountered and which still permeates most of what is being said about Freud or psychoanalysis, it stands in the mainstream of European tradition. Nothing could characterize the personality of Freud better than the following words that were said about his ancestor in spirit, Thucydides:[2] "His was a passionate nature and one of his passions was for self-control, another was for truth" (Gomme, 1954, p. 161). These characters have made their imprint on psychoanalysis, and that at once explains much of the hostility against psychoanalysis—as neither of these two passions[3] is widely shared at any one time—and determines the place which I believe it will occupy in historical perspective as a carrier of the best traditions of our civilization.

The study of theory and of its implications could also, and in particular, be of service for scientific progress because it is the function of theory to suggest what kind of observations, out of an infinite number of possible observa-

[2] I dare call him so because Thucydides, in his *History of the Peloponnesian War*, analyzed the great tragedy of Hellas in his time as an outgrowth of human nature, with the hope that the very understanding of the patterns will weaken their automatic grip on men and will provide men with a degree of emancipation from them.

[3] Because of this sense of dedication of Freud's and of many of his close associates, psychoanalysis has often been called a religion, or pseudo religion, classifications meant to discredit psychoanalysis in the eyes of believer and nonbeliever alike. The dedication of this circle to the ideals of self-control and truth was real, but these ideals are for themselves alone not sufficient to make a complete value system, still less a religion. One hopes that many people—e.g., rulers, educators, healers—have an equal dedication to ideals which they have an opportunity to serve and one will hardly on this ground accuse them of "unscientific" attitudes.

tions, is likely to lead to insights of general significance, to a better understanding of the nature of things.

Ideas without facts are empty, facts without ideas are blind, as Kant put it. As in most other sciences, the most promising avenue of advance in psychoanalysis seems to lie not with pure empiricism nor with daring speculation but in the middle area where observation and theory formation constantly pass the ball to each other.

ACKNOWLEDGMENT

Grateful acknowledgment is made to the following authors and publishers for their kind permission to quote from books and articles published by them:

Freud Copyright, Inc.; The Hogarth Press and the Institute of Psycho-Analysis; Norbert Wiener; John Wiley & Co.; Warren Weaver; *Science; Bulletin of the Philadelphia Association for Psychoanalysis.*

*Many are the wonders, but none is more
wondrous than man*

—Sᴏᴘʜᴏᴄʟᴇꜱ

INTRODUCTION

The Validation of Psychoanalytic

Interpretations and Theories

THE NEED FOR VALIDATION

The question of validation of psychoanalytic results has often been raised—more often by critics of psychoanalysis than by psychoanalysts themselves. As usual, there is a great variety of opinions. Some are satisfied with the validity of psychoanalytic interpretations as made by well-trained and experienced analysts and hence with the validity of the theory which is based on them, and do not see any need for further proof. Others wish interpretations to be subject to more controls within the analytic procedure while rejecting extra-analytic means of verification. Others, for the most part not analysts, request nonanalytic forms of verification as prerequisite to their consideration of analytic claims.

There is also a wide spectrum of opinion regarding the degree of exactitude that is requested. Some merely present their results as products of analytic study, often without clearly distinguishing between the raw material of observation and its interpretation, and without stating the criteria according to which the latter follow from the former. In

3

extreme instances, free rein is given to speculation. On the other end of the spectrum are those, mostly people without passive or active analytic experience of their own, who request for every interpretation or proposition the kind of evidence we expect in the physical or chemical laboratory, i.e., evidence sufficiently conclusive to eliminate every possibility of doubt. With such requirements, of course, nobody could ever claim to be his father's issue, and it would need generations of work and millions of expenditure to establish with this degree of exactitude even the most trivial psychological proposition.

The student of animal behavior, Konrad Z. Lorenz, pointed out that certain features known to the field observers are very difficult to reproduce in the laboratory under controlled conditions: "Should these experiments seem incredible to the animal psychologist who works in the laboratory, he must consider the fact that the experimental animal in a confined space has fewer experiences which he can differentiate qualitatively than does the dog which is always free to accompany his master ... Every dog owner is familiar with a certain behavior in dogs which can never be produced under laboratory conditions ... Imagine what complicated experimental method and how tiresome a training would be necessary to achieve an analogous result under artificial conditions in the laboratory" (Lorenz, 1954, p. 135f.).

Somewhere between uncritical speculation and the insistence on an impossible mathematical certainty, we must look for the degree of certitude that we can at best expect to reach in these matters, a degree of certitude where interpretations and propositions can be established beyond reasonable, though not necessarily beyond all possible, doubt.

In the literature which deals with the problem of validation, one can distinguish between attempts to justify the validity of psychoanalytic interpretations, or to formulate rules which have to be observed so that such interpretations will be valid, on the one hand; and attempts to test psychoanalytic results by nonanalytic means, on the other. In the first group, Bleuler (1910) was an early contributor. In his defense of psychoanalysis, he emphasized the inner consistency of psychoanalytic interpretations: innumerable facts seem to fall in their place, and everything fits in, like in the solution of a picture puzzle. Bleuler pointed at the great improbability that all this should be due to mere coincidence, and he even tried to estimate the mathematical probabilities involved.

Bernfeld (1932, 1934) emphasized that psychoanalytic interpretations, as a rule, cannot be fully proved by induction, but he thought that under certain circumstances valid conclusions can be drawn from a single observation, and he looked toward Gestalt theory to provide the logical justification for such inferences. He referred to certain experiments in Gestalt theory in which a person is given a few words and has to find the story in which they occur (e.g.: cooking stove, kitchen cupboard, glass vials, chemicals, drawing board, inks, money bills, arrest). There is often *only one* plausible solution (as e.g., in this example: workshop for counterfeit money); only one has a "strong Gestalt." This reasoning is substantially identical with Bleuler's.

But on the other hand, Bernfeld was quite aware of the fact that the feeling of evidence by itself alone is not complete proof of correctness. He thought that if the whole clinical material were combed to extract all "invariants" from it, i.e., all features that occur as common denominators of a group of "associations," support or correction of individual interpretations could be found.

In my treatment of the subject (1936, Chapter II; 1939) I was guided by the consideration that inner consistency alone is not a sufficient criterion of correctness, because quite erroneous ideas, and indeed even paranoid ideas, can show a high degree of inner consistence; the whole web of interpretations must, at least in one place, be supported by independent evidence. I also tried to discuss the validity of psychoanalytic interpretation in the simple example of a neurotic symptom of a child caught *in statu nascendi* by the analyst-mother (1936, Chapter VI).

The present stage of the question of validation has been comprehensively surveyed by Kubie (1952). See also the report on a panel discussion at the American Psychoanalytic Association (Brosin, 1955) and the paper by Schmidl (1955) enlarging on Bernfeld's ideas.[1]

A SCIENCE OF THE MIND AND OF HUMAN DESTINY
AND THE EXACT SCIENCES

In recent years there have been instances in which representatives of the exact sciences showed themselves clearly aware of the fact that the exactitude of physics and chemistry and related sciences, which the so-called "behavioral sciences" lack, is due to certain favorable circumstances inherent in their subject matter rather than due to their supposedly greater maturity. The prominent mathematician, Warren Weaver, e.g., said in his Presidential Address at the American Association for the Advancement of Science:

What made possible the great success that the physical sciences have experienced, particularly during the last

---

[1] A Symposium on this subject, chaired by Sidney Hook, was published recently (1959) but appeared too late for discussion in these pages.

century and a half? The explanation appears actually to be rather simple. *Physical* nature, first of all, seems to be on the whole very *loosely coupled*. That is to say, excellently workable approximations result from studying physical nature bit by bit, two or three variables at a time, and treating these bits as isolated. Futhermore, a large number of the broadly applicable laws are, to useful approximation, *linear*, if not directly in the relevant variables, then in nothing worse than their second time derivatives. And finally, a large fraction of physical phenomena (meteorology is sometimes an important exception) exhibits stability; perturbations tend to fade out, and great consequences do not result from very small causes.

These three extremely convenient characteristics of physical nature bring it about that vast ranges of phenomena can be satisfactorily handled by linear algebraic or differential equations, often involving only one or two dependent variables; they also make the handling *safe* in the sense that small errors are unlikely to propagate, go wild and prove disastrous. Animate nature, on the other hand, presents highly complex and highly coupled systems—these are, in fact, dominant characteristics of what we call organisms. It takes a lot of variables to describe a man or, for that matter, a virus; and you cannot often usefully study these variables two at a time. Animate nature also exhibits very confusing instabilities, as students of history, of the stock market, or genetics are well aware [Weaver, 1955, p. 1256].

The phenomena which we study in psychoanalysis are certainly highly coupled. A middle-aged person may suffer from depressions. We may approach this study with ideas gained in prescientific experience, viz., the idea that depressions may hang together with severe frustrations and disappointments, and we may look for them in this person's life. There may be many—in his marriage and family life; disappointments with his children or with their attitude toward him; disappointment in extramarital love relationships; a decrease of sexual prowess or of attractiveness; illnesses or a general feeling of aging; disappointments in work, career, or social recognition; or financial worries. All this may be complicated by organic, perhaps involutionary, processes. Then there are the factors suggested by psychoanalytic theories that would have to be considered, such as, e.g., the loss of an object, abnormal forms of object relationships in terms of introjection and expulsion, loss of love from the superego, aggression turned against oneself, or a feeling of discouragement, fatigue, and defeat (See, among others, Freud, 1917; Abraham, 1924; Klein, 1935, 1940; E. Bibring, 1953). Several of these factors will probably be present in any one case, and many of them can be found in people of the same age group without depressions. In our search for the etiological importance of any one of these factors, or any other factor that may be suggested, we are not able to isolate it, while keeping all others unchanged, and so to study its consequences alone. We will always have many more unknowns than we have equations, so to say, so that no conclusion can be made without the exercise of judgment which may be considered arbitrary.

This factor makes for a very great difference between the physical sciences and such disciplines as psychoanalysis. I do not know whether the two other points which Professor Weaver has advanced as contributing to the privileged condition of the physical sciences—linear, or, in any case, simple laws, and relative stability—are quite as important under the circumstances. Stability is not a universal characteristic of the subject matter of the physical sciences, as Professor Weaver has noted himself. But it is true, in any case, that organic and psychic systems, or social systems, for that matter, show a great instability and that relatively small causes can have radical consequences. A small lesion in certain parts of the brain can completely incapacitate a person. Human behavior is largely the result of inner conflicts, and a small change in the relative strength of the competing forces may lead to an entirely different outcome, just as a shift of a small fraction of the vote can lead to a different outcome of an election—perhaps with great consequences.

Another prominent mathematician, Professor Wiener, also ascribes the enormous success of the natural sciences to peculiar circumstances; his point is different from Professor Weaver's, though not without relation to it.

All the great successes in precise science have been made in fields where there is a certain high degree of isolation of the phenomena from the observer. We have seen in the case of astronomy that this may result from the enormous scale of certain phenomena with respect to man, so that man's mightiest efforts, not to speak of his mere glance, cannot make the slightest visible impression on the celestial world. In modern atomic physics, on the other hand, the science of the unspeakably minute, it is true that anything we do will have an influence on many individual particles which is great *from the point of view of that particle*. However, we do not live on the scale of the particles concerned, either in space or in time, and the events that might be of the greatest significance from the point of view of an observer conforming to their scale of existence, appear to us—with some exceptions, it is true, as in the Wilson cloud chamber experiments—only as average mass effects in which enormous populations of particles cooperate. As far as these effects are concerned, the intervals of time concerned are large from the point of view of the individual particles and its motion, and our statistical theories have an admirably adequate basis. In short, we are too small to influence the stars in their courses, and too large to care about anything but the mass effects of the molecules, atoms and electrons. In both cases, we achieve a sufficiently loose coupling with the phenomena we are studying to give a massive total account of this coupling, although the coupling may not be loose enough for us to be able to ignore it altogether [Wiener, 1948, p. 189f.].

Professor Wiener emphasizes the change that the observer, by the very fact of observing, works on his object, and sees science successful either where this influence is negligible as in astronomy, or where we are interested only in large aggregates. We are all aware of the many objections that have been raised against psychoanalysts on this ground. The crudest version of the argument claims that analytic interpretations are accepted by the patient through the analyst's suggestions, under the influence of a positive transference; analysis appears as a kind of brain-washing. In a less crude form the validity of psychoanalytic results can be questioned on the ground of the subtle but undeniable influence that a combination of various factors—the analyst's personality, scientific interests, opinions or prejudices; the needs of the patient's resistance; and, occasionally, the influence of unrecognized satisfactions in the analytic situation (due, perhaps, to countertransference or to reality factors, unavoidable or not avoided)—can have upon the selection of the material that appears in the analysis and, hence, upon the development of the analytic treatment and the picture derived from it.

Weaver summed the situation up as follows:

In the world of living things, the progress of science was not so rapid, and we ought to be able to surmise why this was bound to be so. As far as its stretching (at a fixed temperature) is concerned, one single descriptive number completely describes a spring. A second descriptive number tells us how the behavior varies with temperature. One single number describes how hard, so to speak, it is for direct current to pass through a certain wire. One single and simple equation describes the temperature-volume-pressure behavior of all perfect gases. One concise law states the gravitational attraction between all particles of matter in the entire cosmos. Although there are indeed great complications and refinements in modern physical and chemical theories, the amazing fact is that enormous and very practical progress could be achieved with exceedingly simple and yet exceedingly general laws.

But how many variables does it take to describe a flower, an insect, or a man? How many subtly interacting and essentially interlocked factors must be taken into account to understand an emotional state? How complicated is the set of influences that affect behavior?

In other words, physical science was able to get started several centuries ago because the world is so built that physics is relatively easy ... Biology, broadly speaking, is several cuts harder. A living organism is essentially more complicated and has many more interacting characteristics. It is much more restrictive (and can be wholly misleading) to study these characteristics one or two at a time, and underneath all this is the massive fact, at once mystical and practical, that when one takes a live organism apart to study it, an essential aspect of the problem has vanished, in that what is on the experimenter's table is no longer an organism and is no longer alive [Weaver, 1957, p. 1227f.].

The psychoanalyst has nothing to add to these words; they clearly state the conditions and limitations, which are imposed upon us by the nature of our subject, the living man. The desire, praiseworthy in itself, for the exactitude of the physical sciences, together with a lack of appreciation of the conditions that had made the latter possible, have produced an enormous amount of literature of a pseudo-exact variety in which *highly coupled systems are treated as though they were loosely coupled.* Interpretations are duly avoided, and a vast amount of data is collected with many apparent safeguards and is statistically elaborated; but every individual item of these data is often an interpretation, made without awareness and, hence, without the criticism to which interpretations consciously arrived at can be subjected. In psychoanalysis as well as in other behavorial disciplines, or in the social sciences, I often prefer the report of an experienced and cautious field observer, or clinical observer, to the semblance of exactitude of the Gallup poll variety.

The conviction that only the results of experiments can be taken seriously while the observation, however prolonged, of the natural course of events with a view to discovering its patterns is hopelessly inexact—at least if these events do not favor us with a display of simple and obvious regularities as do the planetary movements—has greatly influenced, or indeed determined, during the last three or four generations, what problems were considered worth studying; the results of this selection have partly been excellent and partly not so excellent. In medicine, e.g., it has led to a concentration of effort on the study of specific etiological agents and to a neglect of the ecological aspects of disease, viz., the unbalance between the organism and its environment, because the former present single-variable problems that can be studied exactly in the laboratory or with reasonable approximation to exactitude in the clinic, while the latter involve innumerable variables that are particularly difficult to isolate. Thus, apart from surgery, a large part of the progress of medicine in the last few generations has taken place where conditions came closest to being the outcome of single factors such as, e.g., the invasion of pathogenic organisms into a human body as yet without previous contact with them. Successes were least, on the other hand, in dealing with the degenerative diseases of middle and old age—unless they were controllable by surgery—which involved an intricate relationship between the organism and its environment, including the frozen residue of past adjustments and maladjustments.

THE VALIDITY OF HISTORICAL AND
PSYCHOLOGICAL PROPOSITIONS

A discussion about the possibility, or impossibility, to establish psychoanalytic propositions "scientifically" should begin with a consideration of the kind of evidence on which propositions such as those advanced by psychoanalysis, i.e., historical and psychological propositions, are based, and under what conditions we are prepared to admit statements on such subject matter as "scientifically" valid.

Whoever challenges psychoanalysis on the ground of allegedly lacking verification should be asked whether or not, or under what conditions, he believes that the following statements can be verified:

Ia.   John Doe, Jr., is the son of Mrs. John Doe (historical statement based on memories and testimony of witnesses);

Ib.   John Doe, Jr., is the son of Mr. John Doe (historical statement based on circumstantial evidence);

IIa. John Doe loves his wife; he told me so himself (statement about a person's conscious emotional life);

IIb. John Doe thinks that he loves his wife, but he

deceives himself; he does not recognize (or fights against the recognition of) the fact that he has grown tired of her and is interested in Miss X. (Psychological statement about another person's emotional life on the basis of alleged give-away in his behavior, involving judgments about self-deception and unconscious processes.)

Ad Ia. Mater semper certa is a principle of the Roman law, but on what is this certitude based? There is Mrs. Doe who remembers having Junior delivered in the hospital and having brought him home; and he has always been home thereafter until he was grown up; there is a continuity in her memory. So it is in Mr. John Doe's from the day he saw Junior behind a glass wall in the hospital nursery. And there are the neighbors and the friends of the family who have seen Junior periodically throughout the years. All this is of course enough for all practical purposes, but the question is whether it is adequate for scientific accuracy. It is all based on memories or testimony of witnesses, but memories can fail and witnesses can lie or err. Mrs. John Doe, e.g., may not have delivered a child at all but, with the complicity of a few persons, may have presented an illegitimate child of another woman as her own; or she may have delivered and her child was exchanged in the hospital nursery by inadvertence, etc. All these are extremely unlikely contingencies, but they are not entirely impossible. In fact, our judgment that they are extremely unlikely is itself based on prescientific experience or impressions rather than on scientifically controlled investigations, and may therefore be deemed to carry little weight. In order to make the statement Ia exact, it would probably be necessary to have a complete film of Junior's delivery that would keep Junior uninterruptedly in the picture, at least until the footprint has been taken if footprints are considered to be reliable identification marks. But if the latter proposition would, as I fear, have to be proved first, the film would have to run uninterruptedly until the emergency of distinctive features; from then on, perhaps, occasional shots may suffice. Needless to say, there has been no case so far in which maternity has been so established.

Ad Ib. The proof of paternity is, of course, more difficult. In actual life it is based on psychological estimates such as these: It is most unlikely that Mrs. Doe conceived out of wedlock; perhaps she loved her husband, or there was no opportunity for adultery, or nobody has seen her interested in any other man at the time, or adultery would be inconsistent with her character, etc. All this is convincing enough but does not rule out any possible doubt. A fully scientific study may require controlled conditions, with a running cinematographic record, in which Mrs. Doe is kept isolated for a sufficiently long period preceding her delivery, in addition to the data required in the first example.

Ad IIa. The evidence of self-observation has been recognized by many, but others hold that psychic data are purely subjective and, as a matter of principle, not verifiable for others; and universal verifiability, or demonstrability, is alleged to be a fundamental requirement of science. While in the earlier-mentioned historical statements exact conditions can, even though at great labor and cost, be devised for future work, it would seem impossible, if this objection is upheld, to accept any data of self-observation.

Ad IIb. Against the validity of psychological judgments made about others on the ground of their behavior, it can be held that these judgments have never been established. Even if self-observation were admitted, there has never been a comprehensive study to correlate exactly, e.g., facial expressions, described in terms of exact measurement, with reported feelings such as hatred, fear, hope; such investigations, even at the simplest level, would be immensely difficult and time-consuming. On the whole, it could be argued, estimates of things that are supposed to go on in another person's mind and that are not given to his self-observation are speculative and not demonstrable.

To those who are satisfied that valid historical and psychological statements can be made, however, psychoanalytic propositions can be shown to be either valid or invalid; to others, they can probably not be validated.

PSYCHOLOGICAL AND HISTORICAL JUDGMENTS
IMPLICIT IN THE EXACT SCIENCES

At this point one may well stop and wonder whether this is not a semantic question after all. Perhaps, so the argument may run, historical statements based on memories, testimony of witnesses or circumstantial evidence, and psychological statements about an inner life, or about unconscious psychic processes, can be made with a degree of certitude that is adequate *for all practical purposes* but falls short of the standards developed, and lived up to, in the physical sciences. We may then go ahead with our psychoanalytic work, confident about what we are doing as an investigating commission may be confident that it has unraveled the facts of a case; but whether it should be termed science, i.e., whether the representatives of the physical sciences would be willing to recognize that our work can qualify as scientific, or whether we psychoanalysts should actually ask for this recognition, is another question, important for the vanities involved on all sides but entirely irrelevant for an assessment of the validity of the psychoanalytic work itself. Psychoanalysts could go on claiming, if they wished, that they are students of a science of the mind, and practitioners of a technique based on it, while representatives of the older, physical sciences[2] may, if they wished, go on refusing their credentials. But things are not quite as simple as this, and if historical and psychological judgments are inadmissible in science, it is not only psychiatry, psychoanalysis, sociology, or related disciplines, that are excluded, but the physical sciences themselves would face the necessity of re-establishing most of their propositions because *in the work of all scientists a considerable number of things are taken for granted on the ground of historical and psychological judgments.*

Material for experiments has been purchased from a commercial firm and the specifications are accepted because the firm is known as reliable. It is assumed that authors, or at least authors who have an established reputation or work in a respected institution under the supervision of respected scientists, do not deliberately falsify their data, nor suffer from hysterical conditions that would make them doctor their data without being aware of it. The laboratory setup has not been under constant surveillance by machines; there is no guarantee that other individuals have not bribed the night watchman or otherwise got around him and tampered with the setup so as to bring about a certain result, or that the experimenter himself has not done so, with dis-

---

[2] This picture is, in fact not quite correct. The deriding of psychoanalysis does not really come from the representatives of the old, well-established exact sciences, but rather from the representatives of disciplines on the fringe of the republic of science who have themselves to fight continuously for their recognition. The examples, quoted above, of the views of two prominent mathematicians show a full realization of the fact that the success of the exact sciences is largely due to favorable circumstances not duplicated elsewhere, and a full realization of the difficulties which confront those who study man.

honest intent or in a state of fugue. Of course, all these
are possibilities that, practically, need not be taken seriously;
any one of them is enormously unlikely, outside of mystery
stories, and if it should ever occur it would soon be found
out. But this judgment, though sound enough in itself, is
based on a mostly prescientific experience and common-
sense psychology rather than on precisely controlled conditions, and if such judgments are not deemed admissible,
a vast number of scientific experiments would have to be
repeated under conditions in which nothing has been taken
for granted. One cannot have it both ways: historical and
psychological judgments either can, or cannot, be accepted
as valid. If they cannot, many results of physical sciences
which had been won with such judgments being implicit
during the work would have to be re-established under
more exact conditions; or if such judgments are admissible,
they surely can be used not only implicitly by the physical
scientists but also explicitly by the students of human behavior.

And it must be further added that even if all these precautions were taken, it would still remain true that conclusions drawn from experiments rest on the assumption
that the experiments have been carried out as claimed, and
that nobody has tampered with the setup; and this assumption *must*, in some point, rest on the testimony of persons,
and confidence in the reliability of this testimony rests on
psychological judgments. Hence, in the last analysis, the
psychological factors can never be entirely eliminated.

It was probably for considerations such as these that the
philosopher and historian of science, Arthur David Ritchie,
stated recently (1958, p. 7): "... The paradigm or model
type of fact is not the desiccated, artificial fact of the experimental sciences which cannot exist outside the labora-

tory but a more robust if less precise kind of fact, the evidence of the lawyer or historian. This is an affirmation by a person or subject to other persons or subjects about reactions between them ... All public scientific facts depend on these prior affirmations."

A COMPENSATORY ADVANTAGE OF PSYCHOLOGY

But it is time to consider the other side of the coin. It is true that we cannot prove any psychological proposition by viewing it from outside as we do in the physical sciences, with any exactitude approaching the exactitude that is rightly expected from research work in those fields; but it is equally true that *we know a great deal about the proposition from the inside already.* The molecules, atoms and subatomic particles, the cells and viruses we can study only from the outside, but in mental life what we study is *ourselves,* or subjects closely similar to ourselves, and about ourselves we know, or are able to know, a great deal immediately. It is true that the physicist has great advantages over us on account of the loose coupling of his variables, as Professor Weaver has pointed out, and on account of the great difference in size between us and the atomic particles and the consequent concentration of our concern on matters involving large aggregates of atomic particles only, as Professor Wiener has pointed out; but it is equally true that we will never know anything about atomic particles, or large aggregates of them, for that matter, except through observation from the outside, while we know much about the mind from the inside. There is a sense in which one can say that the common man knows more about the mind than the scientist will ever know about gases or atoms. We know that we love or hate, are afraid or panicked or hopeful, jubilant or desperate, tempted or repelled or both. And we know the mood and the feelings of others, too, all the better the more we are in "contact" with them. The sources of our knowledge of the psychic life of others have been said to be an interpretation of their expressions, or an act of intuition (in the sense of the Latin *intueri*—to look inside), or so-called empathy, identification, or a "perception" of the mental life of others (Scheler) in the sense in which we might say that we come to a strange place and "perceive" poverty or provincialism or terror or culture. But whatever the source of our knowledge of psychic processes in another person may be, whatever the mechanisms or processes by means of which we perceive or understand or infer them, there is no doubt that such knowledge exists and is constantly at the bottom of human relationships (or, if you want to use the favorite term of the "neo-Freudians": of interpersonal relationships). The lover either knows that he is loved or is in doubt about it and is anxious to find out, but both imply the possibility of knowing; a part of the game between the two sexes is sometimes to leave a carefully dosed amount of doubt on this point in the partner. The diplomat must be able to gauge the intentions of his opposite number through the deliberately controlled exterior; so does the good poker player. Social life is largely the constant mutual reaction of people to each other's feelings, as swift and, as a rule, unverbalized, as is the reaction of drivers to each other on the road.

And we know, too, that infants and children are highly sensitive reactors to the mood of the adults, particularly their mothers. Infants react immediately to a disturbance not so much in the environment in general as in their biological environment, i.e., their mothers and other adults who take care of them; they react to anxiety or hatred even if the adult tries to conceal them. Neuroses of a severity and tenacity not otherwise easily accountable have often been observed in persons whose mothers went through a depression during their first year of life. The close interaction between mother and child, early observed by analysts (G. Bibring, A. Balint, Peto, et al.) is now the subject of systematic studies through simultaneous analyses of mother and child at the Hampstead Child Therapy Clinic (see, e.g., Burlingham et al., 1955), and at the Child Study Center, Yale University.

It is conceded, or it is not conceded, that this sort of understanding has some validity. If this is conceded in principle, it is not too difficult to prove or disprove specific psychoanalytic interpretations or hypotheses; or it is not conceded and the rules of the game are so set that only external, behavioristic, physical data are admissible, and in that case it is probably impossible, or close to impossible, to verify psychoanalytic propositions or any other propositions involving man's inner life.

In his survey of experimental approaches to psychoanalysis, Professor Hilgard states: "Anyone who tries to give an honest appraisal of psychoanalysis as a science must be ready to admit that as it is stated it is mostly very bad science, that the bulk of the articles in its journals cannot be defended as research publications at all" (1952, p. 44). The latter is true; these articles are not "research publications"; they are mostly clinical papers, comparable to clinical case reports in medicine or to field reports in the social sciences. But my thesis is that *clinical, or field, studies can, and must, be admitted* in a science in which, on the one hand, *research*, i.e., on the whole, the study of one or two variables in isolation, is *impossible* because variables are too highly coupled; while, on the other hand, *introspection* and *perception* are *possible*.

It must be added, however, that the validity which we claim for psychological self-observation and the observations of others is *not absolute*. Just as the perception of the inanimate world through our senses may be misleading, so may our psychological self-observation and our reasoning, intuition, empathy or perception, whichever it may be, about others. We hear the thunder later than we see the lightning, but we would not be justified in claiming, on this ground, that the thunder occurred later. We see the moon disappear in its eclipse, but we would not be right in saying that it had actually temporarily vanished. The wanderer in the desert may clearly see an oasis on the horizon which is not there, etc. And there is the so-called personal equation in all investigations. In the same sense, the results of our self-observation are incomplete and distorted—this is, indeed, the fundamental thesis of psychoanalysis—and we are often deceived in our judgment of others, too. The young man may have erred in thinking that the girl loved him, or did not love him, and the diplomat or the poker player may have been outwitted. What we have to do, however, is not to discard this source of knowledge because it may at times mislead us, just as we do not discard the testimony of our senses because they may produce the desert mirage but to *correct it by comparing data from different sources and cross-checking on all of them.* This is, after all, the way the fallacies of sensual perception have been recognized, made the subject of systematic study, and have become corrigible. This is essentially how psychoanalytic interpretations and evaluations of individual situations, or of persons, are actually arrived at: we take the data of a person's self-observation; and the data of our psychological observation of this person, with the material of our observation vastly enriched by the psychoanalytic rule by which a person commits himself to permit anything to enter his mind and to say everything that did enter it; and the data of outside, physical, observation. We accept none of these sets of data by themselves as necessarily reliable, uncritically, and cross-check each against the others.

The pressure, brought to bear on psychoanalysts, to validate the propositions of psychoanalysis through experiment or statistics, is a predominantly American phenomenon. The situation in the German-speaking countries is almost the opposite and psychoanalysis is far more likely to be censured for any such attempt at validation than for the failure to supply it. This is due to the fact that in the German cultural orbit, a philosophy has been widely accepted which distinguishes sharply between "nature" and *Geist*—an untranslatable word of many meanings which, in this context, means approximately "mind" and "culture" rolled into one. History, according to this philosophy, deals not with nature but with *Geist,* and so does any psychology that goes beyond peripheral problems such as, e.g., sense perception. Nature can be described by a finite number of quantifiable variables, while mind, culture or existence consist of structures, or Gestalts, which can only be comprehended in their totality. There was the famous, endlessly quoted dictum of Dilthey's: We explain nature, but we understand psychic life.

From this point of view, experimental or statistical investigations in matters of "*Geist*" betray a fundamental misunderstanding of the subject; they are something like intellectual original sin.

This dichotomy has dominated German thought for a century, widely accepted not only by philosophers but also by psychiatrists and medical men. An article of mine was recently published in translation in a German periodical; in it I had said that a satisfactory validation of psychoanalytic theory may involve a very detailed, longitudinal

study of a large number of individuals, from the beginning
to the end of their lives; that such a study would be enormously expensive and would probably take a century or two
until the results could become conclusive; but that it may
well be undertaken eventually. Thereupon, the distinguished
chief of a department in the medical school of one of Germany's leading Universities wrote me and expressed his
astonishment at this passage. Was that really what I had
meant to say? Was it not in the very essence of our psychology to claim that the mind was something different
from nature?

The German and the American points of view in this
matter are perhaps a modern edition of the ancient controversy between Platonism and Aristotelianism. It seems
to me that both viewpoints are stronger in their negative,
critical, part than in their positive, constructive, one. The
German philosophy has a strong point inasmuch as the
living organism, and even more the human mind, is more
than any number of physical parameters can describe; there
is, as Warren Weaver called it in the earlier quoted passage," . . . the massive fact, at once mystical and practical,
that when one takes a live organism apart to study it, an
essential aspect of the problem has vanished, in that what
is on the experimenter's table, is no longer an organism and
is no longer alive."

The American view, on the other hand, is strong in its
criticism, too, because it is not quite clear what the criteria of that "understanding" of the mind, of which Dilthey
speaks, are and how one can distinguish between correct
interpretations, on the one hand, and guesswork, speculation or even paranoid ideas, on the other. There do not
seem to be any intrinsic criteria *within* the experience of
understanding itself to sift the one from the others (see
p. 6). In view of the fact that people differ in what they
feel they understand in mental life, Dilthey's formula would
need the setting up of an authority to decide which understanding is, and which is not, correct.

In the light of these difficulties, it seems to me that a

solution can be found only in the integration of both view-points; or that it has to be eclectic, if one prefers this more modest expression.

A PENTATHLON THEORY

The pentathlon was a form of athletic contest in ancient Greece, consisting of competition in five activities: running, jumping, wrestling, throwing the discus, and the javelin. Competitions in five, or in ten (decathlon), athletic disciplines have been revived in modern times. In this kind of contest it is quite possible that the victor is, in any part of the contest, inferior to other athletes who have, or have not, entered the pentathlon competition. The victor's result in running or in jumping, e.g., may fall short of the result of the best Olympic runner or jumper who has not entered into this specific competition, or may fall short of the results of fellow contestants in these branches of the pentathlon itself because it is the average mark that counts. The Greeks have therefore used the term to characterize a type of man whose merits lie more in the width of his pursuits than in his success in a narrow area.

Psychoanalytic interpretations of single events, or a psychoanalytic chart of an individual person, or general psychoanalytic propositions can hardly be proved on the basis of external, physical, measurable data alone. But I submit that the combination of such data with the data of a patient's self-observations (including the self-observations pursuant the tentatively proposed interpretation) and with the data of our observations of his behavior, including his verbal behavior, viewed as expressions of psychic processes, each of these sets of data viewed critically in the light of the other data, form a kind of evidence which is just as convincing[3] as the evidence found in the study of a single variable in such fields where single variables can be meaningfully studied in isolation.

This is actually the way the psychoanalytic practitioner proceeds—or should proceed. The analyst constantly oscillates between an inside and an outside view. There are thoughts and feelings reported by the patient and features in the patient's behavior both inside the analytic situation and in his life, or past memories, which, to the analyst, seem to "click," to tell their story; no sooner is such a hypothetical interpretation won, through the patient's self-observation and/or the analyst's empathy—e.g., in terms of our previous example, about the psychological meaning of the patient's depressions—that the analyst changes his vantage point and looks upon the matter from outside and asks himself: is this hypothetical interpretation in conformity with all the facts; e.g., do conditions with these particular implications always bring about depressions? And he will probably gain further material from the outside view by proposing the interpretation, or part of it, to the patient and watching whether there is any reaction to it. Or, if he has gained any information from the outside, e.g., that depressions always occur at a particular date, or after specific events, he will immediately try to view things from the inside and try to grasp the possible connection of things. In this oscillation the analysis proceeds.

According to newspaper reports, the Water Company in a Midwestern city noticed a few years ago that water consumption rose several times every evening for a few min-

---

[3] Provided, of course, that the analyst has learned to "restrain speculative tendencies" (Freud, 1914a, p. 22) and really practices the cross-checking described above. Carl Becker once spoke of writers of history *sans peur et sans recherche;* it is not astonishing that they can be found among psychoanalysts, too.

utes to a high level. The matter was investigated and it was found that these maxima in the consumption curves coincided with the commercials on television; they were due to the flushing of many toilets at the same time. I do not know whether this has actually occurred in this way or was just a good story. In any case, it is a good analogy for the reasoning that goes on in psychoanalysis. It may be that the Company officials discovered the external fact, i.e., the coincidence of the peaks in the consumption curves with the television commercials, first, and then understood psychologically what was going on; or they may have started with a guess that consumption peaks were perhaps due to the simultaneous flushing of many toilets, then considered the possible reasons for such simultaneity, and thereafter proceeded to search directly for specific situations which many people may consider as proper moments to interrupt their activities. In a similar way, the psychoanalyst may either observe a coincidence first and then understand its meaning; or he may "understand" the meaning of a symptom or behavior trait first and then investigate whether the observable facts are in accordance with it.

There is the further analogy that once the connection has been grasped, it can be further corroborated by predicting the consumption peaks under various schedules for the commercials, in one case, and the occurrence of symptoms or other phenomena under varying conditions, in the other.

THE QUESTION OF UNIVERSAL DEMONSTRABILITY

The admission of "empathy" or perception of psychic processes in others as admissible evidence will meet with the objection that it is subjective in the sense that not all people can "see" what some claim can be seen. Some people are "intuitive," have "empathy," "are in good contact with people," others are not.[4] Some are, indeed, almost blind to psychological material and the incidence of "psyche-blindness" is perhaps in no group as high as among the devotees of the exact sciences—for reasons about which psychoanalysis could venture some guesses. But, however that may be, the fact appears as a serious barrier against using this kind of "perception" because scientific results must be demonstrable to everybody—they must be *intrasubjectiv verifizierbar*—at least in principle, whatever that may mean. So at least it is stated and propositions in the physical sciences are, it is claimed, universally demonstrable.

Yet are they? For one, there are many things that are not demonstrable to those who are deficient in one of their senses—are blind, or deaf, or, to mention minor deficiencies, are color-blind or lack the ability to differentiate between musical tones. A certain area of scientific propositions about nature cannot be demonstrated to them; nevertheless, we do not on this ground question the validity of these propositions but accept it that they are correct and that it is due to personal shortcomings that some people cannot corroborate them.

Then, there are the mentally sick—hallucinating psycho-

---

[4] It is among the desiderata that students of psychoanalysis should have this ability of "good contact with the patient" and "intuition," or "empathy." This requirement may seem particularly odious from an epistemological point of view; we can hardly call it evidence that practitioners of psychoanalysis can "see" certain connections if they have first been chosen for their "empathy," i.e., for their ability to see them. It looks like circular reasoning, but it is no more so than the exclusion of the color-blind from a certain type of work which is discussed farther down in this chapter; and it is not essentially different from what happened in the early years of investigation of the splitting of the atomic nucleus; in those days, research was mainly carried out through observation of extremely minute fluorescence phenomena caused by the impact of individual protons on a zinc sulfide screen, and many students had to be dropped from this kind of work because they did not get the right results (see Waelder, 1955, p. 3).

tics, e.g.—or the intellectually underdeveloped—oligophrenics or morons—to whom many scientific propositions cannot be demonstrated. One might try to circumvent this
difficulty by stating that general demonstrability merely
means demonstrability to the mentally normal. This would
be a satisfactory way out if we could define this group
through characteristics independent of the matter at issue,
e.g., through organic characteristics; in such case, we could
say that it must be possible to verify scientific propositions
to every person except those suffering from a defined anatomical or physiological abnormality. But as things are,
we can characterize the psychotics usually through a lack
in their sense of reality and are therefore in a circular reasoning if we state that scientific laws, an important part of
reality, can be demonstrated to all but the insane, and the
insane are those who cannot appreciate reality.

But let us not belabor the point and assume that a way
has been found to settle this matter in a logically satisfactory
fashion; there still remains the large issue of mathematics.
An understanding of the physical sciences, particularly of
anything beyond the most elementary facts, depends to a
large degree upon the use of mathematical tools. I do not
know how large a percentage of high-school students actually understands algebra or trigonometry as different from
having memorized formulae to the point of being able to
pass the tests; but this is still elementary mathematics. How
great a percentage of the whole population, excluding psychotics and morons, could actually grasp higher mathematics to the point of being able to understand the reasoning
in modern physics? I suspect that there are many more people who could see or feel a great deal of their neighbors'
moods, fears, or aspirations than can understand the tensor
calculus.

Even in mathematics it may happen that a proposition is at a time not universally demonstrable, not only to all people but not even to all ranking mathematicians. J. Hadamard (1945) speaks of the possibility that the "psychology of different individuals may differ in some essential points" and gives the following examples: ". . . a question which, though a mathematical one, was contiguous to metaphysics raised a lively discussion . . . between myself and . . . the great scientist Lebesgue. We could not avoid the conclusion that evidence – that starting point of certitude in every order of thinking – did not have the same meaning for him and for me . . . we recognized the impossibility of understanding each other.

"The subject in question belonged to the theory of 'sets'. Now, when . . . Georg Cantor communicated his fundamental results on that theory (now one of the bases of contemporary science), one of them looked so paradoxical and upset so radically all our fundamental notions that it unleashed the decided hostility of Kronecker, one of the leading mathematicians in that time . . . Of course, the proof of that result is as clear and rigorous as any other proof in mathematics, leaving no possibility of not admitting it" (p. 92).

Thus, the results of physics and chemistry cannot really be demonstrated to everybody; nor even to everybody not insane. They can be demonstrated only to a small fraction of the people at the present time. The others can see or hear the visible or audible *results;* every sane individual who is not deaf can hear that the radio messages do get through the air, but only a few can understand how this happens. The notion that the older, physical, sciences are universally demonstrable boils down to the fact that they have gained a vast prestige, partly because of the demonstrability and usefulness of their technical *applications,* partly because of the relative unity of their exponents, and that the people are satisfied that the structure of science is sound. In this, and only in this sense can one say that the propositions of the physical sciences are universally demonstrable.

The younger psychological and social sciences have nothing of this prestige. They have not yet delivered many applications which people find useful—though the psychoanalytic contributions to education and to preventive psychiatry may in the not far distant future come close to this specification—and their conspicuous representatives do not show the unity which alone can inspire confidence among outsiders. As far as psychoanalysis is concerned, I see no reason, if our free society survives, why a similar state of affairs should not be reached in several generations: that the people at large accept the judgment of experts as correct though they cannot themselves check on it, and that the propositions are thereafter considered as "universally demonstrable."

PART I

The Historical Development
of Psychoanalytic Thought

Psychoanalysis is largely the work of one man, Sigmund Freud, and the most important part of its history is the history of the work and the ideas of Freud. Among the theories of psychoanalysis, we can distinguish between a few basic doctrines, conceived and worked out by Freud around the turn of the century when he was in his early forties; various elaborations and applications developed in the following two decades; and the latter-day additions and modifications worked out in the 1920's when Freud was in his later sixties, additions which cannot compare in importance with the fundamental concepts but are too important to be classified only as elaborations or applications.

The Historical Development of Psychoanalytic Thought

1

The Fundamental Concepts

Freud began his work with the study of the neuroses, particularly, at first, of hysteria. From there, he and other psychoanalysts after him ventured out into other areas—other fields of psychopathology, normal psychology or cultural and historical problems—but the study of the neuroses was the point of departure and has remained the home base of psychoanalysis to which we return from time to time, like Antaeus who regains his strength when he touches the earth.

Neurosis—in the sense in which the word is here used, which is also the sense in which it was generally used around the turn of the century when psychoanalysis came into being—is a circumscribed affliction of an otherwise normal person who is in contact with the world and adequately adjusted except for a limited area; those afflicted with neurosis have feelings, anxieties, thoughts or impulses, or carry out actions, which they *feel as ego-alien but which they cannot help* feeling, thinking or doing—such as, e.g., diffuse anxiety, nightmares, fear of animals, anxiety in places open or in places closed, compulsive thoughts or

35

impulses, or private rituals which a person must observe
though he knows them to be inane; or they show physical
manifestations which are not, as far as can be determined,
symptoms of an organic disease or of a functional disturbance and which conscious volition could not bring about,
such as, e.g., hysterical vomiting, or a *globus hystericus.*
Neurotic manifestations do not seem to be organically produced; they are circumscribed, ego-alien, and unavoidable,
or avoidable only at the price of unbearable anxiety. Those
who suffer from a neurosis clearly differentiate between
their neurotic symptoms and the rest of their personality.
From this core, the meaning of the term has later been extended so as to encompass the so-called character disorders,
etc., to be discussed later (p. 200f.).

BASIC STRUCTURE OF NEUROSIS

The theory of psychoneurosis which gradually crystallized
in the mind of Freud around the turn of the century may be
said to consist of the following propositions:

that psychoneuroses are due to an inner conflict between
an impulse and the interconnected rest of the personality—
the so-called "ego";

that in the case of neurosis, the conflict has not been
solved in favor of one or the other side, nor by a suitable
compromise, but has been "swept under the carpet," as it
were; i.e., the impulse whose claim could not be reconciled
with the interests of the rest of the personality had become
unconscious through a process called "repression";

that the repression, however, has been unsuccessful, i.e.,
had succeeded only in expelling the impulse from consciousness but not in rendering it innocuous, and that the repressed impulse has found its way back into conscious mani-

festations in disguised form (return of the repressed).

Thus, the formation of psychoneurosis follows the pattern: inner conflict—unsuccessful repression—return of the repressed.

INNER CONFLICT AND OUTSIDE PRESSURE

According to the Freudian theory, inner conflict is a necessary condition for neurosis formation. This does not mean that neurosis appears as unrelated to external pressures; but the relation is indirect and is not ubiquitous. External pressure is a factor in the etiology of neurosis either because the threat interferes with the discharge of drives and thereby brings about an inner conflict; or because it forces a person into a situation where he is exposed to temptation, thereby activating a latent desire which is resisted, as, e.g., if a young man with homosexual proclivities is inducted into the military service where he has to live in all-male company and is subordinated to another male, his officer; or because an external event takes on an unconscious meaning and thereby arouses or intensifies an inner conflict, as, e.g., if unemployment is conceived as humiliation and emasculation or as divine punishment. But external pressure is not a *conditio sine qua non* in the formation of neurosis; we know of situations of inner conflict which are not related to external pressures, as conflicts due to the intrinsic contradictions in human aspirations (like the ambivalence of love and hatred or the frictions between masculine and feminine strivings) or the fear of overpowering drives merely on account of their strength and uncontrollability (see p. 160f.). There are even instances in which external pressure can diminish the intensity of an inner conflict and thereby mitigate or even heal a neurosis, e.g., if external re-

straint removes the danger of succumbing to a temptation
or to an uncontrollable instinctual drive.

With its emphasis on inner conflict as a necessary step
in neurosis formation, Freudian theory stands in opposition
to a trend of thought which is both ancient and new. The
ancient, Hippocratic, view of illness as the result of a
disharmony between the organism and its environment has
more recently been revived, in exact terms, by Selye and his
collaborators. Mental illness, insanity, has since time immemorial been attributed to the impact of external events.
In the early nineteenth century, the famous French psychiatrist Esquirol listed a number of factors which in his view
were responsible for a mental break, e.g., loss of property,
insult to one's honor, or frustrated love. In the mind of the
public, mental illness is often attributed to a tragic experience or to overwork. It is tempting to see neurosis in a similar light, as a reaction to unfavorable external conditions.

This view is actually held by other psychotherapeutic
schools, including representatives of the "dissident" or "liberal" schools of psychoanalysis. To these various claims,
psychoanalysts of Freudian persuasion can only reply that
in every case of neurosis they have ever studied the neurosis
grew out of an inner conflict; there is no dearth of examples. If different claims are advanced by other schools of
thought, psychoanalysts think that either the cases on which
others base their claims were not neuroses in the sense in
which the term is here used (see p. 44ff.); or that a more
penetrating study would have laid bare an inner conflict.
But such arguments cannot carry much weight with outsiders.

Behind this lies the larger question of emotional strain,
its nature, its forms, its causes—a wide field for research,
which it will take a long time to map out. Meanwhile, we

may note that the Freudian view of neurosis is supported by an experience, prescientific and easily available, that people usually accept the inevitable and that the greatest strain seems to come from the need to make decisions, from the "agony of choice" (Berlin, 1958).

SEXUAL AND CHILDHOOD ASPECTS OF NEUROSIS

To this scheme, conflict—unsuccessful repression—return of the repressed, two further points have to be added. First, it is not any kind of inner conflict, or any kind of impulse at variance with the rest of the personality, that can start the neurotic process. Careful examination of the pathogenic conflict shows that it is a conflict over a sexual impulse— the term "sexual" being used in a broader sense than was customary in scientific parlance or in common speech, except for many slang expressions; and about equivalent with sensual excitement or gratification. The need for such widening of the concept of sexuality was seen in phenomenological and genetic interrelations between sexual manifestations in the narrow, traditional, sense of the word and those psychic phenomena of a sensual nature which had hitherto not been so called (see p. 104f.).

This is the proposition of the *sexual genesis of the neuroses*. The sexual drives appear as obstacles to adaptation. The reason for this was seen in a rebelliousness and fundamental untamability which appeared to be characteristic of the sexual drives, and which Freud explained in turn by the fact that the possibility of autoerotic gratification and of gratification in fantasy—a possibility which does not exist for the self-preservative drives such as hunger or thirst—has provided them with a kind of wild-life preserve and has thus saved them from the relentless pressure toward adaptation to which self-preservative urges are exposed.

The second addition to the scheme was that neuroses have their root in early childhood—the preschool years—and if they first break out or are first noticed in later years we may be sure that these persons have either passed through a fully developed childhood neurosis over the same or a related issue or, at any rate, through "conditions which may be compared with neuroses" (Freud, 1932c, p. 201), i.e., through very intense conflicts with subsequent unsuccessful repressions. Without such prehistory, apparently, adults can solve their conflicts, if not always in a satisfactory, at least in a nonneurotic, fashion. This is the proposition of the *childhood genesis of the neuroses.*

At this point the question presents itself why the child failed in the solution of specific conflicts. The degree of success in the vast task of adaptation to reality and integration of inner forces during the years of development seems to depend on many factors, but, in general, a child's chances of altogether avoiding any "nuclear neurosis" are not too good. The child, as a rule, has little chance of changing his environment so as to make it conform to his wishes; and he does not bear frustration well, not even temporarily. These factors stand in the way of reaching solutions of conflicts between drives and fears. On the other hand, the child is more flexible than the adult, less settled in his ways, readier to turn to other objects, and this factor facilitates adjustment. But when, for whatever reason, this outlet does not work at the right moment, the child is quite likely to evade the insoluble conflict by mere repression.

Freud described the importance of the early childhood years, discovered by psychoanalysis, for the development of the personality in general and the formation of neurosis in particular in these words:

We came to see that the first years of infancy . . . are
. . . of special importance. This is, in the first place, because they contain the first expansion of sexuality, which
leaves behind decisive determinants for the sexual life
of maturity; and, in the second place, because the impressions of this period come up against an unformed and
weak ego upon which they act like traumas. The ego
cannot defend itself against the emotional storm which
they call forth except by repression and in this way it
acquires in childhood all its predispositions to subsequent
illnesses and disturbances of function [Freud, 1932c,
p. 200f.].

In this way, apparently small causes can have major consequences, a fact which Freud illustrated with this biological analogy:

The damage inflicted upon the ego by its first experiences may seem disproportionately great; but we
have only to take as an analogy the differences in the
effects produced by the prick of a needle upon a mass
of germ cells during segmentation (as in Roux's experiments) and upon the complete animal which eventually
develops out of them [1940, p. 84].

CONSTITUTION AND ENVIRONMENT

When psychoanalysis searches for the seeds of neurosis
in childhood, it studies the experience of the child in his
environment. But that does not imply that the psychoanalytic theory considers neurosis as due exclusively to change-
able environmental conditions. Freud always believed in the
importance of a constitutional factor for neurosis. Constitutional and environmental factors, according to Freud, cooperate in a *supplementary series*:

Are the neuroses exogenous or endogenous diseases—
the inevitable result of a certain type of constitution or

the product of certain injurious (traumatic) events in the person's life? . . . This dilemma seems to me about as sensible as another I could point to: Is the child created by the father's act of generation or by the conception in the mother? . . . From the point of view of causation, cases of neurotic illness fall into a *series,* within which the two factors—sexual constitution and events experienced . . . —are represented in such a way that where one of them predominates the other is proportionately less pronounced. At one end . . . stand those extreme cases of whom one can say: These people would have fallen ill whatever happened, . . . however merciful life has been to them . . . At the other end stand cases which call forth the opposite verdict—they would undoubtedly have escaped illness if life had not put such and such burdens upon them [1916/17, p. 303f.].

There is a widespread belief, particularly in this country, that psychoanalysis stands for an extreme environmentalism in psychopathology; psychoanalysis, e.g., is supposed to hold that neuroses are due to the "mistakes" of the parents in the upbringing of their children. But this is the psychoanalytic view only in extreme, marginal, cases. Whatever the merits of a doctrine of exclusive environmentalism may be, Freud cannot be summoned as a witness for it. His views on this subject have been repeatedly expressed without ambiguity and have not changed during his life. The above quotation was taken from the middle of his psychoanalytic career and may be supplemented by quotations from the early and the late period:

Some of my medical colleagues have looked upon my theory of hysteria as a purely psychological one, and have for that reason pronounced it *ipso facto* incapable of solving a pathological problem. They may perhaps discover from this paper that their objection was based upon their having unjustifiably transferred what is a characteristic of the technique on to the theory itself.

It is the therapeutic technique alone that is purely psychological; the theory does not by any means fail to point out that neuroses have an organic basis . . . [1905a, p. 113].

To look for the aetiology of the neuroses exclusively in heredity or in the constitution would be just as one-sided as to attribute that aetiology solely to the accidental influences brought to bear upon sexuality in the course of the subject's life . . . [1905d, p. 279].

. . . [the psychoneuroses] are serious, constitutionally determined affections, which are seldom restricted to a few outbreaks, but make themselves felt as a rule over long periods of life, or even throughout its entire extent. Our analytic experience that we can influence them to a far-reaching degree, if we can get hold of the historical precipitating causes and the incidental accessory factors, has made us neglect the constitutional factor in our therapeutic practice. And we are in fact powerless to deal with it; but in our theory we ought always to bear it in mind [1932c, p. 210].

On the other hand, Freud and psychoanalysis have often been criticized by some anthropologists and by the "culturalist" school of psychoanalysis for allegedly having overlooked, or not given due weight to, the cultural influence on human behavior. If ignorance of the environmental factor or failure to recognize its importance is alleged, the charge is clearly baseless since Freud pioneered in the study of environmental factors in nervous disease and devoted the greater part of his working life to it. In a passage which was frequently quoted in the environment of my earlier years but which seems to have escaped the attention of present culturalist critics, Freud discussed the different consequences which the early sex play of two little girls, one the landlord's, the other the janitor's child, may have for them in later life on account of the different standards prevailing in their respective milieus (1916/17, p. 308).

On the other hand, if the critics merely mean that Freud attributed less weight to environmental influences than they themselves consider appropriate, the allegation is factually correct since these critics seem to favor unmitigated environmentalism that Freud certainly did not. Extreme environmentalism can hardly be justified on the ground of experience; rather, it seems to be based on a strong will to believe. Our age is passionately in love with equality and, as Alexis de Tocqueville foresaw, the desire for equality feeds on its own satisfaction; the more equal people actually are, the more intolerable the remaining inequalities appear to be. The idea that "all men have been created equal" was called a "self-evident truth"—presumably because so general a statement must be presented dogmatically if it is to be presented at all. But while these words, presumably, meant to the sponsors of the Declaration of Independence merely that all men have been born with "inalienable rights," not that they are actually equal in their native endowment, our age is inclined to give them a literal meaning. That some people should have been born destined to neurosis or other mental or emotional disease while others have come to this world without such impediment, seems intolerable; it should not be true, hence it is not true. Of course, everybody knows that there are congenital *physical* defects; they are too obvious to be denied. But the greater ambiguity of psychopathological phenomena permits us in this area to hold on to ideological prejudices.

SEMANTIC INTERLUDE

The term, neurosis, is now used by many authors in a different sense; individuals are called neurotic who do not show the characteristics, described above, of ego-alien but inescapable affects, thoughts or behavior; rather, they are individuals generally dissatisfied with their lives or disoriented as to what they really want—people who have not found a niche in life and, in Thoreau's words, "live lives of quiet desperation." The application of the term "neurotic" to this group would appear to be justified only if a fundamental identity can be shown to exist between this group and the group which has seniority rights to the title of "neurosis," viz. the hysterias, phobias, and obsessional neuroses.

To a psychoanalyst, such cases of general "malaise" appear sometimes as instances of poor adjustment, due, perhaps, to overprotection in their upbringing (spoiling), and lack of discipline which has starved the ego development of this essential ingredient. Sometimes they are individuals with shallow and unstable object relations. Sometimes they are disoriented with regard to values, a consequence of moral relativism in the climate of their upbringing, be it in their family only or in society as a whole, as a result of which a clear sense of values that would be a source of moral support in the vicissitudes of life was never inculcated, or not inculcated early enough. The psychoanalyst would call neither of these conditions "neuroses" but would prefer to speak of disturbance due to lack of depth in object relations or to abortive ego or superego development.

In some other instances, however, diffuse malaise as described by many contemporary authors appears to the psychoanalyst as a substitute for a real neurosis or as a consequence of the integration of a real neurosis into the ego (character neurosis, ego distortions; see p. 200f.). These cases can be distinguished from the cases of a stunted ego or superego development. In such cases the diffuse unhappiness and disorientation are related to a real, hidden neurosis, but this relation does not reveal itself to a casual glance and can be unearthed only through painstaking study.

When speaking of the Freudian theory of neurosis one should therefore keep in mind that this theory refers to hysteria, phobia, and obsessive-compulsive neurosis, not, or at least not necessarily, to cases of diffuse maladjustment and quiet desperation as they are described by many authors today.

ESSENTIALS OF PSYCHOANALYTIC THERAPY

On the psychoanalytic theory of neurosis is based the psychoanalytic therapy of the neuroses which tries to cure them by rolling the neurotic process back along the road of its development. Psychoanalysis tries to undo the repressions of the present and the past and to restore the conflicts, present and past, to consciousness, thereby offering its patients a possibility of working out a viable, nonneurotic, solution.

In these efforts, psychoanalysis met with two new phenomena. As analysis proceeds, it soon turns out that the analysand does not fully cooperate with the attempt to unravel the knot of his neurosis. On the one hand, the very forces that have caused and maintained repressions appear as *resistances* once the repressed material threatens to enter consciousness. On the other hand, the analysand tries to re-establish and re-enact early childhood situations or longings, with the analyst as object, and thereby becomes personally involved with him (*transference neurosis*).[1] The

---

[1] The above formulation follows closely the analysis of the nature of transference by Nunberg (1951).

latter was discovered by Freud as an unexpected and at first apparently unwelcome complication of a task that was already difficult enough. But Freud soon came to realize that one could turn liability into asset because the transference itself could be seen as an expression, albeit through behavior rather than through words, of live infantile strivings. He thus realized that some of the material was available not in the form of recollection but in the form of behavioral repetitions.

PSYCHOANALYTIC THEORY A PRISON OF THE MIND?

Critics of psychoanalysis have often claimed that once the basic assumptions of psychoanalysis have been accepted, the interpretation of particular data follows practically automatically so that what the analyst does is to apply a few preconceived ideas to everything. The author of a recent study of the psychoanalytic theory of paranoia, e.g., reports, though he does not share in, this argument: ". . . one can argue that it is not surprising that investigators who accept the basic postulates of the Freudian system can find evidence for homosexual conflicts in most cases of paranoia" (Aronson, 1952, p. 399). A former analyst states: "The system of theories which Freud has gradually developed is so consistent that when one is entrenched in them it is difficult to make observations unbiased by his way of thinking" (Horney, 1939, p. 7).

Of all the numerous arguments against psychoanalysis this has always been the most difficult for me to comprehend. Perhaps, Dr. Horney and others who used this argument believed that all interpretations that had ever been made, or considered, by an analyst were "postulates of the Freudian system."[2]

It is, of course, true that psychoanalytic theory, like *any theory*, or indeed *any previous experience*, structures the field and provides us with a perspective, and that may work as a resistance against a restructuring of the field from a different point of view and the adoption of another perspective.[3] Hence the occasional cry, in all disciplines, for a "fresh," unbiased mind.

But the Freudian theories are of a very general character and provide the analyst only with some broad expectations. When the analyst settles down for an analytic interview, he expects that there will be some pattern in the patient's productions, and if the meaning of the patient's train of thoughts is not immediately apparent, he suspects that there are unconscious links. But that merely puts him on the search and does not help him to find the pattern of a single hour. And, incidentally, not even this assumption is thought to be always valid; there are instances in which analysts,

---

[2] I once heard another protagonist of the "liberal," or culturalist, school of thought, in a discussion of "classical" analysis, quote a statement, alleged to have been made by Freud and to constitute a basic tenet of psychoanalysis, and take it as a target of attack. The statement in question, I felt confident, had never been made by Freud, could, in fact, not have been made by him because it was incongruous with his thinking as I knew it. It had, however, been made by one of Freud's older disciples with whom, as it happened, the speaker in this episode had had a very brief period of analysis (which, incidentally, was the only analytic experience, to my knowledge, that he had ever had).

[3] Freeman, Cameron, and McGhie (1958, p. 5) have expressed the argument in these words: ". . . an observer must have some theoretical framework by means of which he can order his clinical observations. With it he is subject to a certain bias; without it he is overwhelmed by a meaningless mass of clinical data. The assumption of a theoretical standpoint must bias the observer to some extent, but the recognition of this factor can lead to a diminution of error."

For the importance of this factor for a theory of prejudice, see Waelder (1949).

unable to find a consistent pattern in their patients' productions, or in some part of them, have thereby been led to suspect the intervention of an organic factor, and have so become instrumental in an early discovery of an organic condition.

The analyst, guided by his theory, will also expect that a neurotic symptom reflects a struggle with a sexual demand, but that again gives him only a very general orientation and does not tell him what kind of impulse is at stake and how the symptom was formed. It takes a long time in analysis until a neurosis appears to be roughly understood, and it often happens that after two or three years of analysis symptoms that had seemed to be understood at an early stage appear in an entirely new light; [4] the understanding is hardly ever complete. And some cases have not been understood at all, even in the hands of the most skillful analysts.

In short, the analytic study of each case, far from being an automatic application of elaborate theories, is rather a piece of original clinical research or field work for which the theory provides only some general directions. A theory can become a prohibition of thought, at worst, only to the degree to which it provides guidance.

THE PSYCHOANALYTIC APPROACH

The psychoanalytic theory of the neuroses introduced three new concepts into psychology:

the existence of an unconscious psychic life which is unconscious not because of a dissociation between various states of consciousness as had been suspected by Breuer

---

[4] For an example, see Nunberg (1932, p. 119).

and others, but because of "the operation of intentions and purposes such as are observed in normal life" (Freud, 1925, p. 40); i.e., because one wants to escape from them:[5] and

[5] The above formulation about the unconscious is in need of some qualifications, however. The repressed is certainly the most important part of the unconscious from the point of view of psychopathology, but there is reason to believe that some parts of the unconscious mind are unconscious not on account of repression. Among them are:

(a) Some kind of instinctive knowledge or wisdom akin to the "instinctive knowledge" of animals—as, e.g., manifested by the fact that very young children often react to a sexual scene as though they had some inkling of its significance (Freud, 1918, p. 120).

(b) Possibly, a residue of important experiences of the race, or of the whole human species, manifested in symbols of a meaning uniform to all men in a culture, or to all men in general. An example is Freud's explanation of the appearance of fire in dreams as a symbol of urination (Freud, 1918, p. 92f.). Freud suggested that this might be understood as a residue of a highly important event in human history, viz., the domestication of fire. Fire had stimulated in primitive man a powerful desire to extinguish it by urinating into it—a challenge still vividly felt by many contemporary males. "The legends that we possess leave no doubt that flames shooting upwards like tongues were originally felt to have a phallic sense. Putting out fire by urinating . . . therefore represents a sexual act with a man, an enjoyment of masculine potency in homosexual rivalry" (Freud, 1930, p. 51). Gratification of this sexual urge stood in the way of the self-preservative interest in keeping the fire alive for the use of the tribe—a gain that was achieved once man had learned to control this temptation. And, as Freud further suggested, man turned the responsibility for the domestic hearth over to the women, whose anatomical build would make it impossible for them to yield to such temptation.

This reconstruction of primeval events found further support by the consideration of a fact, brought to attention by Erlenmayer (1932), that the Mongol *code of Gengis Khan listed urinating into hot ashes as a capital crime, punishable by death—a law that bears witness both to the strength of the temptation and the gravity of the act.

Such experiences, according to Freud's hypothesis, would account for the close association of fire and urine. There is the difficulty, however, that we do not understand how the consequences of such experience could become part of every person's unconscious. Freud assumed that "experiences undergone by the ego . . . when they have been repeated often enough and with sufficient intensity in the successive individuals of many generations . . . transform themselves, so to say, into experiences of the id, the impress of which is preserved by inheritance" (Freud, 1923, p. 52), but this explanation implies the possibility of an inheritance of acquired characteristics which biologists, in recent decades, believe to have ruled

THE FUNDAMENTAL CONCEPTS 51

that this unconscious can send derivatives into consciousness and influence behavior;

the importance of sexual drives for phenomena not overtly sexual;

and the lasting importance of seemingly trifling childhood experiences.

One may say that psychoanalysis found, as regards the unconscious, both its existence and its importance; as regards the sexual factor and childhood experience, it found that their influence reaches farther than had previously been suspected.[6] An alertness for the unconscious, the sexual, and the infantile may be called the *psychoanalytic point of view*.

---

out. Ernst Kris once suggested in a similar case that there may be persistent rituals or games which every generation unconsciously understands. (Oral communication.)

But however that may be, the fact that we do not yet know how it happens that we have these symbols in common does not prove that it does not happen. In the history of science as well as in the investigation of criminal cases, many fundamental relationships were grasped before the whole sequence of events could be reconstructed. Harvey's picture of the circulation of blood was essentially correct although he could not yet say how the blood got from the arterial into the venal system.

This class of unconscious phenomena was later developed by C. G. Jung into his "collective unconscious."

(c) The imprint of the earliest experience of individual life, during the preverbal stage, i.e., an experience that could not be verbalized and consequently was not conscious in the full sense of reflective consciousness, could therefore not be repressed and cannot, in the full verbal sense, be remembered. But there is much to suggest that unconscious imprints of this kind can influence visual experience, bodily sensation or behavior; see, e.g., the residue of early experience with the mother's breast described by Isakower (1936) and Lewin (1946).

(d) The imprint of later experience that did not become fully conscious at its time.

In this connection one might also consider the memory traces of later experiences which have become decathected through loss of interest due to maturation or, in general, to new impressions and challenges of life; but the unconscious of this kind is phenomenologically rather than dynamically unconscious and should therefore rather be termed preconscious.

[6] Except for more or less isolated remarks by philosophers and poets.

THE RANGE OF PSYCHOANALYSIS

The role of these factors was discovered in the study of the psychoneuroses, but it was clear that their application could not be limited to them. If psychoneuroses were due to a distorted break-through of unconscious drives, one could not assume that only the psychoneurotics had an unconscious psychic life; rather it had to be a common human phenomenon, although with differences in content and operation.

In fact, Freud found three areas of normal life for the understanding of which the unconscious provided the key: the *dream;* the common incidents of forgetting or losing, of mistakes in reading or writing—parapraxes—which Freud called the *psychopathology of everyday life;* and the *joke.* Freud developed the theory of these phenomena in three elaborate treatises (1900, 1901, 1905e). These three areas of normal life have something in common; in all of them, the watchfulness of the "ego" is temporarily diminished. The diminution is brought about, for the dream, by the condition of sleep; for the psychopathology of everyday life, which represents momentary "leaks," by, perhaps, fatigue or inattention; for the joke by what Ernst Kris called "regression in the service of the ego" (1936, p. 177), i.e., a playful release by someone who feels himself in safe enough control. In short, these three phenomena occur if the mind works on a reduced level, or, as one might say, in *regressed conditions* of normal life—"regressed" in the sense of a diminution of conscious control and a shift in the inner balance of power.

But if the unconscious is the clue for the understanding not only of the psychoneuroses but also of the psychic manifestations in such states of normal life in which control was lessened, it follows that it must have its part in all psychic phenomena although in the "nonregressed" conditions it shares the field with other, conscious, factors. The borderline between the two respective spheres of influence in full, nonregressed, normal life was, of course, not yet known. Hence, there was room for speculation.

We find in psychoanalysis *maximalistic and minimalistic tendencies* for the definition of the range of application of the psychoanalytic point of view. On the one hand, there is an extreme position, represented, among others, by Róheim's theory, according to which a civilization—including its economic and technological aspects—is due to a specific infantile trauma which is regularly inflicted in the type of child rearing prevailing in this culture, so that all activities, including those manifestly directed toward the fulfillment of conscious, adult, and nonsexual needs, seem to have their root in the unconscious, the sexual, and the infantile. Some anthropologists have followed this lead.

An example from personal experience: Shortly after Pearl Harbor, a small group of noted social scientists, intent on studying the cultural roots of German National Socialism, invited a number of refugee scholars and interviewed them about their experience and ideas on this subject. I was among those invited. I remember that I mentioned among the factors which seemed to me had disposed the German people for a nationalistic dictatorship, the failure of German nineteenth century liberalism, and the subsequent success of Prussian militarism, in bringing about the much-desired unification of Germany; this experience, I argued, had conditioned the German people to distrust the democratic process and to put their faith in strong-arm methods. I also mentioned the impact of rapid industrialization upon a society still almost feudal in its caste structure, without interceding commercialism and without a strong commercial class such as was already established in Anglo-Saxon countries at the onset of industrialization; such a situation seemed to make people more alert to the potentialities of power, rather than the potentialities of welfare, inherent in industry. I was then interrupted by my host, a noted anthropologist; this was not what I had been expected to contribute. As a psychoanalyst I should point out how Nazism had developed from the German form of child rearing. I replied that I did not think that there was any such relationship; in fact, political opinion did not seem to me to be determined in early childhood at all. This view was not accepted and I was told that the way the German mother holds her baby must be different from that of mothers in democracies. When we parted, it was clear that my hosts felt that they had wasted their time.

The idea, allegedly supported by psychoanalytic theory, that social institutions, systems, and creeds have their root in typical family situations and ways of child rearing has borne strange fruits. During the Second World War when many social scientists were engaged in studying enemy "cultures," a school of thought in cultural anthropology claimed that the father in the German family was an autocrat, and this was the reason why the Germans had so readily embraced Nazism. But sometime later another noted anthropologist claimed that the father in the German family was a weak and ineffectual figure, and this was the reason why the Germans had embraced Nazism: German male youth grew up without a strong father as an object of identification, became prey to unconscious homosexuality and thus open to the appeal of Nazism.

Psychoanalysis, it must be clearly understood, can neither claim credit nor accept responsibility for all theories that are advanced in its name or use a psychoanalytic vocabulary.[7]

---

[7] The failure of these theories is well worth studying for its own sake. Perhaps the major reason was that one ventured to interpret phenomena without having first carefully assembled all available facts. In the first

On the other hand, there is the counteroffensive of the culturalists, carried back into the home base of psychoanalysis, the theory of the neuroses; this school of thought is trying to recover for consciousness, adult experience, and nonsexual interests, as large a part as possible in the etiology of neurosis and *a fortiori* in the development of personality.

Freud's statements in this matter are conservative; he was fully aware of the *limitations in scope,* though he insisted on the *importance in weight,* of the new contributions. He said, e.g. (1914a, p. 50):

Psycho-analysis has never claimed to provide a complete theory of human mentality in general, but only expected that what it offered should be applied to supplement and correct the knowledge acquired by other means.

[And again (1924, p. 523):] If one accepts the distinction which I recently proposed, in dividing the psychic apparatus into an ego which is in touch with the outer world and is endowed with consciousness, and an unconscious id which is dominated by the impulsive needs, then psychoanalysis may be designated as a psychology of the id and of its influence upon the ego. Psychoanalysis can thus furnish only contributions to every field of knowledge which must be supplemented by the psychology of the ego. If these contributions, as so often happens, contain the very essentials of a state of affairs, this merely

---

theory, e.g., the authors took it for granted that since Nazism was a tyranny, all things that are associated with tyranny in American consciousness must apply to the case of Nazism; and the American picture of a tyrant is largely shaped by the story of George III as it was seen from the American side. Hence, Nazism was looked upon as an extreme exaggeration of paternal autocracy. Actually, however, Nazism—and fascism in general—grew out of a youth movement that was violently rebellious against, and contemptuous of, parental authority, was opposed to religion and scornful of family values. Unmarried motherhood, if racially unsuspect, was protected; children were encouraged to spy on their parents. Children and teenagers were enthusiastic supporters of the regime at a time when the older age groups were already thoroughly disillusioned.

shows the importance which the so long unrecognized psychic unconscious may claim in our lives.

This estimate of the range of psychoanalysis[8] is also reflected in Freud's remarks about artistic talent:

> Before the problem of the creative artist analysis must, alas, lay down its arms [1928, p. 222]. My friend and disciple, Marie Bonaparte, has in this book focussed the light of psychoanalysis upon the life and the work of a great, pathological, poet . . . Such studies are not meant to explain the genius of a poet but to show the motifs which have stirred it up, and the topics imposed upon it by fate [1933, p. xi].

I once tried to define the *formal* relationship between the conscious, adult, and reality-oriented and the unconscious, infantile, and impulsive (*"triebhaft"*) in the province of the "normal" through what I called the principle of multiple function (1930). The origin of this formulation was probably dissatisfaction with the Freudian hypothesis of overdetermination. The facts which this hypothesis was meant to cover seemed indisputable; psychic phenomena, as a rule, have many "determinants." But I found the notion of overdetermination difficult to accept logically. If $a_1, a_2, \ldots, a_n$ were factors which were both necessary and sufficient to bring about a certain result A, I saw no room for another factor a_{n+1}. It seemed to me to be more satisfying to say

---

[8] Its fundamental conservatism was reinforced by a personal factor, viz., Freud's dislike for sweeping generalizations and for system building. Once, probably toward the end of 1926, the late Dr. Schilder presented a paper on characterology in which he outlined a multidimensional system of classifying character. Freud said in his reply that he felt like someone who had hugged the coast all his life and who now watched others sailing out into the open ocean. He wished them well but could not take part in their ventures: "I am an old hand in the coastal run and I will keep faith with my blue inlets."

that behavior served several functions, or, as one might also say, that it was at once responsive to many pressures, or was a solution at once for many tasks. If this was so—regularly, as the principle of multiple function claimed at the time, or, at least very frequently, as Freud had suggested, and as I, on second thought, would prefer to say—then it followed that reality-directed behavior can be expected to serve instinctual demands, too.

If this is so, it is justified to ask for unconscious, sexual, or infantile aspects in reality-oriented behavior. But this consideration could only provide the *formal* justification for this inquiry; it said nothing about the *relative weight* of the various factors.

THE PARALLELOGRAM OF FORCES

Whether or not the unconscious, the infantile, and the sexual are believed to play an important part in any particular sample of behavior, the psychoanalytic view of human behavior differs from most other views inasmuch as it sees behavior ordinarily not as the result of one all-pervasive motive but as the outcome of many, usually conflicting, forces. In this way, a slight shift within the contending forces can result in radically different behavior, just as a change in the vote of a small fraction of the electorate can lead to the adoption of an entirely different policy. In this dynamic view of human behavior, psychoanalysis is close to the traditional Christian view of man and his temptations and the corruption in his nature—close, except for the supranatural implications of the Christian view—and quite remote from the monistic philosophies of human behavior, as, e.g., the concept of the *economic man*[9] in the older version of classic economic theory, or the determination of man's behavior by his class situation in Marxism.

This picture of behavior as outcome of an inner "parallelogram of forces" has not yet penetrated deeply into public consciousness; most people still think in terms of single motives. There has been, e.g., much discussion in recent years whether "the Germans" have really reformed and can be trusted politically. Apart from the fact that "the Germans" is a meaningless abstraction—the adult population of Western Germany, which alone is in question, in 1959 has only a minority of individuals in common with the adult population of the whole prewar Germany in 1933—it may well be assumed that in the heart of numerable Western Germans of today nationalistic sentiments are present just as it can be assumed that in the heart of numerable Germans of 1933 liberal and humane sentiments existed; but what sentiments prevail depends on circumstances such as opportunity and leadership.

A DIGRESSION ON PHILOSOPHICAL QUESTIONS

A great deal of the criticism of psychoanalysis, by friend and foe, has concentrated not upon the main discoveries of psychoanalysis—the unconscious psychic life, the role of sexuality, and the impact of childhood experience—but on the philosophical writings of its founder and on the philoso-

[9] This does not preclude, however, that simplified models of this kind can yet be useful as ideal, or marginal, types (*Idealtypen*, Max Weber) which reality approximates to a greater or lesser degree without being ever fully mirrored by them. Laws formulated about such ideal types are comparable to theories in physics developed on the assumptions of specific marginal conditions and applicable in the degree to which the real circumstances approach these marginal conditions.

phical implications which various authors find in psychoanalysis. From among the legion of philosophical questions of this kind, we propose to deal with two, viz., the relationship of psychoanalysis to an evolutionist philosophy, and the relationship of a theory of unconscious motivation to a theory of ideology.

It has often been said, as an argument against psychoanalysis, that Freud shared the evolutionist philosophy—in the metaphysical rather than merely the empirical sense of the word—which was so widely accepted in his time. It is the assumption that an organism, or a type of behavior, can be *completely* explained genetically, i.e., by showing the more primitive forms out of which it has developed; it is somehow implied that only the primitive forms have true existence, as it were, while the higher forms have only a kind of derivative existence. Psychoanalysis, it is alleged by some critics, tries to explain the nonregressed in terms of the regressed and the higher forms of life in terms of the lower ones, and is thereby an offshoot of an obsolete philosophy.

In dealing with this argument, it must be said, first of all, that there are signs of such a tendency, particularly in Freud's philosophical writings. An example is Freud's theory of religion. Freud sees the concept of God as a cosmic projection of the father of our childhood. From this hypothesis about the psychogenesis of the belief in God no inference can be drawn about the factual question of the existence of a higher Being; as a psychogenetic hypothesis it may well be correct for the father religions, the latecomers in religious history, but it does not offer a complete elucidation of this psychogenesis. It does not explain why and how a cosmic projection of the father came to pass. Why did the longing for the father of our childhood not remain the longing for the father? And if it had to be displaced for whatever reasons, why was it not expressed in attachment to elders, kings or leaders, or in ancestor worship, as has happened so often in history? Why did it have to turn to an infinite, transcending, God, and how did it happen that such an idea was grasped at all? There is, at least, something like an expansiveness of the mind which cannot in turn be explained in terms of the more primitive elements which are being expanded or transcended.

The evolutionist philosophy is expressed in a letter of Freud's to Ludwig Binswanger, written in 1936:

> I have always dwelled in the ground floor and in the basement of the building. You claim that upon change of the viewpoint one sees an upper story in which there are distinguished guests like religion, art, et al. You are not the only one to do so; most civilized specimens of the *homo natura* think this way. You are in this point conservative while I am revolutionary. If I had another working life ahead of me, I should undertake to find a place in my low hamlet for these aristocrats. [Binswanger, 1956, p. 115].

We may unhesitatingly accept the idea that these aristocrats have a humble origin and yet feel that this does not explain what made it possible for them to rise above their origin.

The implicit assumption, common to most scientists of the nineteenth and the twentieth centuries, is an evolutionist philosophy in the metaphysical sense: the lower forms of life alone have true existence; the higher have developed out of them, and this fact of evolution seems to dispense with the need of making room in the theory for these higher activities. This philosophy is probably not fully understandable without considering also the ethos that used to go hand in hand with it. It was an *ethos of understatement;* one shied away from big words and the "higher aspects" of man that were refused a place in theory were simply taken for granted in everyday life. The philosophical attitude of evolutionism is probably partly due to the suspicion that any other assumption stems from, or will lead to, religious supranaturalism, which one wished to avoid. Also, there was a strong humanitarian resentment of the fact that religious emphasis on the "divine spark" in man could go, and had gone, hand in hand for so long with callousness and cruelty toward the repository of this spark, the real, living man; there was a growing distrust of flag waving of all kind, including moral flag waving, and a tendency to promise less and to deliver more.

All men are part of their time; great, creative men transcend their times—sometimes very far—in and by what they create, but they, too, remain part of their time and social place for the rest of their thoughts and feelings. Freud shared to a large extent the ideas, the hopes, the unwritten philosophy of the scientifically minded men of his age,[10] including some ideas that now appear unsatisfactory.

[10] That Freud's philosophical attitude, or *Weltanschauung*, in general, i.e., beyond the question of evolutionist metaphysics, was a historical rather than an individual phenomenon, part of the outlook of an elite of his age rather than a characteristic personal creation, may be seen from the following quotation from a paper written by George Santayana in 1902. Santayana developed the idea that a religion based on nature, which had followed religion based on revelation, was now in the process of dissolution in favor of a frank naturalism, and he made this prophesy: "The masses of men will see no reason why they should not live out their native impulses or acquired passions without fear . . . while a few thinkers, devout and rational by temperament, will know how to maintain their dignity of spirit in the face of a universe of which they will ask no favor save the revelation of its laws. Thus irreligion for the many and Stoicism for the few is the end of natural religion in the modern world as it was in the ancient" (1902, p. 63f.)

Though these words about "a few thinkers, devout and rational by

This fact should neither be denied nor used as a weapon against Freud or against his discovery, psychoanalysis. For the influence of his philosophical leanings on his *psychoanalytic* work—as different from that on his philosophical writings—is quite *peripheral* and all psychoanalytic propositions can easily be formulated without such philosophical implications. The most important single example of such influence is Freud's formulation that the ego develops out of the id; about the modification of this assumption by Heinz Hartmann, see p. 90.

As to the second question: Since psychoanalysis does not accept a person's own account of his motives as necessarily correct or complete, some authors have felt that a parallel exists between the Marxist theory of ideology and the Freudian theory of unconscious motivation and rationalization.

The analogy is superficial, however, because it does not take fundamental differences into account. Ideology, in Marxism, is determined by the class situation: *das gesellschaftliche Sein bestimmt das gesellschaftliche Bewusstsein,* socioeconomic consciousness reflects socioeconomic realities. In the psychoanalytic view, on the other hand, thought and opinion are only in marginal cases determined by unconscious factors *alone* (as, e.g., in hallucinatory psychosis or in extreme cases of wishful thinking); usually, thought and opinion are the result of an *interplay of forces* (see p. 57), some reflecting unconscious motives, others the impact of reality, with unconscious forces playing a greater or lesser role as the case may be.

Then, in Marxism, the class situation sets inescapable

---

temperament," were written about a quarter of a century before *The Future of an Illusion,* they seem to define accurately the attitude toward the world and toward life shown in this book and in later statements of Freud's in *Civilization and Its Discontents* and *Why War.*

limits to what the people, with few exceptions, can comprehend; the bourgeoisie, e.g., because of its class situation,
cannot fully understand the historical process and its own
inexorable destiny. In the psychoanalytic view, on the other
hand, people *may* become aware of the subjective factor in
their thinking, as a kind of personal equation, and may go
a long way toward correcting it. Some even bend over
backwards and take views opposite to their interests or personal inclinations. In short, unconscious forces, in psychoanalysis, are *influences,* usually important and often decisive; but the class situation, in Marxist theory, is *inescapable
destiny,* as far as the class as a whole is concerned.

Furthermore, Marxists believe that the opinions of *others*
are an ideological superstructure of socioeconomic realities,
but they do not look at *their* views in the same light. Of
themselves they like to think as incarnations of the spirit
of the "proletariat," and the proletariat, by virtue of *its* class
situation, has access to absolute truth, somewhat like in an
earlier eschatology the poor in spirit had access to the
Kingdom of the Heavens. But when Freud discovered the
unconscious, he concluded that self-analysis was his most
urgent task, and the analysis of the analyst has remained
the A and O of an analyst's responsibility ever since: as a
preparatory analysis at the beginning of his studies, as a
constant self-analysis accompanying his later analytic work,
as a reanalysis whenever his self-analysis does not suffice.

What these differences between the psychoanalytic theory
of the unconscious and the Marxist theory of economic
determinism amount to is the difference between a tool of
analysis, carried out with such approximation to objectivity
as one is capable of reaching, and the use of debunking as
a weapon in a struggle for power.

When we look beyond the theory of ideology to the

Marxian view of human events in general, and compare it with the implications which the Freudian theories carry for this wider subject, the differences are even greater. In the psychoanalytic view, conflicts between man and his social environment are a natural state of affairs because man has not been born so as to desire only those things of which his environment will approve, and any homogeneity between him and his environment is the result of adjustment processes and is hardly ever static. And conflicts within man are considered to be unavoidable; they are believed to be rooted partly in the difference between his natural desires and the environmental restraints transmitted to him through education, partly in the difference between the immediate and the long-term consequences of our actions, i.e., the difference between the pleasure principle and the reality principle, partly in the ambivalence of our feelings such as, e.g., love and hatred to the same object; and in other circumstances in addition. The Marxian theory sees conflicts within man and conflicts between men—the latter are its major concern—as exclusively due to the private property of the means of production. Once the capitalists have been expropriated and all means of production have been taken over by the socialist state, the natural harmony of all interests will emerge: "The free development of each is the condition of the free development of all" (Marx).

It is in this point that the theory of Marx and the implications of the theory of Freud are plainly irreconcilable. The Marxian assumption of a preordained harmony of all human interests and aspirations, thwarted in this still "prehistoric" age of man through the institution of private property and certain to blossom forth once private property has been confiscated by a socialist state, must appear to a psychoanalyst as a daydream of great naiveté;[11] on the other hand, the Freudian assumption that conflicts are an unavoidable part of human life and that suffering can therefore not be altogether abolished must appear to a convinced Marxian as a typical "bourgeois" ideology, which has the function to discourage the "proletariat" in its struggle for a classless, and hence conflictless, society by representing this goal as unachievable.

In regard to this, see the recent analysis of utopianism by Sir Isaiah Berlin (1958, p. 53f.): "To admit that the fulfillment of some of our ideals may in principle make the fulfillment of others impossible is to say that the notion of total human fulfillment is a formal contradiction . . . For every rationalist metaphysician . . . this abandonment of the notion of a final harmony, in which . . . all contradictions are reconciled, is . . . an intolerable bankruptcy of reason . . . The world that we encounter in ordinary experience is one in which we are faced with choices between ends equally ultimate the realization of some of which must involve the sacrifice of others . . . if [man] had assurance that in some perfect state, realizable by men on earth, no ends pursued by them would ever be in conflict, the necessity and agony of choice would disappear, and with it the central importance of the freedom to choose. Any method of bringing this final state nearer would then seem fully justified . . . If, as I believe, the ends of men are many, and not all of them are in principle compatible with each other, then the possibility of conflict—and of tragedy—can never be wholly eliminated from human life. . ."

[11] Ignorance and naiveté in some points can, and often do, go hand in hand with great understanding and sophistication in others. E.g., in this case, naiveté in the fundamental ideas has been combined with very great sophistication in political action.

2

The Middle Years

The middle period brought many elaborations and rami-
fications: the more detailed elaboration of the development
of the libido, studies of particular clinical types, the working
out of an analytic technique, the metapsychology; and many
nonmedical applications of psychoanalysis.

NARCISSISM

The most important addition to psychoanalytic theory
during these middle years was the introduction of the concept of narcissism, of a "libidinal complement of egoism"
(Freud, 1916/17, p. 361). It contained the fundamental insight that libidinal urges can take oneself as an object; and
that self-love is not identical with the pursuit of self-interest,
egoism; indeed, that they may be opposed to each other and
that the service of one's self-interest may require a sacrifice
of self-love.

A historical example may illustrate this point. In the last
days of the Byzantine Empire when Byzantium was desperately looking out for help against the Turkish menace, the
last of the Byzantine emperors alienated Francesco Foscari,
the Doge of Venice, which was Byzantium's best prospect

for help. As a prince, Constantine Palaeologus had, for sound political reasons, entered into an engagement with the Doge's daughter which he broke when he unexpectedly ascended to the throne as the bride was not of high enough status for an emperor of Constantinople. Even after the catastrophe had been consummated, Constantinople taken by the Turks and Constantine himself killed in the defense of the city, his courtier and later historian of the tragedy, Georgios Sphrantzes, felt that the emperor had no alternative: "How could the lords and ladies of Constantinople have accepted as their mistress and princess the daughter of a Venetian and have paid their respect to his sons as their emperor's brothers-in-law? He was a noble man, to be sure, and a Doge—but his was only a temporary office."[1]

Another example: The people of this country derive constant gratification from the feeling of being not only citizens of a great country but of a country in which they are convinced everything, or everything that matters, is bigger and better than anywhere else. Even serious national reverses and perils are occasions for self-congratulation; after Pearl Harbor, newspaper headlines announced triumphantly the "greatest disaster in naval history." Indulgence in this kind of satisfaction, while relatively harmless as long as the nation was safely ensconced behind effective ocean barriers, has become a serious danger ever since the nation has been facing a powerful and unappeasable foe without any protection other than it can provide by its own efforts.

---

[1] The fact that vanity, or status, plays so great a role in life, often to the detriment of self-preservative interests, is an important argument against the Marxist theory which sees history largely governed by self-preservative necessities. H. R. Trevor-Roper seems to have this in mind when he says (1957, p. 10) that ". . . status, in spite of all that Marx has said, perhaps still remains the *primum mobile* of social man, at least of those above the starvation line."

The Marxist theory is correct in the sense that unadjusted behavior cannot indefinitely endure—as the Byzantine example illustrates—particularly in times in which the struggle for survival is hard. But with *some* concessions to reality, behavior at variance with self-preservative interests can *long* survive, particularly in easy times with a comfortable margin of survival.

The concept was originally derived from an attempt to take account, in terms of the libido theory, of the behavior of paranoid schizophrenics. Two characteristic features of these patients—the difficulty of establishing contact with them, i.e., a deficiency in their object relations, and the fact that some, though not all of them, produce megalomanic ideas—seemed to be accountable by one single assumption, viz., that the libido had been withdrawn from the objects and concentrated upon the ego. The first part of this process might explain the poor object relationship, while the second part might account for the ideas of grandeur, as a special case of the already well-known phenomenon of overvaluation of the sexual object. The disturbance of reality judgment—loss of the *fonction du réel*, in the terminology of Janet—could then be understood as a by-product of distorted perspective, implied in this concentration of libido upon oneself.

As so often happens in the history of science, the value of the new concept for the problem it was meant to solve is open to question,[2] but its value for other subjects made it indispensable, as, e.g., for the psychology of love or for that of the superego. We will later have to make use of it in the study of anxiety. The application of this fruitful concept by analysts has so far suffered from a carelessness of language that uses the term "narcissistic" equally, without qualification, for the phenomena of satisfied, as for those of frustrated, self-love; the self-contented person who does not seem to need anybody else—self-directed in the sense of

___

[2] Impairment of judgment due to hatred and love—*ira et studium*—is more likely to explain the misjudgments of reality by normals and neurotics than the delusions of paranoiacs because the latter are inaccessible to the corrective influence of experience, while emotional prejudices can be influenced by experience, albeit only very slowly. See Waelder (1951, p. 2), and the later discussion (p. 207f.).

Riesman—is equally called "narcissistic," as is the person in constant need of moral support.

It is often assumed that narcissism is per se, in any form or degree, a pathological phenomenon. This is not the case; there is normal narcissism. A basic acceptance of oneself and love for oneself regardless of one's shortcomings (of which one can all the better afford to be aware the more certain one is of this basic self-acceptance) actually are a prerequisite of psychic health. The lack of them manifests itself clinically as depression. (See Freud, 1923, p. 86.)

METAPSYCHOLOGY

Another addition made in these years is *metapsychology*. As the name suggests, it is a meta-theory, i.e., a theory behind a theory, or a theory on a higher level of abstraction. It is an attempt to do what has been suggested was Freud's ultimate goal in theory building: "Freud's long-term goal . . . was to reduce formulations which describe phenomena qualitatively, in terms of function fulfilled, to quantitative formulations . . ." (Bernfeld, 1932, p. 465). A full realization of this goal would depend on the possibility of measurement, rather than the mere impressionistic estimate, of psychic intensities.

An example may show how metapsychology is related to "ordinary," or clinical, psychoanalytic theory. Repression, one of the most fundamental notions in psychoanalysis, has been described by Freud in the following words: "The ego drew back, as it were, after the first shock of its conflict with the objectionable impulse; it debarred the impulse from access to consciousness and to direct motor discharge, but at the same time the impulse retained its full charge of energy" (1925, p. 54). This is the explanation of repression in clinical psychoanalytic theory. It is a psychologically fully "understandable" process; i.e., empathy with it is easily possible. It answers completely the description with which Freud characterized his own approach to the problem of hysterical amnesias lifted under hypnosis, in contradistinction to Breuer's explanation of this phenomenon: "I was inclined to suspect the existence of an interplay of forces and the operation of intentions and purposes such as are observed in normal life" (1925, p. 40).

In metapsychological theory, on the other hand, the quality of consciousness is seen as due to a hypercathexis. In the system Unconscious are the thing-representations; in the system Preconscious, which contains all contents capable of consciousness, there are the word-representations. An impulse is effective if the thing-representation is cathected; it is conscious (or capable of being conscious) in addition to being effective if both thing-representations and word-representations are cathected. Repression could then be described as a withdrawal of this hypercathexis.

Metapsychology can therefore be said to be the result of attempts to construct a *physicalistic*—or, if you like, mechanistic—*model* of the personality that would reflect all features of the *motivational theory* of psychoanalysis.

Psychoanalysis has often been criticized as a mechanistic psychology, allegedly wed to obsolete ideas of a scientism that uses physics—and a previous state of physical theory at that—as the prototype of all understanding of the Universe. Such criticism has come from various quarters: from the school of *geisteswissenschaftliche* psychology in Germany, from the circles of Adler and Jung, from the Thomists and existentialists, and from some, though not all, Gestalt theorists. The issue is somewhat similar to the controversy be-

tween mechanism and vitalism in biology. Without taking
any stand on this issue—which is probably a moot question
anyhow—it must be said that this criticism, whether right
or wrong with regard to specific questions, does not come to
grips with the main body of psychoanalysis at all; at most,
it could apply to its metapsychological superstructure. And
to the latter, no doubt, applies what Freud has said with
reference to fundamental theories in general, that "these
ideas are not the foundation of science, upon which everything rests: that foundation is observation alone. They are
not the bottom but the top of the whole structure, and they
can be replaced and discarded without damaging it" (1914b,
p. 77).

THE DISSIDENT SCHOOLS

It was also in these middle years that the two main defections from psychoanalysis took place which have accompanied psychoanalysis on its way ever since. They are connected with the names of Carl G. Jung and Alfred Adler.
Their theories are not part of psychoanalysis, but they may
yet be considered in a history of psychoanalytic thought
because of the light they throw upon the potentialities for
reinterpretation and distortion and hence upon the inner
structure of the psychoanalytic model of human behavior.

Both Jung and Adler discarded a large body of psychoanalytic theory and radically reinterpreted what they retained. Neither of them was entirely original in his positive
claims; both had seized upon an element in psychoanalytic
theory which had played a minor role there, had developed
it further and made it the center of their theories.

For Jung the Freudian theory of dream symbols seems to
have provided the original stimulation. When analyzing
dreams, i.e., when trying to translate them into the various

currents and crosscurrents of thought and tendencies which
have produced them and thus putting them in their place
in the dreamer's psychic life, Freud had found certain elements which seemed to defy all efforts to connect them with
individual motifs in the life of the dreamer; on the other
hand, they were few in number and identical with different
people. It made sense to assume that they represented, in
all dreamers, regardless of the variations in their individual
experience, the same thing; e.g., a house standing for a
woman. Freud called them symbols and suggested that they
were a kind of universal primeval language—the same kind
of thinking that lets different nations think of the earth in
which the seed is planted as female, or as mother, or lets
different languages speak of the male and female parts of
machines. Freud, who had no resistance against the Lamarckian assumption, dominant in his formative years, of an
inheritance of acquired characteristics, thought that sym-
bolism, on the whole, was a part of a common heritage, a
residue of the experience of mankind in primeval times
(see p. 50f.). We who came after Freud and who have been
impressed in our day by the warnings of biologists that the
Lamarckian assumption is untenable, may feel the existence
of universal symbols as a challenge to our theoretical powers. But be that as it may: in any case, provision was made,
in Freudian theory, for an unconscious common to all men,
or to all men in a cultural orbit, independent of their experience as individuals, i.e., for a collective unconscious. Jung
expanded what was a niche in psychoanalytic theory into
an enormous edifice.[3] From the beginning, he had been

---

[3] Jung has recognized this origin of his thought. In a recent passage, e.g.,
he said that Freud, after discovering the oedipus complex, had failed to
draw the inescapable conclusion that, in addition to the individual repressed, there must be a "normal unconscious consisting of what he
[Freud] called archaic residues" (1956).

greatly impressed by the similarities between fantasy, dream, delusion, and myth; but while others saw in myth a collective fantasy about nature or human events, Jung put things on their head, as it were, and saw in dream or delusion a manifestation of myth—of the "archetypes" of the collective unconscious.

According to Jung, numerable ideas are deposited in our unconscious mind which have nothing to do with us as individuals; they are part of a vast collective heritage through which we are all bound to our race and to the mystical sources of all being. The analytic investigation of the individual unconscious, as introduced by Freud, still made some sense, in Jung's eyes, particularly for young people; but neurosis and mental illness had not only to do with individual life history but also, and more important, with our collective heritage. On the other hand, the vastness of the collective unconscious which had its branch in every person's mind, so to speak, was also an inexhaustible reservoir of recovery, wisdom, and strength.

The fact that Jungian psychology deals with a "collective" rather than an individual unconscious makes for an important difference between psychoanalytic interpretations and interpretations in the Jungian style. Psychoanalytic interpretations are attempts to fill in lacunae in the train of conscious experience, to undo distortions, and to point out connections—much like the restoration of a doctored text. The content of these interpretations is an inner experience that either was conscious, if only for a moment, or might have been conscious, and in any case can be consciously fully realized. Jungian interpretations, on the other hand, seem to be largely in terms of the archetypes of the collective unconscious or of relations between "the unconscious," conceived as a world of its own, and the individual—in either case a material that has not been conscious and does not normally become consciously felt. They are like interpretations of symbols; the origin of Jungian thought has left its imprint upon it. An outsider whose only source of knowledge is the literature finds it difficult to see by what kind of procedure such interpretations could ever be either proved or disproved.

Adler, also, had his point of departure in an element of Freudian thought, viz., in the secondary gain of illness. Once a neurosis has been formed, there are reactions of the remainder of the personality to this foreign body: partly a struggle against it, an attempt to eject it from the mind, which continues on a new level the original struggle against the disturbing impulse; and partly an attempt to assimilate it. We may think of governments trying to deal in these ways with explosive tendencies in the body politic.

It is part of the second reaction to notice, and to cultivate, potential uses of the illness for purposes of self-preservation. It is well known that people who have been injured in an accident and are now the beneficiaries of insurance payments often prove refractory to efforts at rehabilitation. Freud called such phenomena in the course of a neurotic process the secondary gain of the illness. The adjective implies that the prospect of such gain was not a motive for the formation of the neurosis in the first place but that once the neurosis had been formed, the secondary gain provides an additional motive to hang on to it.

Adler put such utilitarian motives in the center of his theory. People are sick because they want to be sick; they want to shirk their responsibilities. Neurosis is contrived. They shirk their responsibilities because they have (unjustified) inferiority feelings and are profoundly discouraged. The therapist has to see through their subterfuges, undeceived, and to offer them the encouragement they need to face life squarely; he has to lead them out of their selfish isolation into genuine participation in the community.

These two early defections have provided the prototypes for most "revisionism" of psychoanalysis up to the present day. Perhaps that will continue to be so because they represent, in characteristic examples, the two possibilities of radically reinterpreting Freud's central idea, the unconscious.

Freud's basic discovery is that of an effective *unconscious* psychic life, the contents of which are not fundamentally different from those of consciousness, though closer to the infantile than to the adult mind. It is possible to think of the unconscious *either* as something very much *"deeper"*— in the sense of its being more remote from adult conscious content—and more esoteric than the unconscious of Freud, or as something very much *closer to conscious* thought, approximately along the lines of the practical common-sense psychology of the politician, the salesman, and the hotel porter, and thus hardly really unconscious at all. Jung did the former, Adler the latter. Jung thought that "beyond" the layers of the individual unconscious which Freud had explored there is a bottomless expanse through which man is connected with his racial heritage, with the wisdom of the ages, and the life of the eons; there is a window in Jung's unconscious that opens into the cosmic and the absolute. Adler, on the other hand, thought that it meant all the petty deceptions and self-deceptions which cannot really deceive the cool and penetrating mind.

Both Adler and Jung proposed new theories of neurosis. According to Adler, neurosis is an "arrangement," i.e., it is contrived in the service of self-preservative and self-expansive tendencies, a tool in the struggle for *Lebensraum*. Neurosis is therefore, for Adler, a *form of adjustment* to reality

—in radical difference from the Freudian view which holds that while the motive for the flight from an impulse which stood at the beginning of the neurotic process may, though it need not, have been adaptational, viz., concern for external reality, the final neurosis has no adaptational value except as it may be due to the assimilation into the ego of a neurosis already formed (secondary gain). According to Jung, neurosis appears to be the consequence of a kind of imbalance between an individual and the collective unconscious in him.

Adler's psychology is an unmasking, debunking, psychology, something that Freudian psychoanalysis—or, for that matter, Jung's "analytic psychology"—is not. Since in Adler's view neurosis is an arrangement, motivated by the ego, it comes very close to being a lie, a fraud, and the understanding of a neurosis is the uncovering of its secret purpose, hence an unmasking. Adler's view is in this point similar to the Marxist theory of ideology; the relations between the Adlerian school and the moderate, non-Bolshevist, versions of Marxism have in fact been close. Psychoanalysis, on the other hand, assumes a genuine unconscious, and it considers repression a universal phenomenon. The practice of psychoanalysis fosters humility, not supercilious superiority.[4]

Adler's theory of the neuroses does not cover the phenomena as they appear to the observer in the psychoanalytic interview. Every carefully studied case and, in fact, many a single analytic hour seems to us to show that neurotic formations are *not the outgrowth of any single trend but the result of the clash of two*—of ego and nonego, the latter comprising tendencies other than self-preservation and self-ex-

---

[4] There are some practitioners of analysis who have looked upon their work as an unmasking, and assumed the corresponding superior attitude toward their patients; their number, however, has been small.

pansion. The data of observation seem to leave considerable
room for difference of opinion regarding the *nature* of the
contending forces and their *relative importance*—in both
these points there have been differences of opinion among
psychoanalysts at any one time and changes of viewpoint of
psychoanalysts in the course of time; but I can see no possibility of denying the crucial point that *two* forces are
involved rather than one, without losing sight of facts; and
facts have been lost sight of in the Adlerian view.[5]

Against Jung's theory of neurosis Freud (1918) made a
kind of *prima facie* objection; it is based on the simple fact
that *neurosis exists already in childhood*. The categories of
interpretations in the style of Jung are rather abstract and
philosophical and can hardly be attributed to a child of
preschool age. In view of the occurrence of neurosis in childhood and in view of the fact that adult neurosis has often
developed from childhood neurosis in unbroken continuity,
it seems that neurosis must be understood in terms of factors which are already operative in early childhood.[6] The

[5] This point is clearly stated in entries in the recently discovered and
published diary which Lou Andreas-Salomé, the distinguished German
writer who became interested in psychoanalysis in her middle age, had
kept during her stay in Vienna, 1912/13, when the issues raised by Adler
were much discussed; she had participated in the meetings both of the
Vienna Psychoanalytic Society and of Adler's newly formed Society for
Individual Psychology. Looking back on her impressions during several
months, she felt that Freud had modified his views in several points so
that the ego factor had become "more equal" to the sexual factor in the
etiology; Freud, she felt, had thereby bridged a gulf that was beginning
to open between him and some of his disciples: "to all but Adler; because for Adler alone it is not a matter of emphasizing the ego factor
but of eliminating the sexual factor, i.e., of denying the bilateral character of the relation altogether. This alone is the real issue at stake and
here Freud continues to be right" (1912/13, p. 143).

[6] This Freudian argument is equally applicable to a more recent attempt
of explaining neurosis "from above" which has been advanced under the
influence of existentialist philosophy. Modern existentialism is a philosophy

alternative would be to assume that the neurosis of later age is something entirely different from neurosis in childhood even though their manifestations may be almost identical; e.g., that contact phobias, compulsions to wash and similar rituals in a person at the age of fifty are entirely different from the contact phobias, washing compulsions and rituals of the same person at the age of six. Allowance must well be made for the possibility of a certain change of meaning of a symptom during the course of life so that the same symptom may well become an outlet for new conflicts at a later stage in the neurotic process—as if a new neurotic conflict had used an outlet already preformed; but I see no reason to assume that this change of function should be either universal or radical.

Jung's theories gained wide influence in the German-speaking countries, not only in the sense that they found many protagonists there but also in the sense that there has been, in these countries, a considerable infiltration of Jungian thought into the thinking of Freudian analysts. Adler, on the other hand, had his greatest influence in the United States; the number of actual Adlerian practitioners

---

of pessimistic activism, just one step short of despair, that gained much following in Germany in the apocalyptic mood after the First World War when many people could not grasp the possibility of German defeat in the war except as part of a world catastrophe; and gained wide following all over the Continent of Europe after the disasters wrought by totalitarianism and the Second World War, and in the midst of the grave anxieties of the postwar period. Neurosis, according to this philosophy, is a reaction of man to his mortality, and a consequence of the tension, or contradiction, between, on the one hand, the urge to give meaning to one's life and, on the other hand, our unalterable ignorance about the purposes of the Universe—whether purpose there is, what it consists in— in relation to which alone an individual life could become meaningful beyond the acquisition of pleasures for oneself and a few other, equally transient, persons.

Once again, it is difficult to conceive of nightmares of a three-year-old child as being due to concern about the paradoxes of human existence.

in this country is quite small, but Adlerian thought has infiltrated the thinking of numerable psychoanalysts of the "liberal" school of thought. This national distribution should not surprise us. One of the best qualities of the German cultural tradition has been depth of thought, as reflected, e.g., in the fact that Germans have produced the most formidable body of philosophical thought in modern times. One of the greatest qualities of the American cultural tradition is a fundamental sanity, which has prevented the great chiliastic sociopolitical creeds of modern times from ever taking deep roots in American soil, and a sound practical sense. But cultural traditions, like men, like everything, have the vices of their virtues; *du sublime au ridicule il n'y a qu'un pas* and there is only one step from profundity to obscurantism or from a practical sense to superficiality.

Later, in the middle twenties, a third defection took place which had nothing to do with the two possibilities of reinterpreting the unconscious. Otto Rank was apparently greatly impressed by the phenomena of transference and, in general, by the possibility of strong emotional attachments of a patient to his therapist. Before his development led him away from psychoanalysis, he once spoke of the formation of a *masse à deux,* a group of two, as a characteristic feature of the psychoanalytic treatment. From this point, he later developed the idea of treatment as a school of human relationship, completely discarding the very essence of psychoanalysis as an exploratory therapy. He has thereby probably provided the basic inspiration for a new form of psychotherapy, viz., relationship therapy.[7]

Rank's ideas, like Adler's, have been tremendously influential in the United States, not through winning many out-

---

[7] For a discussion of the possible effectiveness of this therapy, see p. 228.

right disciples, but through infiltration into analytic thought. The number of practitioners who are professed Rankians is infinitesimal, but a large number of psychoanalysts has accepted the view that psychoanalysis works through a relationship experience, as, e.g., the so-called corrective experience in the transference; they often are no longer aware of the fact that this is not the idea of psychoanalysis as invented by Freud.

In view of the fact that the term "psychoanalysis" is at the present time often used to refer to psychotherapeutic procedures which derive from the theories and practices of Adler or Rank, the following definitions can be suggested.

Psychoanalytic treatment is based on the theory of the etiological importance of unconscious psychic life for psychopathology, particularly the psychoneuroses; it is a procedure designed to explore the unconscious factors involved and to bring them to the patient's consciousness.

Adlerian psychotherapy is based on the theory that psychopathology is due to faulty adjustment to the outside world; it is a procedure designed to re-educate the patient with regard to his life adjustments.

Rankian psychotherapy is based on the theory that psychopathology is the consequence of inadequate relation to other persons; it is a procedure designed to let the patient have the experience of a deep human relationship and of its termination.

The Adlerian and the Rankian theories and treatment procedures can easily be combined and usually are.

Psychoanalysis does not question the validity of the adjustment and the relationship aspects in psychopathology, nor the therapeutic usefulness of re-education or relationship therapy for certain conditions, but it holds that the Adlerian and Rankian theories of neurosis and of personality are inadequate for the reason that adjustment and object relations are only *partial aspects* of a more complex situation; that, in particular, adjustment to the outside world and object relationships are closely interwoven with *intrapsychic* processes(as the relations of the organism to its external and internal environments are interwoven in Claude Bernard's view of the healthy organism); and that adjustment and relationship cannot be understood in their full significance without considering the powerful urges of *psychosexuality* and the equally powerful *counterforces* which they bring into play.

It looks as though Jung, Adler, and Rank had exhausted the main possibilities of misinterpreting or misapplying psychoanalytic thought; no new such doctrine or practice[8] has appeared during the almost thirty-five years that have passed since Rank's turn. All the reformist and revisionist efforts of the last decades have been working with the ideas supplied by Jung, Adler, and Rank.

---

[8] Some readers may wonder why this or that divergent trend has not been mentioned in this context. There is, of course, no dearth of ideas that have not been widely accepted by other analysts. But it seems to me that the term, dissident school, should be limited to consistent systems which took their point of departure from psychoanalysis, radically reinterpreted some part of it (as Jung and Adler did with the unconscious, Rank with transference) while discarding the rest. In this sense, only Jung, Adler, and Rank, and their successors, can qualify.

3

The Later Additions

Freud's writings 1920-1926 contain additions to, and modifications of, psychoanalytic theory through which the theory has been brought into its present form. These latter-day additions have been the point of departure of most psychoanalytic work since. They are:

the concept of a repetition compulsion, i.e., of persistent repetitions beyond, and sometimes to all appearances against, the requirements of the pleasure principle;

a revision in the theory of instinctual drives, introducing destructive drives as an independent class and substituting the classification of instinctual drives into erotic and destructive drives for the old classification of self-preservative and sexual drives;

the revision of the older view that identified the ego and ego ideal with consciousness, to the effect that parts of the ego and of the ego ideal are unconscious, as unconscious resistances and unconscious tendencies of self-punishment, respectively;

the notion that repression is only one, though the most important, representative of a whole class of defense mechanisms; and

a revision of the theory of anxiety to the effect that anxiety in psychoneurosis should be understood as basically similar to normal fear, i.e., as a reaction to danger, and not, as had hitherto been the case, as a toxic product of libidinal tensions accumulated and undischarged.

Most of these propositions will be discussed in more detail in the latter part of this book. It may be said at this point that they were not entirely new concepts but that germs of these ideas can be found in much earlier writings of Freud. But it was only now that Freud took them up and developed them further. At least two of the innovations— repetition compulsion and unconscious need for punishment —seem to owe their existence to the observation of cases particularly refractory to therapy, and a third one—unconscious resistance—also stems from the study of therapeutic difficulties.

THE MODEL OF THE PERSONALITY

It was also at this time that a model of the personality was introduced which distinguished three systems, or provinces, of the mind—id, ego, and superego. Two of these terms—id and superego—were freshly adopted while the ego had been talked about from the beginning, though not too much, since it had not been in the focus of psychoanalytic interest. The model has been in general use in psychoanalysis ever since, and id, ego, and superego have almost become household words in the English language.

In the use of this model with its different agencies, or provinces, of the mind it should be kept in mind that it has been developed in the study of inner conflict, and that the three systems of the personality are clearly defined only in the case of conflict; only then can we distinguish between ego and id, or between ego and superego. In the numerous activities of life which we perform without conflict, dis-

tinction between ego and id, or between ego and superego,
is a questionable undertaking. If John Doe has his morning
breakfast, it is doubtful whether there is any meaning in
trying to distinguish between the part that the various
systems play in it. Perhaps, one can say that there are id
impulses—partly hunger and partly oral desires—and that
they have been accepted and approved for gratification by
ego and superego; but one may also, and perhaps more
correctly, say that John Doe wants his breakfast and en-
joys it, and that the various agencies of the mind are not
differentiated in the act. The situation changes if, e.g., John
Doe has been put on a diet by his doctor; in this case, his
hunger and his oral desire may be opposed by concern for
his health and by conscience reminding him of his responsibilities. There is then a conflict, and we can see id,
ego, and superego clearly, apart from each other, each with
its own business.[1]

---

[1] I believe that this was essentially Freud's view. He stated once that
ego and id "belong together and in a healthy case there is in practice no
division between them" (Freud, 1926b, p. 44). Sometime in the fall of
1930 a paper was read in which, as was fashionable at that time, the
phenomena under discussion were described by the author as being
brought about by an intricate sequence of interactions between id, ego,
and superego, which behaved like a three-person cast of a drama. In his
comments, Freud developed the view of the agencies of the mind which is
outlined above. For purposes of illustration he referred to Dutch seventeenth century painting. There were Dutch painters of the period who carefully and exactly worked out every detail of the subject; in contrast to
them Freud mentioned as closer to his own liking the style of Rembrandt,
in whose pictures it may sometimes be difficult to distinguish whether
a limb belonged to one person or another; a few things come out in bold
relief while the rest fades into darkness. When you paint your own pictures, Freud concluded, you will follow your own style; but when you
report on what I have done, remember that my watchword has always
been: more darkness. (The latter was a humorous allusion to the fact
that a few weeks before this meeting Freud had been awarded the Goethe
prize of the city of Frankfort; and as every person educated in the German
cultural orbit knew, Goethe's last words are said to have been: "More
light.")

A model whose parts are distinguishable only at certain times and which blend into each other the rest of the time may seem unsatisfactory or unacceptable to many people. But something quite similar seems to have been adopted in modern physics: apparently, an electron can be allocated a place only when it sends a message, i.e., when it emits a ray, in transition from one energy level to another. In the stationary condition of the atom, when no ray is emitted, it is meaningless to ask for the place of the electron in the atom; it is then everywhere in the atom, so to say.

Theoretical constructs such as these will be resented only as long as we feel entitled to expect that models have the qualities of objects of our daily experience.

Many people seem to think that a fundamental change came into psychoanalytic thought in the 1920's with the structural model of the personality. Change undoubtedly there was, but in order to evaluate it one must distinguish between change in substance, change in emphasis, and change in vocabulary.

As far as substance is concerned, psychoanalysis has dealt from the beginning with the dichotomy of id and ego. It was not called this way. There was talk of the "incompatibility of the ego and some idea presented to it" (Breuer and Freud, 1895, p. 122), or of nature versus civilization, of instinctual drive versus ego, or sexuality versus ego. Moral sentiments have always been taken into consideration; they were implicit in the ego as it was then conceived, or in the civilization (*Kultur*) which the ego represented. Since 1914 a separate term—ideal ego or ego ideal —has been used to designate the reflective activities (1914b, p. 93ff.). The structural model introduced in the 1920's did not bring any substantial change in these aspects. What was, indeed, substantially new about the model was the proposition, formulated above, that ego and superego were not in their entirety capable of consciousness but that there were unconscious parts of the ego (unconscious resistances) and of the superego (unconscious need for punishment).

There was also a certain change of emphasis inasmuch as the ego aspect was accorded, on the whole, more weight than it seemed to carry in the early years of psychoanalysis; it became an equal partner of the id in the genesis of neurosis and the development of personality (see p. 77).

The new vocabulary, finally, was more plastic than the old one and has therefore gained wider coinage. It has dramatized the relationships. Whether this was an unmixed blessing is a moot question.

4

Current Trends

The great variety of work that is being done in psychoanalysis and its applications to related disciplines cannot be reduced to a number of "trends." Yet it is instructive to consider *two polarities* in psychoanalytic thought and the developments to which they have given rise.

First, we meet again the two different trends that had been stimulated by the fundamental propositions of psychoanalysis: on the one hand, interest in the "deeper" unconscious, the earlier infantile stages, the preoedipal sexuality, i.e., in effect, in *early infancy;* and, on the other hand, a *trend away* from the unconscious, the sexual, and the infantile. These trends show the same tendencies, or differences of emphasis, which in extreme cases have led to the formation of the two main dissident schools.

Among the many efforts to dig down "deeper" into the unconscious, the work of Melanie Klein and her collaborators and disciples is most impressive. It has brought much stimulation to psychoanalysis. But, on the whole, the harvest from the study of psychic life at the *earliest* stages has, to my mind, not been as rich as might have been hoped. The difficulties of research into the psychic life of infants are formidable. Later memories of earliest experience are few and not necessarily reliable, and the direct observation of infants has one source of information less to draw on than the psychological study of older children or adults, viz., verbal expressions. The observer is therefore in a situation similar to that of the animal psychologist, and restraint in inferences about the inner life seems equally advisable.

On the opposite end of the spectrum there is a widespread trend which appears to be a moderate version of the opposition which Freud's fundamental propositions had originally encountered. It is an enthusiastic rediscovery of consciousness, of the importance of adult experience, and of nonsexual activities—all supposedly overlooked by Freud. We are told, e.g., that the important thing for neurosis lies in "interpersonal relations," presumably not seen by Freud; from the writings of this school of thought, one could get the impression that Freud had set up a solipsistic psychology.[1] Or, we are told that clinical material has to be studied not in terms of instincts—whatever that may mean —as it is allegedly done by psychoanalysts of the Freudian persuasion, but in terms of "adaptational psychodynamics," i.e., a system based on psychoanalysis but rejecting its sexual aspects as well as ideas about deeper unconscious layers.

This may be the place to refer to the contention, often heard from the same quarter, that it is the earmark of a mind interested in the advancement of knowledge that he does not accept too many of Freud's ideas, and that those

[1] Many people may not realize that in earlier years Freud was accused of precisely the opposite error, i.e., of having introduced nonmedical subjects such as human relationships into medicine. Organicists in psychiatry looking toward physiological processes for an explanation of mental illness considered psychoanalysis as irrelevant precisely because it had introduced interpersonal, social, factors. These critics, whatever the merits of their position, can be credited with a better understanding of the fundamental position of psychoanalysis than is shown by the current culturalist criticism.

who have accepted the bulk of the Freudian theories are thereby proved to be opposed to innovation. The oddity of this view becomes apparent if we translate it into any other scientific field. Has anybody ever suggested that a physicist who does not discard a substantial part of the theories of Einstein and Planck, Bohr and Heisenberg is a standpatter, opposed to progress in physics? In other sciences it is well understood that advance does not necessarily imply the overthrow of ideas of one's predecessors but that it may, and in any sound science usually does, lie in fully assimilating their achievements and carrying the frontier of knowledge beyond the limit which they had reached. *Science* is naturally *cumulative*. It is *only in non-cumulative fields*—as, on the whole, in religion, philosophy, and art—that the *new* often *implies* the *discarding of the old*.

Copernicus proposed a heliocentric system of planetary motion. It aroused bitter controversy which lasted for generations. In the course of this debate Tycho Brahé developed a kind of compromise system which won many followers in the seventeenth century; according to him, many planets circled around the sun somewhat as Copernicus had suggested, but the sun itself circled around the earth as Ptolemy had thought, carrying with it its planetary satellites; in this way the earth was still the center of the Universe.

The current revisionist theories around psychoanalysis seem to be related to Freud's ideas somewhat as Tycho Brahé's system was to Copernicus's. They are attempted compromises with pre-Freudian thought. At the same time, they claim to be revolutionary developments going beyond Freud; in short, they are *restorations masquerading as revolutions*.

We do not think today that it was through Tycho Brahé's system that knowledge advanced beyond Copernicus but rather through the work of Kepler, who, *on the basis of the Copernican theory*, found his laws of planetary movement, and through Newton, whose theory of gravitation united in one comprehensive theory the movement of the heavenly bodies and the fall of bodies under terrestrial conditions.

Then, there is *another polarity* of interest in the cultivation and development of *theory*, on the one hand, and in the collection of *empirical* data, on the other—trends which are the more useful the closer they cooperate. In the field of theory, there is an impressive attempt by Heinz Hartmann, partly in collaboration with Ernst Kris and Rudolph M. Loewenstein, to construct a comprehensive psychoanalytic theory encompassing not only unconscious mental life and its impact upon conscious phenomena but all mental phenomena. This involves the necessity of a threefold synthesis: of the various stages of psychoanalytic theory; of the clinical, or motivational, theories of psychoanalysis with the physicalistic theories, the metapsychology; and of psychoanalytic theory as a whole with nonanalytic psychology. The studies in question have led to formulations which have much clarified matters, such as, e.g., the distinction between dynamic and genetic propositions, or between apparatus and stimulation, or the concept of the autonomous ego, as well as to concepts which will yet have to be tested, such as, e.g., that of neutralization of aggression in analogy with the neutralization of sexuality (desexualization) previously known (see p. 152f.). In some instances, there is an improvement over the traditional formulations, as, e.g., when the notion of the ego developing out of the id is replaced by a formula according to which both, id and ego, develop out of an undifferentiated matrix. Some hypotheses, finally, appear to be rather difficult to verify, such as, e.g., the proposition that neutralized aggression is used in the defensive process.

Proof of this hypothesis has been sought in the observation that a person in analysis sometimes, though by no means always, experiences an aggressive impulse after accepting a correct interpretation—a reaction which could be understood in the light of this hypothesis as due to aggression previously used in the maintenance of repression and set free when the repression was lifted.

But there are many possible motives for an aggressive response to an interpretation, which can be analyzed in the context. The patient may react to a narcissistic blow implicit in the interpretation. He may feel it as criticism. He may try to forestall criticism that he may feel is forthcoming. He may feel that the interpretation proves the analyst's superior wisdom and may resent this real or supposed fact. Or, on the contrary, he may have expected a great revelation and may feel disappointed and scornful that the mountains had given birth to a mouse. The aggression may be a revenge for the anxiety about being found out which he had felt when the analyst began to speak. There are many more possibilities. It is difficult for me to see how all these possibilities could ever be effectively ruled out.

On the opposite end of the spectrum, much work has gone into therapeutic trial-and-error experimentation. One changes the external arrangement such as the frequency or the length of interviews, divides the analysis over several periods, replaces the recumbent position with a sitting or reclining one, etc., and one mixes at different points various forms of educational influence with the analysis; the number of possible combinations is enormous. The result of these variations has practical interest though, in view of the large number of variables involved, their value lies more in a kind of general stimulation than in any formulation of readily applicable rules.

The so-called "orthodox" analysts have not been overly enthusiastic over therapeutic experimentation of this kind;

for this, the proponents of so-called "liberal" views have castigated them as reactionaries, opposed to innovation.

"Orthodox" analysts feel that the best hope for greater therapeutic effectiveness lies not in more or less random experimentation but in a better understanding of the disease processes. In this expectation they feel backed up by the whole history of human knowledge. The great triumphs of modern medicine and technology were due to increased knowledge of the disease processes and of the working of nature rather than to trial-and-error empiricism. "Orthodox" analysts also believe that this holds true for the neuroses, too, not only in the sense that future patients will profit from the present studies, in which case it could still be argued that the interests of present patients are sacrificed to those of the future if their therapists give priority to prolonged study; they believe that the present patients, here and now, will also profit from a deeper study of their conditions. And they also think that while this is clearly true, to their minds, if the treatment is psychoanalysis, i.e., consists of helping the patient to acquire and to make his own the understanding won by his therapist, it is also often true if the treatment is psychoanalytically oriented psychotherapy, i.e., consists of various forms of influence and manipulations based on such understanding.

It so happens that the therapeutic variations of the "classical" setting usually make it much more difficult to learn more about the patient; whatever their therapeutic merits may be, they are scientifically sterile. The real difference between "orthodox" and "liberal" analysts is therefore not that the former cling to tradition while the latter are open to innovation, but rather that "liberals" seem to assume that all problems are already fundamentally solved, so that the structure of a case can, at least in its outlines,

be understood in a relatively short time, and all that remains is the task of influencing a condition already properly
understood; while the "orthodox" analyst looks upon a new
case as a new enigma that will yield its secrets only very
slowly and hardly ever entirely. In short, the "orthodox"
analyst stands *more in awe of the unconscious*. He is, so to
say, less at ease in Zion . . .

PART II

SURVEY AND DISCUSSION OF
BASIC CONCEPTS

5

Introductory Remarks Concerning
Instinctual Drives

INSTINCTUAL DRIVES AND INSTINCTS; THE TYRANNY OF WORDS

Neuroses, according to Freud, are due to inner conflict between the *Triebe* and the ego. The understanding of psychoanalysis in the English-speaking countries has, I believe, been seriously threatened by the lack of a word in the English language that corresponds to the German *Trieb;* the English word, instinct, that appears in most translations, carries implications which are alien to the idea of *Trieb.*

Triebe are powerful strivings within living organisms which are rooted in their physical nature, like sexuality, hunger, self-preservation. The word may also refer to the shoots of a plant—a meaning related to the same basic idea.

This is also the meaning of the term in psychoanalysis. One may describe *Triebe* in psychoanalysis by saying that actions expressive of a *Trieb* fall in the class of goal-directed behavior, and that within this class they differ from other goal-directed behavior by their close connection with somatic sources;

by their *vis-a-tergo* character, i.e., the fact that a compulsion is felt whenever the action is thwarted; and

by a great persistency (except for a change in the somatic sources, through maturation, decline, illness, or somatic destruction) and the possibility that long-abandoned strivings are revived under conditions of regression.

The English "instinct," on the other hand, suggests an innate as against an acquired character rather than a force pushing from behind. The Oxford Dictionary of current English usage gives three meanings of the term: "innate propensity, especially in lower animals, to certain seemingly rational acts performed without conscious design; innate impulse; intuition, unconscious skill."

Of these three meanings, the latter two (innate impulse; intuition, unconscious skill) are those already distinguished by Lord Herbert of Cherbury (1625); the first ("innate propensity . . . to certain seemingly rational acts performed without conscious design") came into the foreground in the nineteenth century, particularly through Darwin, and has probably become the dominant meaning of the term; hence it is mentioned first in the Dictionary. Only the second meaning comes anywhere near the psychoanalytic concept of *Trieb*, though even it does not exactly correspond to it because "innate impulse" does not necessarily imply the imperative, majestic, power of *Trieb* nor its *vis-a-tergo* character. But while the Oxford Dictionary does at least include something roughly similar to *Trieb* among the possible meanings of "instinct," the Webster Collegiate Dictionary gives only the following definitions none of which comes near the meaning of *Trieb*: "2. A natural aptitude or knack; as, an *instinct* for order—3a. A tendency to actions which lead to the attainment of some goal natural to the species; natural and unreasoning prompting to action; as, the web-building instinct of spiders. b. The native or hereditary factor in behavior; as, habit is based upon *instinct*."

The English "instinct" carries the implication of an inherited, unlearned behavior and usually also that of biological usefulness for the species—like the nest building of birds or the avian migrations to warmer climates—the kind of thing that made people speak of the unconscious wisdom of nature.[1] It carries an implication of preformed (inherited) order while *Trieb* suggests a power that defies organization.[2] It is difficult to discount completely such deep-rooted implications. The word in the English language that comes closest to *Trieb* is, perhaps, "oestrus," in one of its meanings. But it is an esoteric word and does not have the familiar, casual, ring that *Trieb* has for a German ear. I have been following the prevailing American usage in rendering *Trieb* as "instinctual drive," or sometimes "drive" for short, but this is not ideal and one must always remember that it is *Trieb* that is meant, whatever the translation, and beware lest undertones of the English word may influence our thought.

Misunderstandings on this score occur constantly. One example may show the type. In a Symposium on the Libido Theory, held at an annual meeting of the American Psychoanalytic Association (see Brenner, 1955), a noted student of animal behavior rose to attack the libido theory as "an incorrect biological conceptualization." To prove his point, he reported experiments about so-called instinctive behavior

---

[1] See, e.g., Lorenz (1952, p. 126): ". . . . that unconscious omniscience which we call nature."

[2] It may not be without cultural significance that the English language has no proper word for *Trieb*, while German lacks a term for "integration."

in mammals and, in particular, a study which showed that if the female rat had never been allowed to lick its anus, it will not mother its young but eat them. He was convinced that these observations cut the ground from under the libido theory, and that psychoanalysts lacked the proper instruction about the facts.

The experiments suggest that even as fundamental an instinct—in the sense of an "innate propensity . . . to certain seemingly rational acts without conscious design"—as maternal behavior subsequent to delivery is not completely rigid but subject to previous environmental influences; they therefore militate against the traditional theory of instincts in animals and are certainly of great interest in this connection. But they have no bearing on the psychoanalytic libido theory, i.e., on the proposition that neurotic and psychotic disorders should be described "in terms of the economics of the libido" (Freud, 1905b, p. 218)—on a theory which has to do with the range of the sexual, not with its congenital or environmental roots.

Our critic presumably believed that it was the thesis or the presupposition of the libido theory that sexuality, its forms and its development, are manifestations of rigid, congenital, patterns which are not subject to influence by experience. Actually, psychoanalytic theory, far from making such assumptions, has always held that sexual drives, as different from self-preservative ones, have a considerable degree of *plasticity*, an assumption which is an integral part of the psychoanalytic theory of the neuroses.

It is possible that the concept of instinct, in the sense of inherited, unchangeable, patterns of behavior, will be discarded by biologists and students of animal behavior. This possibility is one more argument against the use of the term, instinct, in psychoanalysis; for if it should come to pass, psychoanalysts speaking of instincts will be widely regarded as harboring obsolete notions, as they were regarded by the discussant in the reported episode. Of course, the psychoanalyst can reply that he uses the term in a different sense to which the objections to the instinct concept in biology do not apply; but in view of the fact that hostility against psychoanalysis is widespread while the ability to distinguish between word and thing is not, such protests will probably not help him any more than it helped Cinna the poet to protest to a Roman mob that he was Cinna the poet, not Cinna the conspirator: "It is no matter, his name is Cinna."[3]

"TRIEB" AND "INSTINKT"

Freud referred only very rarely to instincts in the sense in which the English word is commonly used and which would in German be called "*Instinkte*." There is no direct relation between *Trieb* and *Instinkt*. One such reference of Freud's to *Instinkt* is this: "If inherited mental formations exist in the human being—something analogous to instinct [*Instinkt*] in animals . . ." (1915b, p. 195). In another passage, Freud speaks of the "far-reaching *instinctive* knowledge of the animals" and continues, "if human beings too possessed an instinctive endowment such as this . . ." (1918, p. 120). In these instances, the German words used by Freud are *Instinkt, instinktiv,* not *Trieb, triebhaft,* and then, the English words, instinct, instinctive, convey the right meaning.

The obvious necessity to keep the concept of *Trieb* free from implications and fringe meanings which belong to the Darwinian instinct does not mean that it is not legitimate

[3] Shakespeare, *Julius Caesar*, Act IV, Scene III.

to ask whether there is any relation, genetic or otherwise, between the instincts of the student of animal behavior and what the German language calls *Triebe*. Such relations may well exist. Darwinian instincts—or whatever inherited dispositions may take their place as result of the current biological criticism—seem to combine, at least under species-typical conditions, automatic actualization and strength with usefulness for the survival of the individual or the species. Man is probably poorer in this respect; it is as though in him these behavior structures were split into halves, *one* of which inherited the *strength*, the *other* the *usefulness* of the animal instincts. Man has instinctual drives (*Triebe*) of great compelling strength, but they are not necessarily useful for individual or species preservation and will often bring either in jeopardy; and he is equipped with great intelligence that can deal not only with typical challenges in a wholesale fashion but with any problem in an individualized, appropriate, fashion but which is no longer equipped with automatic executive strength. Phylogenetically, *instinctual drives and intelligence* may be the *differentiation products of animal instincts*.

DEFINITION OF INSTINCTUAL DRIVES

Instinctual drives, in psychoanalysis, are defined by Freud as follows:

By an 'instinct' [*Trieb*] is provisionally to be understood the psychical representative of an endosomatic, continually flowing source of stimulation, as contrasted with a 'stimulus', which is set up by *single* excitations coming from *without*. The concept of instinct is thus one of those lying on the frontier between the mental and the physical [1905b, p. 168].

[And again, he defined it in similar words as] a concept on the frontier between the mental and the somatic, as the psychical representative of the stimuli originating from within the organism and reaching the mind, as a measure of the demand made upon the mind of work [*Mass der Arbeitsanforderung*] in consequence of its connection with the body [1915a, p. 121f.].

This definition fits well enough the sexual and self-preservative drives, i.e., the two classes of instinctual drives which Freud distinguished in the early version of his theory, guided by the distinction of hunger and love, and by the clues which the study of the neurotic conflict provided. Later Freud substituted for it the classification of erotic and destructive drives in which he saw, in a further step of psychobiological speculation, manifestations of life and death instincts. The latter would be ultimate characteristics of living matter, not reduceable psychologically to simpler elements.

Does the definition of instinctual drives which was formulated at an early stage of psychoanalytic theorizing and which fitted the self-preservative and sexual drives well enough apply to erotic and destructive drives, and the life and death instincts, of a later stage of the theory, too? Erotic and destructive drives are psychological concepts derived from clinical observations; life and death instincts are biological concepts, one further step removed from psychological observation. Erotic and destructive drives seem to fall within the scope of the above-quoted definition. But the definition does not seem to apply any more to the assumed life and death instincts; they are no longer a "psychic representation of an endosomatic . . . stimulation," nor a "concept on the frontier between the mental and the somatic"; they are biological forces or trends as the comparison with metabolism and catabolism indicates.

6

The Sexual Drive

Among instinctual drives, the sexual drives have been studied most, because of their role in the psychoneuroses. The term, sexual, is used in a broader sense than had been customary, encompassing all sensual desires. It would probably be difficult to define sexuality in such a way that the definition includes everything that is so called in scientific or popular speech (including slang)—copulative behavior, perversions, courtship behavior—and still keep the concept much narrower than Freud's. The justification for Freud's insistence on treating all the phenomena covered by his broader concept together and on calling them *a potiori* sexual lies in their genetic relationship. One interferes with the genital masturbation of a child—a sexual manifestation in the common sense of the term—and the child may take up nail biting, nose picking, or hair curling. Heterosexual desires in the ordinary sense of the term may decrease in later age and we may see a marked increase of interest in bowel function and other features classified by psychoanalysis as anal—a fact most simply described as a regression of the libido. Helene Deutsch (1925) has pointed

104

out that neurotic illness of women breaking out some years
before the onset of the menopause is usually hysterical
(i.e., due to the struggle against sexual temptations in the
common, genital, sense of the word), while later menopausal and postmenopausal illnesses are usually of the depressive and paranoid type, having partly to do with oral
or anal strivings; these facts are most simply described as
manifestations of, or reactions to, a premenopausal increase
in the demands of genital sexuality, on the one hand, and a
menopausal and postmenopausal regression to pregenital
stages, on the other. These are but a few examples of the
countless interrelations between what is called sexual in
ordinary language and phenomena not ordinarily so called
but included in Freud's concept of sexuality.

Sexuality, in the Freudian sense, does not begin in
puberty, after an asexual childhood, nor does it end with
the end of genital discharge; it starts at birth or nearly so,
and ends with death. Sexuality penetrates most of our
activities which are to a large extent, though by no means
only, satisfactions of sexual drives, at one or more removes
from the original goal (displacement, sublimation). When
the demands of sexuality are opposed but neither conquered
nor controlled, they may give rise to neurotic symptoms.
"The sexual life of the persons in question [sc. neurotics]
is expressed . . . in these [sc. neurotic] symptoms" (Freud,
1905b, p. 163).

GENERAL CHARACTERISTICS

Sexual drives can be described in terms of goals, objects,
and (somatic) sources. They have a considerable degree of
plasticity; under the influence of stimulation or the lack
of it, of satisfaction or frustration, or promise and intimida-

tion, sexual drives are subject to change in object, goal, and intensity.

We are far from having a complete map of these relationships. On the whole, stimulation or the lack of it seem to influence, above all, intensity. Stimulation may awaken a drive before its appointed time in the maturational scheme and condition the individual to certain specifications as regards object and goal; the lack of stimulation may long postpone the appearance of a drive. Satisfaction has a more complicated influence on intensity, making it disappear for the moment while intensifying it in its periodical recurrence, i.e., appeasing for the moment and appetizing in the long view. There is also often a long-term effect of diminution when satisfactions often repeated grow stale and a desire for a somewhat different stimulation or form of satisfaction develops.

Persistent frustration often leads to the abandonment, permanent or temporary, of a desire, subject, however, to existing fixations. The latter may come about through previous conditioning to satisfactions as well as through the frustration of the "needs" of a particular age such as maternal love or oral gratifications in childhood, i.e., through too much or too little.

If an object or goal is abandoned under the influence of frustration, one usually turns to other objects or goals. If they are not available, or not immediately available, the result is often regression, i.e., the return to former goals and objects that had already been abandoned: the six-year-old that had been denied a wish may put his finger in his mouth again, and the prisoner whose sexual life had been normal prior to his arrest may with time indulge in pre-genital fantasies or practices. Sometimes, for unknown reasons, the result may be progression, i.e., a premature activation of a later developmental stage (Greenacre, 1952).

The result of intimidation in childhood is usually the flight of the ego from the drive, i.e., repression or another defense mechanism (see p. 179ff.).

An important special case of change of goal in a sexual drive is *desexualization*. A drive that was originally a fully psychosexual phenomenon with bodily and mental manifestations, loses its physical aspects and becomes an exclusively psychic phenomenon. The hierarchy of the manifestations of Eros, in Plato's Symposium, from the physical to the spiritual, is an example of desexualization.

A special case of reaction to stimulation which is particularly important for social relations is what in want of a better term might be called *complementarization*: behavior expressive of a drive tends to elicit in the object the complementary drive, a mirror image. Sadism, e.g., calls forth masochistic urges in the object and *vice versa*. The assumption of leadership by a person will increase in others the inclination to subordinate themselves, and, conversely, subordination will encourage the assumption of mastery in the object. The phenomena of relative sexuality (Max Hartmann) are based on the encouragement of complementary attitudes in the object.[1]

Phenomena of complementarization rarely appear in pure culture, as it were; usually they are mixed with other reactions due, e.g., to anxiety or to moral sentiments, and these other reactions may go in different directions and

---

[1] Anna Freud once pointed out (oral communication) that we rarely meet in analysis with the pure manifestations of a *Trieb*—most of what we encounter being anxieties, defenses, conflicts, and compromises—but that on the rare occasions in which an unopposed *Trieb*, pure and simple, manifests itself, the impression upon other people is that of something imperative, majestic, that does not tolerate contradiction, and people are "instinctively" inclined to give away . . .

thereby cover up the complementary reaction, particularly if the person that provided the stimulus had "gone too far." Then, e.g., brutality and oppression may stimulate hatred and rebellion rather than meekness and obedience.[2]

Complementarization is the basis for a trend in human affairs that has been a source of despair or of cynicism since time immemorial—the common experience that the ruthless often prosper and that if they come to fall, they appear to be ruined not by their sins but by their mistakes; and that the peaceful and meek are often abused and exploited. Apparently, drives of which ruthlessness is an expression encourage in many people the corresponding attitudes of submissiveness, and as long as the top dogs do not overplay their hands, their road is easy and successful, while meekness turns even ordinarily well-intentioned persons into abusers. People, said Woodrow Wilson, will endure their tyrants for years, but they will tear their deliverers to pieces if a millennium is not created immediately.

SEXUAL DEVELOPMENT

As far as objects are concerned, the development of the libido is seen as starting from an objectless autoerotic stage and to develop from here to narcissism (with oneself as object) and then to object libido. The final stage will be a mixture of narcissism and object libido in individually varying proportions. Everybody returns partially to narcissism in sleep. There are regressions to narcissism, in individually varying degrees, under conditions of frustration or danger.

[2] The totalitarian experience seems to show that if oppression goes even farther and stops short of nothing, the reaction may again be subordination, on account of mechanisms more complicated than mere complementarization (Waelder, 1951, 1960).

With regard to goals, the development of the libido in the male is seen to follow approximately this scheme: the oral, anal, and phallic stages in earlier childhood, culminating in the oedipus complex; a latency period (the earlier school years); a brief prepubertal stage, showing a revival of pregenital (oral and anal) strivings; puberty, starting with a phallic revival and possibly, though not necessarily, moving toward a so-called postambivalent (i.e., non-sadistic) genital stage; adulthood, with a slight diminution in the intensity of genital drives and a continuing trend toward postambivalent genitality; a decline, sometimes slow and sometimes sudden, of genital drives, which may happen at any time between early middle age and late old age.

The development of female sexuality is assumed to proceed roughly in these stages: pregenital stages (oral and anal) as in boys; a phallic stage, of short or long duration, characterized by penis envy, emulation of the male and masculine fantasies and attitudes; a genital stage manifesting feminine behavior and including the feminine oedipus complex, sometime between the later preschool age and the early school years; a latency period, somewhat shorter than in boys because, as a rule, entered into later; puberty consisting of an earlier stage which revives the phallic phase (the tomboy age) and a later, feminine, stage in which the feminine position is, however, still honeycombed with phallic remnants and therefore rarely complete; adulthood, continuing the development toward femininity, with pregnancy, delivery, and child rearing normally furthering it and heterosexual attitudes increasing toward a maximum at about the end of young adulthood; sometimes, though not always, an intensification of heterosexual desires in the years preceding the menopause, producing occasionally something like a second adolescence;

after the menopause, a decline of genital urges which may range from a slight diminution to a complete stoppage, and a renascence of pregenital urges.

Female sexual development is thus more complicated than masculine development. The latter deviates from a straight line only through the biphasic onset of sexuality, i.e., through the interruption of latency and the at least partial change of direction, which is necessary both at the onset of latency and at the onset of puberty. Female sexuality, in addition to this deviation from the straight line of development common to both sexes, is further complicated by an imprint of bisexuality deeper than in the male, i.e., by the fact that woman does not develop straight toward femininity but makes a detour through masculine attitudes, in childhood and often in puberty, too; and by the probably closely related fact that only the outside part of the genitals—part of which corresponds to the male organ—is exposed to stimulation, accidental or voluntary, in childhood or youth, while the organ of adult feminine sexuality, the vagina, is closed and hidden and has to take its place in adulthood without previous preparation. The arrival at a feminine sexual attitude is therefore jeopardized not only by the zig-zag of the biphasic onset but also by the detour over masculine attitudes and the required transfer of excitation from the external genitalia, particularly the clitoris, to the vagina.

There is one further point in which the feminine sex appears as the victim of discrimination. The caricature of male sexuality is sadism, that of female sexuality is masochism; the former is much more likely to be ego-syntonic, acceptable to the ego, than the latter; and even if it is not, it is unlikely to arouse as much anxiety as the latter. Masochism is a frequent accompaniment of femininity, and

the fear of masochism often interferes with the assumption
of feminine attitudes: the woman cannot give herself because she notices with terror the temptation of giving herself up completely and to fall, so to say, into infinite space.

Because of all these factors frigidity, total or partial, in
women is much more common than impotence in men.

This is a most cursory picture and there are wide variations. Here is an auspicious area of research, not only for
psychoanalytic studies but also for direct observations.
We have only a very general idea of the time span of these
stages, of the variations in their intensity, and of the transition from one stage to another.

There is also the problem of culture dependence and
culture invariance: how much of the described typical development is characteristic of a particular culture only from
which the objects of observation happened to come, and
how much can be found in any culture?

As far as the fragmentary data at the present time permit, one might conjecture that the oral and phallic stages
have a large culture-invariant core, while the anal stage
may be to a large extent variable with the time and procedure of bowel training. Latency is perhaps to a great
degree a cultural phenomenon (Freud, 1905b, p. 177),
although there is reason to believe that a measure of delay
of sexual maturation in man as compared with other
mammals is common to all men and may have something
to do with man's ability to produce civilization (Freud,
1905b, p. 234; Levy-Suhl, 1933; see also p. 127f. below).

As far as puberty is concerned, there is a great deal of
evidence which indicates a considerable and significant
difference between American and European (or Canadian)
puberty. The type of puberty, described in Anna Freud's
early work (1936, Chapters XI/XII), in which balance

is precariously upheld by emergency measures in the face of great inner danger, is common in Europe but rare in the United States, and my experience suggests that when it occurs here we had better watch out for signs of schizophrenia. It seems likely that this difference is due to the difference in external conditions: there the adolescent is, or at least was, surrounded by a wall of obstacles, with little or no outlet other than masturbation or occasional sexual contact with prostitutes or near-prostitutes, both guilt-laden and neither fully satisfactory, while here society, through institutionalized dating, not only permits but actively encourages, facilitates, and sanctions, within broad limits, the sexual activities of adolescents, with social disapproval attached to nonparticipation. Thus, the difference between the two kinds of puberty appears to be of cultural origin.

Generations of anthropologists have refuted Freud's alleged theory of the universal validity of the oedipus complex[3] according to which the sexual love for the parent of the opposite sex and jealousy of, and rivalry with, the parent of the same sex, are strong and permanent influences in all peoples' lives, at all times. The theory so pictured is then attacked by citing examples of behavior reported of primitive tribes which seem to be at variance with the pattern at one point or another. Such an example is, e.g., the habitual sharing of one wife by several brothers without apparent jealousy, which is reported of a South Indian tribe (J. M. Smith, 1958, p. 291f.).[4]

[3] Much criticism of Freud is based on the assumption that what Freud did not expressly say, he did not know or did not acknowledge. Actually, Freud, like any other author with the possible exception of logicians and lawyers, has often failed to mention certain points, or to make qualifications, not because he was not familiar with them but because he either took them for granted or they did not seem relevant in the context of the argument.

[4] This author concludes: "Thus the Oedipus Complex, believed by Freud

These critics need not have recourse to reports from remote tribes, reports which usually rest on the authority of
a few observers only. Variations from the pattern which is
typical in our climate can be found in any reasonably sized
city block in any major American city. Some variations were
mentioned by Freud, as e.g., the "negative oedipus complex,"
i.e., the attachment of the child to the parent of the same sex
and rivalry for his affections with the parent of the opposite
sex (Freud, 1926a). All that the theory of the oedipus
complex claims to be universally valid is the proposition
that at the height of childhood sexuality—the phallic period
—the boy's inborn phallic desires and his inborn or acquired
aggressive or competitive strivings—are attached to the
adults who rear the child, or to fantasied objects with which
he may fill in the vacancies. The same applies to the girl's
oedipus complex, which occurs somewhat later.

The oedipal period may come earlier or later, with sensations stronger or weaker, and may last long or end soon;
and the end, the dissolution of the oedipus complex, may
be sudden or long drawn out. There may be a change of
objects within the oedipal phase, as, e.g., from a normal to
a negative oedipus complex, or a fluctuation between the
two. There may be a regression to preoedipal stages while
the oedipus complex was still at its budding prime. The
later consequences, too, may show great variety. In short,
there is a variety of forms, not only in different cultures but
in our own diversified culture, and, indeed, in any fair-sized
population sample. If a child grows up in a setting in which
several men habitually share in the sexual favors of the
mother—a situation which occurs in our culture too, albeit

---

to be an unchangeable feature of human nature, seems to depend on the
existence of feelings aroused only in a society with a particular type of
family."

very rarely—his attitude in matters of sharing and competition will be different from that of a child growing up in a monogamous family.

But an oedipus complex in the generalized sense, i.e., a kind of premature rehearsal of the future sexual role with parents or parent substitutes as objects, and with details varying with the child's environment, is probably universal.

Out of the multitude of problems about the sexual drive, I should like to touch upon those that have to do with the difference in sex.

PHALLUS WORSHIP

The early genital stage is called the phallic stage because the little boy appears to be dominated, or obsessed, by phallic impulses. The penis is now the seat of strivings and pleasant sensations; masturbatory activities are enjoined, and the fantasy life indulges in penetration and shooting. There are competitive urinary games ("putting out the church fire"). The penis is the proudest possession, narcissism is mostly concentrated on it. Any threat of loss or damage causes severest anxiety, any unfavorable comparison with peers severest shame, and intense desires to restore equilibrium. Phallic attitudes remain throughout life.

Phallic object relations—penetration, with its possessive and sadistic implications—must be distinguished from the "postambivalent" attitudes (Abraham) which may later take their place, by their sadistic and their narcissistic character. The narcissistic character of phallic sexuality is particularly apparent in the reaction to castration threat when the function of the organ is surrendered to ensure its continued possession. Postambivalent attitudes are free of sadism, the penis is no longer conceived as a weapon but as a messenger of love, and the narcissistic elements of possession and display are less important than the achievement of sexual union.

The worship of phallic prowess and the contempt for phallic weakness or emasculation, running the gamut from the triumphant Petruccio in the *Taming of the Shrew* to the cruelly ridiculed Falstaff in the *Merry Wives of Windsor* —not to mention more barbaric manifestations—and the satisfactions, frustrations, ambitions, and anxieties of men in this respect contribute much to the color and the noise of life. To trace all their social manifestations could fill a sizeable volume. One example may suffice to characterize the class: the current attitude to the automobile. The amount of the national income spent in this country on automobiles and their maintenance is out of proportion if viewed merely as expenditure for transportation. Size and ornateness of cars often interfere with, rather than contribute to, their effectiveness as carriers; their luxuriousness in many cases far exceeds the living standards of their owners in other respects. Their fuel consumption is a serious drain on limited natural resources and, in particular, a source of dependence on foreign conditions, hence a factor of national weakness. All this suggests that automobiles are not merely treated as tools of transportation. They are objects of display, like the fan of the peacock. Students of traffic safety have reported that the average person has a feeling of personal safety behind the wheel— a feeling which is incomprehensible on the basis of the reality of three or four tons of metal moving at considerable speed on crowded highways, but which becomes easily understandable as a reaction to the symbolic meaning of the car as a token and display of phallic strength.

But not only the life of the boy or man is under the

sign of the phallus; girls are under the same spell. Psychoanalytic reconstructions and, later, direct observations in
childhood have led to the conclusion, mentioned before,
that the sexual development of the little girl does not go
on a straight path from pregenital to the genital stage, culminating in the oedipus complex as a kind of early rehearsal of her later sexual role, but that little girls reach
their oedipus complex, i.e., their female attitude toward
the father, only after a long detour in which the girl's
development is parallel rather than complementary to
the boy's, in which the girl wants to be a boy and tries herself in that role as best she can. This constitutes the stage
of "penis envy." It is only through biologically unavoidable failure of these attempts that the masculine strivings
are, in the average case, given up and the child turns toward feminine attitudes, substituting the interest in, and
attachment to, the male phallus-bearer for the unrealizable aspiration of possessing the phallus herself.

There is no doubt about the ubiquity of penis envy and
of frustraneous movements toward masculine development
in little girls, particularly around the third and fourth year.
It has occasionally been suggested that there is no difference in the social behavior of the sexes in early childhood, before the end of the period of the female castration complex. This is an exaggerated notion and not ten-
able; significant differences in activity and aggressiveness,
on the average, exist from the beginning. But on this
early, inborn, differentiation, there is superimposed a
masculine urge which becomes apparent with the onset of
the phallic phase and has a great, though individually varying, influence on the development of the feminine sexual
function and on the woman's social and intellectual life.
Individual variations as regards duration of the phallic

period in childhood, the violence of its manifestations, or its lasting consequences are considerable, but the importance of masculine trends in women is never negligible.

This aspect of Freudian theory has encountered fierce opposition, particularly from women authors. The proposition that women should generally desire to be men—or have so desired at a junction in their development—was said to be a reflection of male arrogance, or at least of the male inability to understand women. Karen Horney thought at one point that female development is in all stages complementary to the male, so that the two compare like the photographic positive and negative. According to this scheme, the little girl moves toward a female oedipus complex of attachment to the father and jealousy of the mother when the boy develops his masculine version. Horney did not deny the phenomena of penis envy, but she saw in them a regression from an already attained feminine, oedipal, position, and she suggested that envy of the possibility to give birth to a child was an exact parallel to penis envy in the boy's development. She seemed to overlook, or not to give sufficient weight to, the fact that envy of the female ability to bring a child into the world, though existing, is far from being a universal phenomenon among men, as is penis envy among women. Also, there is no parallel between the two; the girl has reason to envy the little boy, her contemporary, his possession because he has it here and now and can use it for quite amazing tricks, such as urinating in erect position, but the little boy has no reason to envy the little girl an ability of giving birth to a baby which she does not now have. The fact that the little girl may give birth to a baby in the distant future is too far beyond the horizon of a child to have much of a discount value at present and therefore to become an object of envy.

"Phallus worship," or something very much like it, seems to be widespread in subhuman nature, too. Polygamy of the dominant males, and enforced celibacy of the weaker males, is reported of many species, e.g., of baboons (Zuckerman, 1932). A somewhat extreme case is reported by J. W. Scott (1942): in a large flock of sage grouse 74 per cent of all matings were performed by about 1 per cent of the cocks—the so-called master cocks—and a further 13 per cent by about 2 per cent of the cocks; that left only 13 per cent of the matings to 97 per cent of the males who were thereby destined to practical celibacy. The great majority of the males has thus been functionally castrated, as it were, by a small number of males with the greatest sexual prowess. Human analogies are easily on hand; monogamy, by limiting at least the number of legal mates of the stronger males—stronger in a physical or in a socio-economic sense—works as a protection of the weaker ones, by giving every male a chance to find a mate.

There are cases reported in the literature of male animals losing male characteristics in the presence of an aggressive, dominant, male; e.g., of a male dove which abandoned its display and showed feminine reactions though it was in a separate cage and no physical contact with the aggressive animal took place (Craig, 1909), or of an Asiatic white pelican who lost the nuptial knob on its bill (Steinbacher, 1938).[5]

Although there seems to be no simple relationship between sex and the social order that is valid for all species, it is reported of many that the weaker animal presents to the dominant one, i.e., assumes the feminine position, to

[5] One is reminded of the fairly common symptom of men who cannot urinate in the presence of other, supposedly stronger, men.

avert attack, e.g., to get away with taking a morsel of food. Maslow and Franzbaum (1936) reported that among macaques the dominant animal assumes the masculine position in copulation regardless of sex.

Vernacular expressions in many languages show that submission to an alien will is regularly seen as assumption of the feminine role. This idea is expressed, e.g., by King Kreon in Sophocles' drama when he deals stubbornly with the defiant Antigone:

> Now if she can thus flout authority
> Unpunished, I am woman, she the man.

R. B. Onians suggests in his extensive linguistic study of the origin of European thought (1951, p. 472ff.)[6] that "liberty" and "libido" come from the same root, "lib," which appears in the Latin *libare,* or the Greek λείβειν and is preserved in the English "libation." Its meaning is "to pour liquids" and it originally carries the implication of the outpouring of semen, hence of sexual desire (Greek λίπτεσθαι = to desire); the German *lieben* and the English *love* are believed to be related to the same root. "Liberty" stems from it because free, in fundamental thinking, is the potent, procreative, male. Onians considers it possible that the name of the Roman fertility god, *Liber,* may come from this root, too, and he sees similar linguistic relationships between potency and freedom in Northern European languages (Anglo-Saxon *freó* = having desire, joy; *freón* = to love, friend; German *Freier* = suitor; *Frig,* the goddess of sexual desire and fertility; and "freedom").

Relations between freedom and manhood and between unfreedom and castration or womanhood abound. Long

---

[6] I am, of course, not competent to judge the validity of any of these etymological connections. But I can say that they would fit very well with the psychological connections observed by psychoanalysis.

hair was the privilege of the free man among the ancient Germans. It was always felt to be one of the most characteristic features of slavery that the slave lost the right of decision in sexual matters and had to serve the will of his master. Lewdness, said Seneca, is a crime for free men but a necessity for slaves. The basis for this association of manhood with freedom and womanhood with unfreedom is presumably the fact that woman can be forced to cohabitation against her will but not man,[7] and it is man who can so force her. The consciousness of this situation becomes blurred under civilized conditions which give the female effective protection so that she does not face the possibility of rape unless under exceptional circumstances, when stripped of this legal or cultural protection; the fundamental possibilities continue in dreams and fantasies, in anxieties and neurotic symptoms, or are playfully used in flirtation. But in times in which woman was not effectively protected by taboos or laws, the ever-present possibility must have colored all relations between the sexes.

Most, if not all, human societies have been dominated by men. Until fairly recently, this fact was accepted as part of the natural order of things, ordained by God, perhaps as punishment for the sin of the first woman, or inherent in the physical and mental weakness of the feminine sex. More recently, people were no longer willing to take these things for granted and questioned the validity of time-honored institutions. Since then, various theories have been advanced to explain these conditions, some in biological, others in environmental terms. One Victorian author, e.g.,

[7] There is a characteristic exception to this which only illustrates the point; man can be forced, too, not by a woman but homosexually by another male who may forcibly enter one of the orifices of the body, thus putting the object into the feminine position.

spoke of the "physiological feeble-mindedness" of women. But the more "advanced" opinion rejected the idea of a biological inferiority of women and sought to explain male dominance in terms of "culture"—which is no explanation at all as long as one does not know what makes culture the way it is. Yet, men must all the time have known it in their bones what the cause of male dominance is: the relative physical weakness of women, their frequent physical incapacitation due to their childbearing functions, and, above all, the *sexual helplessness* of women, i.e., the fact that woman is without adequate defense against a man's determination to use her as a sexual object. Nature has thus left the choice of the object to man and denied it to woman. This need not make for any dominance as long as there is no discrimination between partners, hence no desire to exercise any choice; but once there is discrimination, it makes for male superiority and for woman's need of male protection. Equality—or, *a fortiori*, a superior position—of women is therefore, for the great majority of womanhood, possible only under certain cultural conditions, i.e., if physical strength has become less important than other qualities and if law and custom provide adequate protections against sexual attack. Whenever contemporary men live under conditions in which the struggle for survival is fierce and physical strength is the most important asset, male dominance has full sway again and the survival chances of women often depend on their ability to secure for themselves physically strong and aggressive men as husbands or lovers.[8]

Perhaps we can now understand the extraordinarily high estimation of the penis by children of both sexes.

---

[8] For such conditions in Arctic labor camps, see, e.g., Weissberg-Cybulski (1951, p. 699f.).

There is, first of all, the fact that the male genitals can be seen and touched while the female reproductive organs are hidden to view and that it takes imagination and abstract thought to understand and appreciate their function; and the child's capacity for abstract reasoning and appreciation of its results is still very limited. More specifically, there is the fact that children of both sexes, in any case from the phallic stage on, have experienced genital sensations, and they take it for granted, in their unsophisticated thinking, that pleasure must be a linear function of size; if there was such pleasure on the clitoris, the little girl surmises, how much more must there be in something that much bigger? Finally, and most important, there is the "instinctive" knowledge that the *phallus* is the *master of the sexual act*, that man can force the female to his will. Phallus worship, by the female, will of course facilitate consummation and one might be tempted to speculate, teleologically, whether it could not be seen as one of the wholesale institutions which secure the propagation of life.

SUBLIMATION

This subject could be treated in a chapter of instinctual drives as well as in one on the ego; it is a kind of condominium between the id and the ego.

Few psychoanalytic terms have become as popular as has "sublimation." Friends of psychoanalysis, embarrassed by the emphasis which psychoanalysis put on sexuality, have held on to sublimation—as they have to the superego and to the ego—to show to the world that psychoanalysis does recognize the existence of higher things in human life. Opponents of psychoanalysis, on the other hand, have protested against a theory which, by "deriving" these higher activities from instinctual ones, seemed to offend their dignity and, perhaps, to move in the circular reasoning of evolutionistic philosophy (see p. 59ff.). Thus, a recent critic states: "As to the Freudian interpretation of intellectual passions as a sublimation of appetitive drives, it leaves unaccounted for everything that distinguishes science and art from the instinct of which these are supposed to be sublimates. 'Sublimation' is a circumlocution which relies for its meaning entirely on a previous understanding of the things which it is supposed to explain" (Polanyi, 1958, p. 309).

One must, of course, beware of the fallacy of thinking that a thing is explained if one knows its origin—that the egg explains the chicken. But in presenting the idea of sublimation, Freud had steered clear of this fallacy. For one, he had always insisted on the distinction between id and ego, or between sexual and nonsexual energy: "We distinguish [the] libido in respect of its special origin from the energy which must be supposed to underlie mental processes in general" (1905b, addition 1915, p. 217). And he introduced sublimation in these words:

> We know of a far more expedient process of development [i.e., more expedient than repression] called *"sublimation,"* in which the energy of the infantile wishful impulses is not cut off but remains ready for use—the unserviceable aim of the various impulses being replaced by one that is higher, and perhaps no longer sexual. It happens to be precisely the components of the *sexual* instinct that are specially marked by a capacity of this kind of sublimation, for exchanging their sexual aim for another one which is comparatively remote and socially valuable. It is probable that we owe our highest cultural successes to the contributions of energy made in this way to our mental functions [1910a, p. 53f.].

This is quite unambiguous language; the expression, "contribution of energy . . . made to our mental functions" should leave no doubt that Freud did not look upon mental functions as created by this process.

Freud made this point on several occasions as, e.g., when he said:

A portion of them [i.e., the sexual instincts] remains associated with the ego-instincts throughout life and furnishes them with libidinal components, which in normal functioning easily escape notice and are revealed clearly only by the onset of illness. They are distinguished by possessing the capacity to act vicariously for one another to a wide extent and by being able to change their objects readily. In consequence of the latter properties they are capable of functions which are far removed from their original purposive actions—capable, that is, of "sublimation" [Freud, 1915a, p. 126].

Or, we may remember Freud's earlier quoted words about artistic talent and the functions and limits of a psychoanalytic study of literary works: "Investigations such as these are not intended to explain the genius of the poet but they show what motifs have stirred it up and what topic has been imposed on it by fate" (1933). Similarly, sublimation is not intended to explain the existence of "higher" activities but rather some of the driving force behind them.

The idea of sublimation remained in Freud's mind as general, on the whole, as the quoted passage from his early lectures indicates. In one of the previously mentioned small scientific meetings in the late 1920's a systematic paper on sublimation was presented. In his discussion, Freud took the view that "sublimation was not a well-defined psychic mechanism like repression or reaction formation[9] but rather a loose characterization of various processes that lead to socially more valuable activities. He also mentioned two things that had stimulated him to the idea of sublimation. One was the story that the famous nineteenth-century surgeon Dieffenbach was, as a boy, the terror of his town because he was wont to cut off the tails of unattended dogs. Next, Freud was impressed by a set of three cartoons in a then popular magazine (*Meggendorfer Blätter*). In the first picture one could see a little peasant girl marching in front of a flock of geese and somewhere in the background an elderly gentleman making an entry in his notebook—as though he had taken pleasure in the little girl and planned to do something for her. The consequences of his intervention could be seen in the second cartoon; the little girl was now a student in a boarding school, dressed in the uniform of the institution and marching among her peers while a middle-aged spinster led the whole class, in a setting which in outward appearance was not unlike the setting in the first cartoon. In the third and last one, the story had been fully consummated; the little girl, now herself an elderly spinster, was a teacher in such an institution and marched at the head of a class of girl students in a picture which but for the difference in the subjects fully matched the first one.

This may indicate the slightly ironical flavor in the idea of sublimation which seems to have escaped both friendly and antagonistic critics. The implication for Freud was not only how much things had changed but also how much

[9] This differed from his position taken on another occasion (1915a, p. 126) when sublimation was mentioned among the vicissitudes of the instincts.

they had in essence remained the same.[10] *Plus que ça change ça remène la même chose.*

Among the observations that support the sublimation theory there are, first, many data about displacement. If a child likes to smear his feces and the environment puts a stop to it, he will probably smear with his food, or *vice versa.* Neither of these changes is sublimation as neither has any social value; they are almost equally obnoxious. But if the environment interferes both with the smearing of feces and the smearing of food and offers the child a set of paints and sheets of paper, he may take the suggestion up and cover the surface with paint. This, of course, has as yet nothing to do with art; it is still smearing. Artistic quality does not come into play unless there is a sense of form. While there is nothing in the setup to create such a sense, the use of durable paints and durable surfaces provides a better opportunity to bring out whatever sense of form potentially exists. Hartmann's distinction between apparatus and stimulation can here be usefully applied; talents belong to the equipment of the apparatus, the urge to smear provides the stimulation. Enthusiasm cannot create talent where there is none, but it can activate whatever talent there is. This is only a simple example of a common phenomenon.

Some psychoanalysts who have had an opportunity to study analytically one or a few very creative individuals

[10] This ambivalent attitude toward sublimation, however, was fully preserved in a paper presented by Anna Freud to the XV. International Psychoanalytic Congress in Paris, 1938 (unpublished) in which was pointed out that what was sublimation from the point of view of the id was sexualization from the point of view of the ego. Sexual drives were put into the service of ego purposes and the latter had gained mighty succor but at the price of possible embroilment in the conflicts to which sexual drives are prone.

have some very detailed information about the close similarity between childhood and adolescent fantasies of such individuals and what might be called the prefigurations of their scientific thought or artistic inventions. In scientists, e.g., there is a close similarity between the scientific fantasies[11] of what they hope to achieve and/or the more or less preconceived ideas which they are out to test, on the one hand, and the sexual fantasies of their childhood and adolescence, on the other. This kind of material which would demonstrate, if not the validity of the theory of sublimation, at least the existence of an intimate connection between the motifs of their thought and those of their sexual fantasy life, can, however, not be published because the details of a scientist's work, together with other facts that would have to be revealed—at the very least, his domicile that would be given away by that of his analyst— would make it possible to trace the person in question and would thereby violate his anonymity. This kind of experience will therefore, unfortunately, be available only to those who are willing to undergo psychoanalytic training themselves and who will thereafter study such creative individuals.

Finally, there is a considerable body of experience to suggest a close relationship between the level of intellectual achievement and a retardation in sexual maturation or in the assumption of an adult sexual life. *Homo sapiens* whose cerebral capacity vastly surpasses that of any other mammal is comparatively retarded in his sexual development. Mammals, with the exception of the elephant, need only a few

---

[11] It is quite true, as Professor Polanyi said, that science and art are very different from the instincts "of which [they] are supposed to be sublimates" (l.c.); there the realms of truth and of beauty, here the driving forces of living matter. But the statement is not relevant for the issue at stake because the scientific *fantasies* are quite commensurable with the personal sexual *fantasies* which are an expression of instinctual drives.

per cent of their life span to reach maturity. If man were to mature at the same speed, he would become capable of procreation at the time of his oedipus complex. Actually, he spends about one fifth of his life span in the sexually immature stage. It is suggestive to think of man's extraordinary cerebral development as related to the retardation of his sexual maturation.

It is all the more suggestive as we find the same relation again among humans if we compare the sexual maturation of people of different educational levels. Those who reach higher levels of education have been retarded in their teens both as regards their total genital output and the form which their sexual activities take. While those whose education stops with the high school, and even more those who do not go beyond elementary school, usually engage in early regular sexual intercourse, the teenage activities of the future college graduate are far more often limited to masturbation and petting; many have had little or no intercourse until the time of college or later, and among those who had such experience, regular sexual intercourse in the teens is rare.

Kinsey, Pomeroy, and Martin (1948) have supplied ample data on this subject. They found, e.g., that

. . . in the later teens, 85 per cent of the grade school group and 75 per cent of the high school group is having pre-marital intercourse, while the figure for the College group is still only 42 per cent [p. 347]. Varying with the age period the College group derives 4 to 21 per cent of its pre-marital outlet from intercourse; the high school group derives 26 to 54 per cent of its outlet from that source; but the grade school group depends on coitus for 40 to 70 per cent of its total pre-marital outlet [p. 348f.]. Between adolescence and 15 years of age there may be 15 times as much intercourse among males of class 3 [the group of semi-skilled workmen] as there is among boys who will ultimately go to College and whose occupational ratings will ultimately be in class 6 or 7 [upper white-collar group and professional group]. If the parental occupational class is 5 [the lower white-collar group] there is 122 times as much pre-marital intercourse among the boys who regress to class 3 as there is among those boys who will ultimately go into the professional group [p. 351].

The relationship is certainly not simple as there are probably many superimposed phenomena and secondary adjustments to be considered, but the data seem to favor a strong correlation between sexual retardation in adolescence and higher intellectual development.

The idea of sublimation is probably of Hellenic origin; it permeated much of the thought and the art of the classic age of Greece. In Aeschylus's *Eumenides,* Athena had put a stop to the endless sequence of blood revenge asking for ever more revenge. Orestes who had killed his mother Clytemnestra to revenge the slaying of his father Agamemnon is persecuted by the Furies and comes as a fugitive and supplicant to Athens; Athena has his case brought before the new court, the Areopagus, and Orestes is freed through a tie-vote. The Furies, goddesses of an unfathomable past, deprived of their legitimate prey by the new Olympic gods, are spitting outrage and hatred. Athena tries not only to appease them but to make friends of them and she invites them to settle in Athens as protectors of her city; the Furies eventually accept the invitation and become the Eumenides, the well-intentioned. The bloodsucking spirits of a merciless talion come to serve an ideal of justice tempered by mercy.

In a similar way, the Muses, goddesses of the arts and

sciences, may have developed out of the Maenads, the orgiastic female entourage of Dionysus, as Jane Ellen Harrison has suggested: Muses may be "Maenads repentant, clothed and in their right mind . . . The shift of Maenad to Muse is like the change of Bacchic rites to Orphic; it is the informing of savage rites with the spirit of music, order and peace" (Harrison, 1903, p. 463f.).

Although the classic age of Greece has emphasized the nobility of man and tended to idealize him, it has never, like the classicistic age of Victorian Europe, tried to deny or to denigrate sexuality. The trilogy of the classic tragedy with its gods, demigods, and heroes is regularly followed by the satyric play in which the scene is taken by the satyrs.

Whenever sublimation occurred, there had been an obstacle in the way of instinctual gratification, a frustration or an inadequate satisfaction (which may have been due only to inner ambivalence). But the concept of sublimation, as has already been emphasized, cannot explain the existence of higher activities any more than the theory of evolution can explain the appearance of higher forms. *Ordo renascendi est crescere posse malis.*[12]

Various theories have been suggested to explain the process—or "mechanism"—of sublimation in detail (see, i.e., Sterba, 1930; Bernfeld, 1931; Deri, 1939; Hart, 1948; Alpert, 1949; Hartmann, 1955; Kris, 1955).

---

[12] It is the rule of rebirth to be able to grow through misfortune (Rutilius Namatianus, *De reditu suo,* I, 140).

7

Destructiveness and Hatred

The role of destructiveness and hatred in human affairs in general and in psychopathology in particular was not a discovery of recent days. As early as 1909 Freud discussed at some length the part played by hatred in the make-up of obsessional neurosis. What happened in the 1920's was therefore not that factors previously not recognized found recognition; rather factors that hitherto had been peripheral were allocated a greater share in the total canvas of psychic life and given a different place in theory. While they had previously been thought of as explainable in terms of sexual and self-preservative drives—the dichotomy of the early psychoanalytic instinct theory—and in terms of the ego,[1] they now came to be seen as manifestations of a destructive drive.

PREJUDICES PRO AND CON

Whenever it is suggested that we abandon a well-established theory in favor of a new theory, the assets and

[1] For a detailed account of the development of psychoanalytic thought on this matter see Edward Bibring (1936).

liabilities of both should be carefully weighed against each other. What are the phenomena with regard to which the old theory seemed to fail? Is the new theory the only possible one that can account for these facts? Or, if not, in how far is it preferable to other possible hypotheses? Can the new theory account for everything that seemed satisfactorily explained by the old theory, without any loss? Or, if not, what are the losses? What are the implications of the new theory, and can they be verified by observation or experiment?

If we compare this ideal picture of a critical examination of a new theory with the reception of the new psychoanalytic theory of Eros and Destruction, we see that the course of events did not quite correspond to rational requirements. The new Freudian concepts were widely accepted and widely rejected on the ground of factors which bore little relationship to methodology.

It must be emphasized, however, that the ideal way of handling scientific matters is approximated only in certain disciplines and then only in certain periods. It is predicated upon two conditions, viz., that hypotheses are relatively easily accessible to decision by experiment, and that the propositions are either not related to passionately held philosophical beliefs, or else that all workers in the field agree on matters of fundamental philosophy. Should one of the conditions, or both, be absent, subjectivity has a wide scope. The theory of evolution is a good case in point. A noted contemporary biologist has put the matter in these words:

The problem of evolution in its entirety cannot be decided on the basis of the experimental data. The results of non-experimental research on fossils, on the other hand, almost too vast for any one individual to oversee, and the data derived from the comparative study of living organisms, are facts of a very different kind. They require interpretation and it is in the formation of interpretations that the personality and the philosophy of a scientist plays a decisive part. Philosophical and religious convictions, sometimes hardly conscious, sometimes with all the force of an ingrained dogmatism, influence thought in the most different directions [Portmann, 1953, p. 246].

Many analysts were quick to accept the new theory on impressionistic grounds. It seemed to fit so well with the display of human aggressiveness which had been conspicuous in the world at large in recent times and had become conspicuous in the microcosm of the analytic couch ever since analysts had ventured out from their original area of study and therapy, the psychoneuroses, into fields such as delinquency, psychopathy, or psychosis. But unorganized impressions, while often the guide for the first formulation of an idea, cannot be its final arbiter.

The easy acceptance of the new theory by many analysts may have had something to do with a factor to which Bernfeld had called attention (1935, p. 125ff.): the apparent ease with which the new theory can be applied as compared with the difficulty of application inherent in the old one. The old theories could *not* be *directly* applied to the phenomena; the latter had first to be analyzed, i.e., their unconscious meaning had to be investigated. Only after this had been done, could the theoretical concepts be applied, as a further step of abstraction, to the meanings, distilled by analysis, of the raw material of observation. But classifications such as "erotic" or "destructive" could be applied directly to the raw material of observation, without any previous analytic work of distilling and refining (or with a bare minimum of it); they could be applied, as Bernfeld put it, according to physiognomic rather than psychoanalytic criteria, i.e., judging from their outward appearance rather than from the meaning they yield to analytic study. It is easy to say that a patient is hostile, much easier than, e.g., the reconstruction of an unconscious fantasy from transference behavior. Could some of the popularity of the concept be due to the deceptive ease of its application (or misapplication)?

There is another factor to be considered, though in view of the universal involvement of all of us, it seems hardly possible for anyone to pronounce judgment on this score, viz., the fact that the introduction of primary destructiveness has made it possible, perhaps imperative, to allocate less space to sexuality in the total canvas of human life. Some may feel that the reluctance to recognize the power of sexuality may condition people to welcome any idea that helps to de-emphasize its role. But as psychology is "a knife that cuts both ways,"[2] others may counter with the suggestion that a bias for things libidinal or a resistance to the recognition of human destructiveness may make people refractory to the idea of primary aggressiveness.

But, above all, the introduction of an instinctual drive of destructiveness bears upon the same loaded philosophical and political issues that are involved in the question of constitution and environment and in the question whether human conflict is intrinsic or merely the consequence of transient social conditions. The concept of an instinct of destruction, or of a death instinct, was vigorously rejected by those who either were outright Marxists or at least belonged to that branch of Western liberal tradition of which Marxism itself was an offshoot, i.e., the school of

[2] The expression in Dostoevsky's *Brothers Karamazov* which Freud used to quote (e.g., 1931, p. 258).

thought which passionately believed that man is "good" by nature and that whatever ills and evils there are in human affairs are due to rotten institutions—perhaps to the institution of private property or, in a more recent and more moderate version, to a so-called "neurotic culture." Once these institutions have been changed, man will be restored to his original goodness and cooperativeness, and whatever conflicts there will still remain will be easily settled through mutual good-will.

The evil social institutions are seen as due to a combination of ignorance and vested interest. The more moderate in this school of thought have set their hopes for salvation on the growth of enlightenment which they expect will overcome the resistance of vested interest, while the more violent among them hold these expectations in contempt and are working for the destruction of our kind of society. But whether gradualist or revolutionary, no believer in the fundamental goodness of man and in the exclusive responsibility of external causes for human suffering could help being disturbed by a theory of an instinct of destruction or a death instinct. For if this theory is true, potentialities for conflict and for suffering are inherent in human affairs, and attempts to abolish or mitigate suffering appear to be not hopeless undertakings, to be sure, but far more complicated ones than the social reformers or revolutionaries had fancied them to be. In fact, the reformers might even appear in the somewhat ridiculous position of the husband in a story popular in my youth who, having surprised his wife in the arms of a lover, made up his mind to forgive her but, to insure against repetition, disposed of the living room couch at auction.

But psychology is a knife that cuts both ways, and what makes the theory of a destructive drive unacceptable to believers in the goodness of human nature, makes it more attractive to conservatives and to the other branch of Western liberal tradition whose view of man is rooted in the Christian doctrine of original sin;[3] this school of thought considers man as corruptible and has therefore staked its hopes on institutions that would either check or harness the evils of human nature. The Founding Fathers of the American Republic belonged to this group as did the philosophers of private enterprise. From this viewpoint, selfishness, greed, and destructiveness are part of the human make-up, and the economic system of competitive enterprise, far from creating them, merely channelizes them into directions which are, at worst, far less noxious than the outlets they would otherwise find, and at best highly useful. Without economic channelization, the world we would be living in would not be the Peaceable Kingdom

[3] Freud discussed the possibility of emotional resistance against the assumption of a destructive drive and he pointed out that faith in the benevolence of human nature is a factor in this, but he also, erroneously, thought that optimism about human nature was a religious prejudice: "Why have we ourselves taken so long to bring ourselves to recognise the existence of an aggressive instinct? Why was there so much hesitation in using for our theory facts which lay ready to hand and were familiar to every one? . . . to introduce it into the human constitution seems impious; it contradicts too many religious prejudices and social conventions. No, man must be by nature good, or at least good natured. If he occasionally shows himself to be brutal, violent and cruel, these are only passing disturbances of his emotional life, mostly provoked, and perhaps only the consequence of the ill-adapted social system which he has made so far for himself" (1932, p. 142).

This criticism of a shallow optimism hits home, but the latter can hardly be ascribed to *religious* prejudices. In particular, Christianity, the dominant religion of the European world, has maintained that, in consequence of the Fall, man was born a sinner. The idea of a benevolent nature of man is decidedly un-Christian and fairly new: it made its appearance in the eighteenth century. "It is essential not to have faith in human nature. Such faith is a recent heresy and a very disastrous one" (Butterfield, 1949, p. 47).

but the jungle. This view was expressed, among others, by Keynes (1936, p. 374):

> . . . dangerous human proclivities can be canalized into comparatively harmless channels by the existence of opportunities for money-making and private wealth, which if they cannot be satisfied in this way may find their outlet in cruelty, the reckless pursuit of personal power and authority and other forms of self-aggrandizement. It is better that a man should tyrannize over his bank balance than over his fellow-citizens; and whilst the former is sometimes denounced as being but a means to the latter, sometimes at least it is an alternative . . .

Those inclined to this point of view may add that there are more reasons to think that economic oppression is a modification — and mitigation — of savage destructiveness rather than its cause. Barbaric tribes have practiced wholesale slaughter of their victims when they might have exacted tribute from them had they been willing to spare them. Asiatic nomads transformed civilized lands in Central Asia into deserts. In order to make a whole oasis liable to tribute, the raiders "only need seize the main canal; and the nomads often blindly plundered and destroyed everything. A single raid was enough to transform hundreds of oases into ashes and desert" (Peisker, 1911, p. 327). Gibbon said of the Mongols that "from the Caspian to the Indus they ruined a tract of many hundred miles which was adorned with the habitations and labor of mankind, and five centuries have not been sufficient to repair the ravages of four years." Savage tribes have usually behaved in this way. It is only when aggression weighed less than avarice that man enslaved his victims or exacted tribute from them instead of slaughtering them; or even learned to prefer trade to piracy and loot.

The view that brutality was not created by the profit motive but rather, on the whole, mitigated by it, is actually the more ancient one by far. Joseph was hated by his brothers because they "saw that their father loved him more than all his brethren," and they decided to kill him. But Judah said to them: "What profit is it to slay our brother and conceal his blood? Come and let us sell him to the Ishmaelites, and let not our hand be upon him; for he is our brother, our flesh." The psychoanalytic view of these matters is the same as the view that is latent in this Bible story.

The difference between these various attitudes to the conquered, or the weaker ones, seems to be due not merely to the experience that enslavement is more profitable than slaughter and free labor more profitable than slave labor, or trade more profitable than piracy or plunder, but to a *genuine change of attitudes* or desires which in terms of Freud's later theory would have to be seen as a libidinization of aggressiveness (see p. 151f.)—albeit for the most part on phallic and anal levels only.

This development is not universal. Most Americans expected the newly "liberated" nations to behave as, on the whole, Americans did after gaining their independence, i.e., to try to "work out their own destiny" and to improve the very low standards of living of their own people through the ordinary time-consuming processes of industry and trade; and they were amply prepared to offer a helping hand in this. But we see that, for many nations, political goals such as catering to national pride through humiliation of their former masters, and the satisfaction of hatreds at whatever cost to themselves, has priority over economic and social improvement. This is but one example of the many miscalculations of Western nations in the last decades which were based on the tacit assumption that all men will prefer the gratification of libidinal desires to the satisfactions of hatreds.

There is a story of a man to whom a good fairy appeared in his dream, offering to grant him one wish; but on the condition that the man's neighbor would receive twice that wish. The man did some hard thinking until he made up his mind; his wish was to lose the sight of one eye.

DESTRUCTIVENESS SUBORDINATE TO THE STRUGGLE FOR
SURVIVAL AND THE PURSUIT OF HAPPINESS

The principle of simplicity and economy in scientific concepts formulated by William of Occam is still a good guide for theory building. *Entia non sunt multiplicanda praeter necessitatem.* The number of abstract concepts should not be increased without compelling need. We should therefore investigate first to what degree we can explain the manifestations of destructiveness as by-products of ego activities or of libidinal drives, or as reactions to provocation, without recourse to the assumption of an inborn propensity operating without provocation and basically independent of ego and libidinal activities. At least it should be useful to know how far the phenomena of destructiveness can be accounted for on the basis of the older, presumably simpler, theories and at what point the old theories fail us.

A destructive attitude, action or impulse may be

    I.   the reaction to

        (a) a threat to self-preservation or, more generally, to purposes usually attributed to the ego; or the reaction to

        (b) the frustration, or threatened frustration, of a libidinal drive.[4] Or

---

[4] This aspect was intensively studied by Dollard et al. (1939).

II.   it may be a by-product of an ego activity such as
      (a) the mastery of the outside world, or
      (b) the control of one's own body or mind. Or
III. it may be a part or aspect of a libidinal urge which
      in some way implies aggressiveness against
      the object, such as, e.g., incorporation or pene-
      tration.

In the first case, we may feel hostile to those who
threaten our lives or thwart our ego ambitions (Ia), or to
those who compete with us for the same love object (Ib).[5]
In the second sense, the normal attempt of the growing
organism to acquire mastery of the outside world implies
a measure of destructiveness as far as inanimate objects
are concerned, and a measure of aggression with regard
to man or animal (IIa).[6] Or it may manifest itself as a
by-product of the control, gradually required, of one's body[7]

---

[5] See the famous lines by Hobbes: "... if any two men desire the same
thing, which nevertheless they cannot both enjoy, they become enemies;
and in the way to their End (which is principally their owne conservation,
and sometimes their delectation only) endeavour to destroy, or subdue one
another."

[6] I am, of course, aware of the fact that the drive toward mastery (Be-
mächtigungstrieb) is in later Freudian theory described as a mixture of destructive and libidinal strivings and in this sense as an erotization, or
domestication, of original destructiveness. No doubt it can be so described, and once we have accepted the assumption of the later theory,
this explanation of the drive toward mastery becomes imperative. But we
are now engaged in an attempt to examine the situation naively and to
ask whether there is a compelling need for the assumption of a destructive drive. The drive toward mastery displayed, e.g., in the child's play,
does not in itself make this assumption unavoidable. A drive toward mastery or something equivalent to it would have to have a place in the
normal equipment of living beings, regardless of whether or not there
is an inborn need to destroy. If we make room in our theory for such a
tendency and classify it, presumably, among the ego activities, we have
to recognize that this involves a measure of aggressiveness.

[7] At one point in the development of this thought, Freud derived aggression from the experience of muscular control (E. Bibring, 1936). Anna
Freud called attention to a class of martinets, sometimes encountered

or as a by-product of our struggle to acquire control over
our mind (IIb), related to the fear of being overwhelmed
by the strength of the id. Finally, it may be part and parcel
of a libidinal urge, or an aspect of it, such as in oral biting,
oral incorporation, anal sadism, phallic penetration, or
vaginal retentiveness (III). In all these instances aggression
appears, sometimes a very dangerous aggression; but there
is no compelling need to postulate an inborn drive to
destroy.

Of course, provision would have to be made in any
theory to account for the fact that aggressiveness appears
among the reactions to frustration or to threat, or as a by-
product of self-preserving or self-expanding ego activities,
or as an aspect of the libido. But that could be done without postulating a drive toward destruction per se. The
latter hypothesis would not be unavoidable in the case
of reactive, or provoked, aggression because it comes into
play only upon provocation, while instinctual drives have
their source in inner tensions and do not necessarily need
external stimulation. Nor would the hypothesis appear
necessary in the case of aggression as an accessory to ego
activities because the goal is not destruction; destruction
is incidental to the achievement of ego purposes.[8] Finally,
the cases in which aggressiveness is part and parcel of a
sexual drive require the assumption that sexuality has some

---

among educators, who are intolerant of any sign of independence in the
children under their care, or are thrown into panic by it. This disciplinary
rigidity was seen as an outgrowth of childhood experiences of anxiety
and terror at the occurrence of erections independently of one's will and
not responsive to efforts at controlling them. (*Ein Beitrag zur Pädagogen-
analyse.* Vienna Psychoanalytic Association, June 17, 1936. Unpublished.)

[8] The "law of the jungle," in Kipling's *Jungle Book*, distinguishes clearly
between killing for food and killing for other reasons, the former permitted,
the latter outlawed.

aggressive elements; but as, in these cases, sexual pleasure is always derived from the respective practice, it is not necessary to postulate aggressive forces that operate independently of sexual drives, still less that they have destruction as goal.

ESSENTIAL DESTRUCTIVENESS

There is thus a wide area of aggressive or hostile manifestations for the explanations of which it is not necessary to postulate a destructive drive.

However, there are also destructive manifestations which, through their character or their intensity, lie outside of this area; manifestations of aggression which cannot be seen as reactive to provocation because they are so vast in intensity or duration that it would be difficult to fit them into any scheme of stimulus and reaction; which cannot be seen as by-products of ego activities because they neither are accompaniments of present ego activities nor seem explainable as derivatives of former by-products of ego activities; and, finally, cannot be seen as part of sexual drives because no sexual pleasure of any kind appears to be attached to them.

Paul Federn has repeatedly pointed at these activities and he saw in them the real basis for the assumption of a destructive drive. He mentioned, above all, certain extreme forms of suicide which occur among psychotics. A psychotic may strike his head with an axe with full force, and he may repeat the assault if he has the strength left to do so;[9] or the sudden outbursts of catatonics, reaching out

[9] During a discussion of this subject, Dr. M. Katan felt that the argument was not conclusive. It may well be, he pointed out, that such patients experience anxiety far beyond anything we can imagine (see p. 206f.),

without warning from what had seemed to be a state of indifference, to a lightning attack, from which they may with equal suddenness return to their previous appearance of apathy. The epileptic attack, too, has been mentioned in this group.

Behavior of this type makes an uncanny impression on us; we find it difficult to identify ourselves with it—a difficulty which we do not encounter in the earlier mentioned examples of aggressiveness. This strangeness has been thought to be due to the fact that they are expressions of pure, or almost pure, nonsexual destructiveness.

To these examples may be added examples of aggressiveness in individuals who do not appear to be psychotic and whose aggressiveness could be understood along the lines previously discussed were it only less intense and less enduring; in these cases it is the intensity and the inexhaustibility of aggression that poses the question as to its origin.

We have witnessed in our own day powerful rulers whose hatred of opponents seemed unappeasable and whose need for revenge against those who had ever touched their sensibilities—extremely vulnerable as they were—proved impervious to the passing of time and the change of conditions. Stalin has been credited with the remark that revenge must be eaten cold. He settled accounts with luckless opponents of a day long past who fled from the advancing German armies into Russia, apparently in the expectation that little quarrels of bygone days had become obsolete

---

and that their extreme destructiveness is in proportion with their extreme anxiety. This is probably a genuine alternative to the assumption of a destructive drive, at least as far as these phenomena are concerned. What transcends the requirements of self-preservation and the pursuit of happiness may not be the aggression itself but the anxiety. A *general* application of this idea, beyond the realm of psychosis, would probably run into difficulties with childhood destructiveness.

through the passage of time and in the face of a common peril. They were mistaken.

Perhaps the most monstrous case of insatiable hatred was Adolf Hitler's hatred of the Jews. It is difficult to see how it could be explained on a reactive basis because of its limitlessness and inexhaustibility. Hitler's hatred of Jews has sometimes been said to have been caused by the rejection of his application to the Academy of Fine Arts in Vienna, which he attributed, in a quasi-paranoid fashion, to Jewish influence. But why was this hostility still fresh so many years later when he had become the autocratic ruler of Germany, and the conqueror of most of Europe, and when the very frustration of his early artistic ambitions, supposedly the work of Jews, must have seemed to have turned out all to his good? Or why, at least, could his resentment not be allayed by taking revenge against a few individuals supposed to have had a hand in the resented experience? Why did it have to be the total expropriation, deportation, infinite degradation, and eventual extermination of a whole people? Psychoanalysts, of course, will feel that childhood experience rather than the grievance of a later day provided the fuel for his aggressiveness. But that raises the same question: what should we assume these childhood frustrations to have been, so that they could account by way of reaction for this insatiable destructiveness?[10]

----

[10] It is, of course, impossible to establish a diagnosis with regard to historical personalities for whom clinical records do not exist. There can be only impressions and conjectures. It is in this sense that I should like to mention facts regarding Adolf Hitler to which Dr. Bertram D. Lewin called my attention many years ago: a temporary blindness at the end of the First World War (October, 1918) had been reported by various authors (e.g., Heiden, 1936, p. 61) and was attributed to a gas attack or to hysteria; a tremor of his hands in 'his last year of life was observed by the President of the International Red Cross, Count Bernadotte. Both facts

There are also cases in which hatred is provoked and its intensity seems understandable but in which the reaction is nevertheless strange because hatred is satisfied at enormous cost in terms of libidinal sacrifices such as "we" would not have considered to pay, however much we may have felt aggrieved. What sets these cases apart from the psychic economy of the average man in our civilization is the fact that hatred and destructiveness have priority over even the most important libidinal satisfactions. Destructiveness in these cases is therefore not, or is no longer, subordinate to the requirements of the ego and of the libido.

The classical example of this type is shown in Euripides's *Medea;* in order to take revenge on Jason, who is about to desert her for a young bride, she kills her and Jason's children whom she loves. None of the Greeks in the tragedy would have done anything like that; they are pictured as quite capable of ruthlessness, but, with them, libidinal satisfaction has priority over the satisfaction of hatreds. But Medea is a barbarian, a sorceress, perhaps an immortal; all this removes her from the human fold.

Phenomena like these and like the previously mentioned manifestations of destructiveness in psychoses and epilepsy make it doubtful whether the *whole* of aggressiveness can ever be explained in terms of reactive behavior. They seem strongly to suggest that allowance must be made for the existence of some inner needs of destruction.

To sum up: while it is possible and indeed indicated to explain many manifestations of aggressiveness—most

---

together suggest, though of course they do not prove, that Hitler may have had encephalitis at the time of the great epidemic. That encephalitis is often followed by a marked weakening of inhibitions need not be emphasized.

of those that can be observed in normal individuals and in
psychoneurotics—as reactions to frustration or danger, or
as by-products of self-preservation or self-expansion, or as
sexual manifestations, an attempt to explain *all* destructive
behavior along these lines becomes strained. There seems
to be an irreducible remainder of destructive phenomena
which suggest the existence of destructive forces in man—
at least in many men. Perhaps we might call this irreducible
rest *essential* destructiveness, borrowing from the psychi-
atric distinction between essential and reactive alcoholism.

Essential destructiveness is explained, in Freud's later
theory, as expression of a destructive instinctual drive,
which in turn is seen as a derivative of a death instinct.
The drama of life appears as the result of an interplay of
constructive and destructive forces, of Eros and Thanatos.

It is necessary to distinguish between the postulation of
a destructive drive and the assumption of a death instinct
of which the destructive drives are manifestations. The
former is a clinical, or psychological, the latter a biological
theory which cannot be discussed and evaluated on the
basis of psychological experience *alone*.

Whether we do, or do not, accept the hypothesis of a
death instinct, makes no difference in our conduct of an
analysis; the death instinct itself does not appear as element
of psychological interpretations suggested in analysis. Interpretations may refer to destructive or aggressive strivings,
but their biological root is not relevant for psychological
investigation and treatment, just as the assumption, made
by some theoretical biologists, that the mortality of all
living organisms is ultimately due to the principle of
entropy, the second theorem of thermodynamics, has no
direct bearing upon the study and treatment of cardiac
failure.

DESTRUCTIVENESS AND THE ANIMAL KINGDOM

Expressions such as "inhumanity," "brutality," or "bestialism" suggest that cruelty is commonly associated with the animal world, and evolutionist theory may see destructiveness in man as a survival from prehuman stages.

In a recent article on this subject, Ludwig von Bertalanffy argues that "intraspecific aggression . . . in wild life and under severe interspecific competition would soon be eliminated by selection" (1958, p. 52). He looks upon essential destructiveness as a kind of luxury that men can afford because they no longer live under the pressure of interspecific competition, and he thinks that "only a minor part . . . such as crimes of violence, the destructive mob, the self-mutilation of the maniac, is purely on the level of the primary process," that most of man's essential destructiveness is due to his ability of symbolic thought, i.e., is committed in the service of ideas. Another biologist, Adolf Portmann, is equally emphatic in insisting on the human, rather than subhuman, nature of destructiveness (1943, p. 63f.):

The idea that the nature of man could be deduced from pre-human animal stages has led to nasty illusions. One of the worst is the idea of a slow but inescapable improvement of human nature. Very slowly, so many people thought, must the base and mean be left behind in the gradual upward development from animal to man. A superficial way of thinking has thus successfully attempted to explain the evil that we find so powerful in man, as a survival from an earlier animal stage that is slowly but certainly overcome in continuous progress. And when terrible things, cruelties hardly conceivable, occur among men, many speak thoughtlessly of "brutality," of bestialism, or a return to animal levels . . . As if there were animals which inflict on their own kind what men can do to men. Just at this point the zoologist has to draw a clear line: these evil, horrible things are no animal survival that happened to be carried along in the imperceptible transition from animal to man: this evil belongs entirely on this side of the dividing line, it is purely human . . . He who searches for the borderline between man and animal and thus for the nature of our own kind, must know that he has to find a place for evil in our human world; he must fully realize the difficulty of the task that is hereby presented to us.

Jacob Burckhardt called Henry VIII "that slab of bacon in gold brocade, half boer, half fiend." Himmler and his kind were not animals but fiends and a fiend belongs to the human world.[11]

There are other views, too, and Schjelderup-Ebbe, the discoverer of the pecking order, said that "despotism is the basic idea of the world, indissolubly bound up with all life and existence" (1931).

I am not competent to judge whether there are sufficient reasons for assuming that destructiveness for its own sake exists among animals. From such view as an outsider may gain from a distance, it seems to me that biologists, on the whole, are more inclined to see the destructive behavior

[11] In Goethe's *Faust*, Mephistopheles, speaking to the Lord, says about man:

Ein wenig besser würd' er leben,
Hätt'st du ihm nicht den Schein des Himmelslichts gegeben;
Er nennt's Vernunft und braucht's allein,
Nur tierischer als jedes Tier zu sein.

Life somewhat better might content him,
But for the gleam of heavenly light which Thou hast lent him:
He calls it Reason—thence his powers increased,
To be far beastlier than any beast.

in animals as contingent upon the struggle for survival, or other activities not primarily destructive, rather than in intraspecific destructiveness per se.

DESTRUCTIVENESS AN INSTINCTUAL DRIVE?

Essential destructiveness that goes beyond the requirements of the ego and the libido may either be due to a force of its own, or, following Dr. Katan's suggestion about the suicide of psychotics, to paroxysmal degrees of anxiety. In the first case, an inborn instinctual drive of destruction may be assumed. This was done by Freud, who derived this drive from a death instinct which was thought to form, together with its counterpart, the life instinct, the fundamental proclivities of living matter. To see in essential destructiveness the manifestation of an inborn instinctual drive is probably the simplest hypothesis; it permits us to give account of the known facts, both in children and in adults, and to organize them in a way that has predictive and manipulative value; and the dualism of Libido and Destruction, or of Life and Death Instincts, which promises to open new perspectives for a deeper understanding of all life, may some day become physiologically demonstrable. The hypothesis of a self-destructive death instinct which is turned outward and mitigated through the workings of Eros may then, perhaps, explain phenomena such as the frequent sudden transition from health to illness in people who have retired from active life or have been retired by circumstance.

But the theory of a destructive drive is not the only way in which essential destructiveness could be understood. There is, for instance, also the possibility that we may have to do with a debris of the mental apparatus, i.e., with a part of the equipment of the organism which is ordinarily integrated in the personality as part of the hierarchy of the ego but may take on an independent existence and play havoc with things if it manifests itself outside of such integration, on leave from the organism, as it were—like plundering soldiers when army discipline has broken down. That might happen either in early childhood before enough of an integrated ego exists; or at any time later in the case of regressive disintegration. This hypothesis would fit in with those observations which suggest that essential destructiveness appears in early childhood and under conditions of regression (including regressions due to brain damage).

We may expect that future experience will decide between the various possible hypotheses.

AN ASYMMETRICAL CLASSIFICATION

In using the theory of erotic and destructive drives it is necessary to keep in mind that there is no real parallelism, or mirror-correspondence, between the two; the classification is asymmetrical. Eros and Destruction may be thought to represent the polarity of building up and tearing down, of life and death. But there is an infinite variety of structures that can be built up while destruction, negation, is always the same.

Because of this lack of symmetry the same processes mean something different in one case and in the other; the same mechanisms have different consequences when applied to destructive urges than when applied to sexual ones. Persistent impossibility of satisfying heterosexual drives, as, e.g., in a prison, will lead to substitute gratification of any kind that can be found, probably on a regressed level. The same impossibility of expressing aggressiveness would probably lead to a change of object only: either one "lets it out" on something available, or if this possibility does not exist, for external or inner reasons, aggressiveness is likely to be turned against oneself, in the form of self-accusation or depression. The plasticity of the sexual drives makes it possible to find substitute gratifications, but negation can only negate, and can change only its objects. Any other possibility in the area of aggression implies the *cooperation of the libido.*

There is no parallelism between the development of the erotic drives and the development of destructiveness, either. Let us take the sexual drives as example (although the concept of Eros is wider). The sexual drives have a clear pattern of maturation: from prodromal stages to a precocious prime of genitality; then over a period of (relative) latency to the maturation period in puberty, ending with adult genital sexuality in which full satisfaction, within broad limits, is physiologically and psychologically possible and socially permitted. There is no parallel maturation of the destructive drive. Destructiveness is probably at its most perfect in early childhood and all later manifestations are, for most people, dilutions or mitigations. As a rule, there is no full satisfaction socially permitted at any time—although the hunting of animals has been provided as an outlet in many societies and the hunting of a class of humans has been permitted in some.

THE DETOXIFICATION OF DESTRUCTIVENESS

If there is an inborn destructive drive, the question arises how it happens that the great majority of adults do not have violent destructive urges most of the time. Their destructiveness must have been mitigated, and Freud ascribes this mitigation, or detoxification, to the influence of the libido, i.e., of love. The job of detoxifying destructiveness is done the more efficiently the higher on the developmental scale the intervening libido is.

This theory has been of very great usefulness. It made us understand, e.g., why children become more aggressive when their object relations have been disturbed, and it advised the child therapists that only a progress of the libido will cure the aggressive child. But the theory has been expressed in somewhat unprecise terms. Freud spoke of the *Mischung* and *Entmischung* of erotic and destructive drives, their mixing and unmixing—terms which in English translation have been rendered as "fusion" and "defusion." The fusion of the erotic and destructive drives brings about the mitigation and domestication of destructiveness, while the disintegration of such combinations—defusion—is said to set destruction "free."

This picture seems to me to be in need of clarification. When various ingredients are mixed—e.g., different kinds of fruit in a salad—we expect that as a consequence of unmixing them we will recover the ingredients; after defusion of instincts we should find both, libido and destruction, unadulterated. What we find in fact is destructiveness plus *low* developmental *stages* of the libido.

What this suggests is not so much a process of mixing and unmixing ingredients but rather something like a detoxification of destructiveness through the intervention of erotic drives—the more so the higher on the development scale the sexual drives are—and the reappearance of aggressiveness when the libido regresses.

More recently Hartmann, Kris, and Loewenstein (1949; also Hartmann, 1952, 1953; Kris, 1955) suggested that destructiveness can be mitigated not only through the inter-

vention of the libido but also, independent of such intervention, through a process that is the exact counterpart of
the desexualization of sexual drives (deaggressivization).
They proposed the term "neutralization" to cover both the
desexualization of libidinal drives, and the deaggressivization of destructive drives.

This hypothesis is, of course, contingent upon the assumption that destructiveness is the manifestation of an instinctual drive. And since every mitigation of destructiveness
implies a degree of conservation of the object, it would
have to be shown either that this conservation contains no
elements of love, or if it does, that love is only a consequence, not a cause, of the process.[12]

---

[12] The following statement of Freud's on desexualization may be interesting in this connection: "By . . . obtaining possession of the libido
from the object-cathexes, setting itself up as sole love-object, and de-
sexualizing or sublimating the libido of the id, the ego is working in opposition to the purpose of Eros and placing itself at the service of the
opposing instinctual trends" (1923, p. 65). Freud thus thought that desexualization took place under the influence of the death instinct; presumably, he would have considered deaggressivization to occur under the
influence of Eros. There is no conclusive evidence, so far, to decide
between this view and the hypothesis suggested by Hartmann, Kris, and
Loewenstein.

8

Anxiety

THE TWO THEORIES OF ANXIETY

The story of Freud's old theory of anxiety and its revision has often been told. Freud believed that there was a distinctive type of neuroses which he called *"Aktualneurosen"* —"actual neuroses," i.e., "nervous states which . . . depend on the somatic factor in sexual life" (1910d, p. 224), which show in all cases the same symptoms, viz., diffuse anxiety, palpitation, fatigue, intestinal upset, without individual variations such as psychoneurotic symptoms show; and he thought that these symptoms had no psychic etiology but were due to practices in a person's current sexual life, practices which led to an accumulation of sexual tensions without adequate discharge, and that these symptoms were therefore consequences of a toxic influence of dammed-up libido. The treatment of these symptoms should consist, not in psychoanalysis as there was no psychogenesis to disclose and to repair, but in the discontinuation of the nocuous practices in the patient's current life. It seems that Freud maintained up to the end of his life that cases of this kind, responsive to this kind of treatment, did exist. Psychoanalysts who were a generation or more younger than Freud did not follow him in this point but claimed that they had never themselves encountered a clear case of "actual neurosis"; they were inclined to think that this was a diagnosis of the early days when the clinical eye had not yet sharpened enough to spot more hidden neurotic features and that the cases classified as actual neuroses at the beginning would have qualified as full-grown neuroses at a later date.[1]

Thus, anxiety in the "actual neuroses" was interpreted by Freud as a toxic product of undischarged libido.

On the other hand, there was no question about the fact that normal fear is a reaction to danger: " 'objective anxiety' [*Realangst*] must be regarded as an expression of the ego's instinct for self-preservation" (Freud, 1916/17, p. 356), and Freud distinguishes "neurotic anxiety (abnormally utilized libido) and 'objective anxiety' (which corresponds with the reaction to danger)" (ibid., p. 351); the term "neurotic anxiety" refers to the anxiety of the actual neuroses.

What remained was the problem of anxiety in psychoneurosis: should anxiety be seen as a reaction to danger like normal fear, or as a transformation product of the libido like anxiety in "actual neurosis"? It is well known that Freud's views have changed in this point, i.e., that he was at first inclined to see psychoneurotic anxiety in the light of the actual-neurotic one, and later as a response to a danger. What changed his view was the realization that the first assumption led to a circular reasoning (1926a). If anxiety was due to the damming up of libido, and the damming up of libido was due to repression, then repression had to pre-

---

[1] It may be remarked in passing that this virtually unanimous rejection of a Freudian hypothesis by psychoanalysts shows how little basis there is for the widespread contention that analysts—particularly the so-called orthodox analysts—echo their master's voice, and that their acceptance of most of Freud's ideas is due, not to the fact that their experience has corroborated them, but to an uncritical adherence to authority.

cede anxiety. That left the question of what had caused repression. Anxiety must have been the motor of repression and could therefore not have been its consequence—although it was, of course, thinkable that a preceding anxiety which had led to repression was then increased by the damming up of libido caused by the repression. But a part, at least, of the anxiety could not be explained toxically. It had to be seen as a reaction to a danger, like *Realangst*.

Since Freud continued to believe in the existence of *Aktualneurosen* and hence of anxiety due to an accumulation of sexual tensions without adequate discharge, he faced the question of how the two views of anxiety could be combined and a unified theory be developed. Freud made such an attempt, along the following lines: he analyzed the meaning of danger and proposed that danger was the anticipation of a future trauma; trauma appeared as an overflooding of the organism with need-tensions, way beyond the degree that can be assimilated, or digested, in the given time. Realistic fear and the anxiety of the psychoneuroses appeared then as an anticipation, in small doses, of such future need-tensions; a small anticipated dose of the threatening trauma sets, through the working of the pleasure-pain principle, the defensive operations into motion and thereby forestalls the actual realization of the trauma, somewhat like in vaccinations a small sample of the disease prevents the real disease. Then, perhaps, one could see in the anxiety of the *Aktualneurosen* the consequences of the real traumatic situation that had come to pass, i.e., the consequences of the flooding of the organism with need-tensions, here and now.

This attempted unification does not seem quite satisfactory because the need-tensions that rapidly increase in a traumatic situation are not all of a sexual nature; some are self-preservative. The toxic anxiety of the *Aktual-neurosen,* on the other hand, had been attributed, in the old theory, not to an accumulation of any kind of tensions but specifically to the accumulation of sexual tensions. Since the new unifying formula did not distinguish between libidinal and nonlibidinal tensions, it does not seem capable of including, without further elaboration, the old view of toxic anxiety as a transformation product of the libido.

But since psychoanalysts no longer believe that actual neuroses exist, and either do not believe in the existence of anxiety caused by undischarged sexual tensions, or have withdrawn their interest from this matter, the question of a unified theory has, for psychoanalysts, lost much of its urgency.

It could be clearly shown that anxiety is the motor force of repression, hence a necessary condition for the formation of psychoneurosis. This insight has thereby given the psychoanalyst a new dimension in his study of the neuroses; hitherto merely oriented toward searching for the goals and objects of his patient's drives, he was now alerted to look for his dangers, too.

But the new theory reopened a question that had seemed to be settled, viz., the question of the difference between *Realangst,* realistic fear, and neurotic anxiety. Things had seemed to be clear as long as the old theory had prevailed. Realistic fear was a response to danger; neurotic anxiety was a transformation product of overflooding libido. They were altogether different things. But if, as the new theory has it, neurotic anxiety is a response to danger, too, then the question arises: what distinguishes realistic fear and neurotic anxiety? The difference between them could be sought in differences in the content of the threat (as, e.g., real or imagined), the source of danger (as, e.g., inner or outer danger), or the intensity of the response.

Current psychoanalytic theory sees the difference between realistic fear and neurotic anxiety merely in the source of the danger: "We know the difference between them [viz., *Realangst* and neurotic anxiety]; a real danger is one which threatens from some external object, neurotic danger from an instinctual demand[2] . . . the seemingly extremely intimate relation between anxiety and neurosis derives from the fact that the ego protects itself against an instinctual danger in the same manner as against an external reality danger, but that in consequence of an imperfection of the psychic apparatus this defensive activity eventuates in neurosis" (Freud, 1926a, p. 115f.).

It is merely this "imperfection of the psychic apparatus" that lets us treat instinctual dangers as though they were external ones, i.e., makes us try to flee from them, through repression, and thereby starts the neurotic process.

FORMS OF ANXIETY

Freud (1926a) discussed four major anxieties in childhood:

1. As the earliest, the fear of losing the object; the

---

[2] It is interesting to note that this possibility was already considered by Freud about a decade before *The Problem of Anxiety* (1926a) in which the switch from the old to the new theory was clearly made. Freud wrote in the *Introductory Lectures* (1916/17, p. 351): "As we know, the development of anxiety is the reaction of the ego to danger and the signal preparatory to flight; it is then not a great step to imagine that in neurotic anxiety also the ego is attempting a flight, from the demands of the libido, and is treating this internal danger as if it were an external one. Then our expectation, that where anxiety is present there must be something of which one is afraid, would be fulfilled." This passage is one of many which show that the changes in psychoanalytic theory in the 1920's were less abrupt than is generally assumed, and that the new ideas had actually been under consideration for quite some time.

child is afraid of being left alone with his imperative needs, with nobody to satisfy them.

2. Somewhat later, there develops the fear of losing the object's love, which may bring about the same result as the loss of the object. Under ordinary circumstances, the fear of losing love will take the place of the fear of object loss after the earliest infancy.

3. In the phallic phase, there is castration fear in boys and its equivalent in girls. In boys, it is fear of losing the penis or of damage to it; or fear of being overpowered by the stronger male and thereby forced into the feminine position, of being put into a lower place in the scale of "relative sexuality" (Max Hartmann), a fear that can, in the last resort, be traced back to the fear of losing the penis; or fear that, on comparison with one's peers, one will turn out to have the smaller membrum, to be less virile.

In girls, castration fear is originally the fear of a repetition, or symbolic repetition, of the violent intervention that had made them females in the first place; and later, after a successful development along the feminine line, i.e., after acceptance of their femininity, the fear of being deprived of the very qualities or possessions of femininity, particularly the integrity of the female organs, attractiveness as women, and satisfactory children.

4. Finally, after the establishment of a superego, the fear of conscience.

Of these, the first three should ideally disappear in the course of development, while the fourth has a permanent place in our ideal of normal adulthood.

To these four types of anxiety two more have been added. One was mentioned by Freud somewhat casually in the same context (1926a, p. 116) and later elaborated by others, viz.:

5. Fear of one's own masochism, which may manifest itself, e.g., in fear of high places.

A special case of this fear appears in the case of a sexualization of danger (Laforgue, 1930; also regularly treated in Anna Freud's Seminar on Child Analysis at the Vienna Psychoanalytic Institute at that time). One "flirts with danger," as an English idiom aptly calls it; it is a masochistic enjoyment of danger and anxiety. But, as is usually the case with masochism, this is pleasurable only as long as it does not go too far and does not get really serious, i.e., as long as it is a play which one can always stop to reassume control. The game often takes the form of an oscillation, or seesaw, between states in which one permits anxiety to mount and gives in to it almost to the point of being overwhelmed by it, and the resumption of control at the danger point.

But it is hardly possible to keep such flirtation always within safe bounds. If it gets out of control, or if it goes on unconsciously, which amounts to the same thing, the original external danger is increased by the danger of masochistic surrender and the anxiety may become intolerable.

A taste for the thrill of sexualized anxiety is both stimulated and exploited by a large industry—the suspense story in literature, the comics and the movie, and the treatment of news in the popular press. It is a source of enjoyment as long as one is at a safe distance from the danger and feels anxiety in identification only.

Finally, there is a type of anxiety which was described somewhat later, viz.:

6. The fear of the intensity of one's own instinctual drives, i.e., the fear of being overwhelmed by uncontrollable forces and thus disintegrating, as it were, as a person. It

was extensively described by Anna Freud for puberty and for a prodromal stage of schizophrenia (1936, Chapter XII).[3] This assumption of a direct fear of instinctual drives, independent of any outside punishment they may invite, has not been generally accepted in psychoanalysis. Like the constitutional factor in neurosis, like the assumption of intrinsic sources of inner conflict, like the assumption of an inborn destructive drive, it goes against the philosophy of environmentalism and its picture of a harmonious human nature and a potentially ever-happy human existence, only temporarily thwarted by social institutions.

All these anxieties are common in childhood and in later life, too; they all appear in the psychoneuroses; they all can be motives of repression. But the list does not include other fears which do not take on such large significance.

Some of the types of anxiety enumerated above can be reduced to others. Fear of the superego can be traced back either to fear of losing love or to castration fear, because the superego is the product of an internalization of parental commands and prohibitions to which one has submitted either out of fear of losing love or out of castration fear.

---

[3] It seems that Freud's thought had veered in the same direction though his frequent references to *Triebangst*, fear of instinctual drives, were ambiguous, open to two interpretations: that the fear was due to the consequences in the outside world which their expression would bring about, or that it was due to a danger implicit in the drive itself. Freud stated that the former was "often" the case (1926a, p. 116) without discussing what other possibility there might be. However, in his last statement on the subject (1940, p. 111) he clearly described both possibilities of instinctual danger, one due to repercussions in the outside world, the other to the strength of the drive: "[The] id is a source of similar danger, and that for two different reasons. In the first place, an excessive strength of instinct can damage the ego in the same way as an excessive 'stimulus' from the external world. It is true that such an excess cannot destroy it; but it *can* destroy its characteristic dynamic organization, it can turn the ego back into a portion of the id. In the second place, experience may have taught the ego that the satisfaction of some instinctual demand that is not in itself unbearable would involve dangers in the external world. . . ."

The fear of one's own masochism is a derivative of castration fear, as masochism is, in the main, sexual enjoyment of playful castration; in the man, of being treated like a woman; and in the woman, of being rendered totally defenseless and being penetrated in any depth, i.e., of symbolic supercastration.

The various types of danger discussed above can therefore be reduced to these apparently elementary ones: loss of object, desertion, emasculation, and ego disintegration. These anxieties vary greatly in strength in different individuals, and in different periods in the life of the same individuals. The fear of losing love is particularly marked in depressives, castration fear in phobics, the fear of psychic disintegration in incipient schizophrenics or in people who sense in themselves a threat of psychosis.

There is a kind of complementary relationship between the fear of losing love and castration fear; one can be diminished at the expense of an increase of the other. Those who have great anxiety in one direction can thus protect themselves to a degree by retreating, if they are not too afraid of the other danger which must increase in consequence of their retreat. The depressive, e.g., desperately afraid of not being accepted, or of being abandoned by his love object, may try to win, or to keep, his object by catering to his will and whims, by humbling himself before him, in short, by accepting symbolic castration in relation to the object. Equally, those with overpowering castration anxiety can protect themselves to some degree by violent self-assertions, which will not increase their popularity, or by withdrawing from people; they can do one or the other if they are not too afraid of losing love. Those, however, who are *equally afraid* of both dangers cannot retrench in this way; they are *trapped*.

ANXIETY   163

ANXIETY AND TRAUMATIC NEUROSIS

It is common knowledge that shock and sudden fright have pathological consequences, the so-called traumatic neuroses. Among their symptoms is anxiety.

In many instances, the pathological reaction to an external event which was conceived as trauma follows the pattern of a psychoneurosis, i.e., the anxiety is due to an inner, instinctual, danger, as, e.g., in the case of the celebrated war hero who faints in a doctor's office at the sight of a hypodermic needle; the instinctual danger is, in this example, represented by a feminine impulse.

But in other cases we seem to be dealing with the effect of shock. As mentioned before, Freud explained it as a consequence of an accumulation of need-tensions beyond the assimilating capacity of the organism within the given time.

That leaves the question whether it makes any difference if these accumulating need-tensions are of a self-preservative or libidinal nature. The situation can be illustrated by a trivial example. A three-year-old child plays in a pool, falls in and swallows some water before he is pulled out again; he is badly frightened. The normal child will after a while go back in the pool and be more careful. The time interval that will pass between the accident and the child's return will vary according to individual and circumstances, perhaps from a few minutes to a few days, and so will the degree of caution that the child will show from now on; but, in the normal case, the result will be a resumption of the pleasurable activities with some modifications and restrictions which represent the lesson learned from the experience.

But the picture is changed if, e.g., the child is very clinging and greatly fears desertion, and interprets the little accident as evidence that the mother is not taking care of him, that she allows such things to happen; or if the child is in a period of an intense castration complex and interprets the experience as a token of castration. In such cases, the resulting anxiety may be unbearable and the child may stay away from the water for a long time, perhaps forever.

It all depends whether the threat takes on the meaning of the four great dangers discussed: loss of object, loss of love, castration, or ego disintegration. Of these, the loss of the object represents a danger both of rising need-tensions of a self-preservative nature and of rising libidinal need-tensions; it is, for the very young child, an all-around catastrophe. Desertion, emasculation, and ego disintegration are dangers of rising libidinal need-tensions—of the unsatisfied longing for the object and for his love; of the urges of frustrated genital narcissism; of the need for a cohesive, integrated, psychic existence, the need of being master in one's house, respectively. They are *narcissistic catastrophes.*

It seems that the threat of painful consequences which do not take on any of these implications is taken in stride and leads only to adaptive behavior; it starts a learning process. But if the threat, in addition to endangering these self-preservative interests, implies a narcissistic catastrophe, too, the resulting anxiety is often intolerable and the reaction nonadaptive. In this way, there may be a nucleus of truth in the old theory which related neurotic anxiety to sexuality.

Freud considered at one point the possibility that the behavioral response to danger—such as fight or flight—may be due to the self-preservative instincts, while the emotional

aspect, viz., the anxiety affect, may be due to the ego
libido, narcissism:

> . . . . the relation between anxiety and libido, otherwise
> so well defined, is with difficulty harmonized with the
> almost indisputable assumption that objective anxiety
> in the face of danger is the expression of self-preserva-
> tive instincts. But how if the anxiety-affect is provided,
> not by self-interest on the part of the ego-instincts, but
> by the ego-libido? The condition of anxiety is after all
> invariably detrimental; its disadvantage becomes con-
> spicuous when it reaches an intense degree. It then in-
> terferes with the action that alone would be expedient
> and would serve the purposes of self-preservation . . .
> if we ascribe the affective component of objective anxiety
> [Realangst] to the ego-libido, and the action undertaken
> to the ego-preservative instincts, every theoretical dif-
> ficulty will be overcome [1916/17, p. 372].

It is perhaps not accidental that these words were written toward the end of the First World War when Europe
was full of shell-shocked soldiers. The appearance of these
so-called war neuroses was greeted by numerable psychiatrists as the final disproof of psychoanalysis; for psychoanalysis claimed a sexual etiology of the neuroses and the
"war neuroses" seemed to be clearly unrelated to matters
sexual but rather expressions of the desire of soldiers to
get out of the trenches, back from the firing line, at virtually any price—hence expressions of a self-preservative interest. In his introduction to a psychoanalytic study of
this subject, with contributions by Ferenczi, Abraham,
Simmel, and Jones, Freud (1919b) pointed out that since
the formation of the theory of a narcissistic libido, a sexual
energy concentrated upon the ego, it could no longer be
taken for granted that ego conflicts did not involve the
libido; i.e., the wish to escape from the trenches could

have been the motive of the traumatic neurosis, and the neurosis formation may yet have to do not just with self-preservative tendencies but with the narcissistic libido. Freud then looked forward to later investigations, by psychoanalysts, of the traumatic neuroses, and of the probable relationship between shock, anxiety, and narcissism.

But there was little follow-up along this line. The war neuroses disappeared with the war, and the interest of psychoanalysts was concentrated on the psychoneuroses, from there to expand, later, to character neuroses, behavior disorders, and the border area between the neuroses and the psychoses, rather than to the traumatic neuroses. But whenever we approach the subject of traumatic neurosis, we seem to be led back to the ideas and problems of Freud's early theory of anxiety.

Various additions to and modifications of the Freudian theories of anxiety have been suggested by Federn (1929), Rado (1933, 1949), Blau (1952), Schur (1953), Brenner (1953), and Rangell (1953).

9

Analytic Ego Psychology

PRECURSORS OF THE CONCEPT

Psychoanalysis began with the study of neurosis, which it understood as manifestations of unsolved conflicts; attention was thereby focused on the main possibilities of conflict, and we find certain polarities, or dichotomies, in Freud's earliest concepts. "Instinctual drives," or in the earliest version, certain "ideas," confront an "ego."[1] "The basis for repression," says Freud (see Breuer and Freud, 1895, p. 116), is "the incompatability between the single idea that is to be repressed and the dominant mass of ideas constituting the ego"; or Freud speaks of the "incompatability . . . between the ego and some idea presented to it" (ibid., p. 122) or of the "refusal on the part of the patient's whole ego to come to terms with this ideational group" (ibid., p. 166).

A similar polarity is then upheld by Freud in his theory of the two psychic operations, the primary and the secondary process (1900), or of the "two principles of mental func-

---

[1] Freud's earliest ideas on this subject are comprehensively described by E. Kris (1950).

167

tioning" (1911a), the pleasure principle and the reality principle. While an organism operating according to the former presses toward immediate satisfaction, regardless of the consequences, the organism operating according to the latter has learned to restrain the urge toward immediate discharge, to stop, look, and listen, and consider the future consequences of action. The difference between the two *modi operandi* is illustrated by Freud (1911a, p. 18) with a quotation from George Bernard Shaw: "To be able to choose the line of greatest advantage instead of yielding in the direction of least resistance." Both the secondary process and the reality principle take in the early versions of Freud's theory the place that is later occupied by that elaborate structure, the ego.

THE CONCEPT OF THE EGO

Freud's latest definition of the ego is as follows (1940, p. 15):

> The principal characteristics of the ego are these. In consequence of the relation which was already established between sensory perception and muscular action, the ego is in control of voluntary movement. It has the task of self-preservation. As regards *external* events, it performs that task by becoming aware of the stimuli from without, by storing up experiences of them (in the memory), by avoiding excessive stimuli (through flight), by dealing with moderate stimuli (through adaptation) and, finally, by learning to bring about appropriate modifications in the external world to its own advantage (through activity). As regards *internal* events, in relation to the id, it performs that task by gaining control over the demands of the instincts, by deciding whether they shall be allowed to obtain satisfaction, by postponing that satisfaction to

times and circumstances favorable in the external world or by suppressing their excitations completely.

In such words ("in control" — "task" — "avoiding" — "dealing with" — "to bring about appropriate modifications" — "gaining control" — "postponing") the ego is described as a *problem-solving agent*. It is a teleological concept.

THE USE OF TELEOLOGICAL CONCEPTS

Teleological concepts can be used merely descriptively or with a view to explaining a phenomenon.[2] We use them descriptively, e.g., when we classify machines according to their function and speak of washing machines, printing presses or computers. No claim is implied that their useful-

---

[2] For the following treatment of the subject, see, among others, the view of Tinbergen (1951, p. 152): "The adaptiveness or directiveness of many life processes is a matter of fact and can be revealed by objective study; however, a description of the directiveness of life processes is not a solution of the problem of their causation. Once the survival value of a process has been recognized and clearly described, the biologist's next task is to find out how its mechanism works."

Similarly, Harold F. Blum speaks of different meanings of the term, teleology: "Many a biologist . . . has asked himself . . . what is the purpose (or function) of such and such an organ? If pressed he will no doubt have explained that what he really meant by purpose was the fitness of the organ with respect to the organism as a whole . . . Such thinking has often, no doubt, led to fruitful discovery, for reasoning in terms of purpose we may discover fitness and so be led to understanding of underlying mechanisms, but it has also, perhaps, led us frequently into error. Is this teleology? If so, I am afraid many of us are teleologists though I do not like the term applied to myself.

"The kind of teleology which assumes purpose and goals as realities is another sort, and is perhaps more deserving of the name. Since it is based upon extra-physical concepts this kind of teleology lies beyond the confines of science. And there, too, belong attempts to explain evolution as guided by purposes towards a goal of perfection, such as the concept of 'tele-finalisme' . . ." (1951, p. 210f.).

What I call the descriptive and the explanatory use of teleology seems to coincide with these two meanings of the term, teleology.

ness explains how they operate, except in the sense that their utility may have been a stimulus for the inventor.

But teleological concepts have also been used as explanatory tools. Aristotle's explanations of both inanimate and animate nature are teleological. Since the so-called scientific revolution in the late sixteenth and in the seventeenth century, they have fallen into disuse, which is fairly complete in the sciences of inanimate nature and somewhat less complete in the biological disciplines where they turn up occasionally or implicitly.[3]

Teleological explanations have been discarded because they did not seem to explain anything. Aristotle explained the development from the fertilized egg to the full-grown animal by assuming that the form of the mature animal, the *entelechy*, is represented in the fertilized egg, guiding the development to a realization of the form. But that seems to us merely to reword the known facts without teaching us anything new.

What might serve a particular end does not necessarily exist. If a man is trapped, it would be a good thing for him to be able to fly, but that does not make him grow wings. The chameleon takes on the coloring of its environment, but other animals who would be just as well served by this ability do not, etc. Like children who are not satisfied to enjoy what their gadgets can do but take them apart to see how the thing works, we want to know the mechanism of

[3] As, e.g., homeostasis, the "wisdom of the body" (Cannon, 1932) though these concepts, on the whole, are used descriptively, i.e., to group together a number of physiological processes the mechanism of which has been understood in physicochemical terms. Selye's concept of an alarm reaction, an unspecific organismic response to a variety of nocuous agents which have nothing in common except their noxiousness, implies that the organism, or a special organ, analyzes various stimuli with regard to their future implications—a teleological concept, though presumably also used only descriptively.

the various processes in question—hence, the attempt to reduce teleology to causality. The historically most important examples of such attempted reduction are probably the explanation, or attempted explanation, by Darwin and Wallace, of evolution in terms of natural selection from chance variations, and the explanation, by Boltzmann and Gibbs, of the second theorem of thermodynamics, postulating the tendency in an isolated system toward maximization of entropy, in terms of mechanical systems moving toward more probable molecular distribution.

Without such explanation of "how it works," teleological explanations explain nothing; they merely add to a description of a process the information that it is useful for a purpose, implying that its existence is due to its usefulness. Walter Rathenau once said that it has always been a privilege of theory builders to explain a fact by postulating a faculty. Nothing is added to our understanding of the nest building of birds or the migration of birds and fish by ascribing them to animal "instinct". The fact that most people, by and large, can perceive and appreciate reality, and that psychotics, within a large area, cannot, is not explained by attributing the former to a function of reality testing, the latter to the breakdown of this function. Nor is intolerance to frustration explained by attributing it to weakness of the ego. If, as Hume said, explanations are places where the mind comes to rest, one may say that our mind no longer comes to rest when we are told that a thing exists because it is useful—as presumably the minds of our forefathers did.[4]

---

[4] It is interesting in this connection that Seneca considered it the characteristic difference between Etruscans and Romans that the former thought teleologically, the latter causally: "We believe that because clouds collide, lightning is discharged; they think that clouds collide in order to discharge lightning" (*Quaestiones naturales*, II, 32, 2).

A phenomenon is *"explained"* if it is seen as a *part of a more comprehensive order* of things; and, in addition to mere explaining, it is also *"understood"* if this order of things can be shown to follow logically from what we might conceive to be the *essence,* or the nature, of the matter.

It is in line with this reasoning that teleological explanations would be genuine explanations if the purposes served were seen as part of a hierarchy of purposes of a plan of the Universe. In that case the assumption would be that God had bestowed the various organisms with their respective faculties as part of the plan of His creation; this plan is then the ultimate frame of reference. Teleological explanations would then become fully meaningful, but this fact would not make them acceptable to scientists today because science is an attempt to understand the universe *immanently,* without recourse to extramundane influences.

At the present time, the reduction of teleological to causal explanations is usually brought about by describing goal-directed behavior with the help of models which are equipped with feed-back mechanisms, such as, e.g., projectiles directed toward their target by a built-in radar, or the thermostats which regulate the temperature of our homes. Information about outside events is continuously fed back into the apparatus and the apparatus is regulated on the basis of this information. Such mechanisms, of course, are planned and designed by engineers, and give to changing conditions those answers which their designers have built into them. The new scientific study of governing agents, called cybernetics, operates largely with the feed-back principle.

The teleological concepts of psychoanalysis are used

only descriptively and are not meant to be explanations.[5] Freud tried to study their mechanism. His metapsychology is an attempt to build a physicalistic foundation, or super-structure,[6] for his theory of motivation.[7] Also, his later theory of anxiety contains an attempt to reduce teleology to causal terms. When Freud looked upon anxiety in psycho-neurosis as fundamentally like normal fear, viz., a reaction to danger, his interest was turned toward that reaction which up to that point, like other phenomena of conscious life, had apparently been considered to be in the province of the "academic" psychologist. Reaction to danger was a teleo-logical concept; it implied that the organism had reacted to the possibility of future damage with a view to avoiding it. Freud proceeds by examining the meaning of "danger" (1926a, Chapter VIII). Danger, he suggests, is the possi-bility of a trauma in the future; trauma is a sudden increase of need-tensions, beyond the assimilative capacity of the organism within a given time. Hence, "danger" is reduced to a sample anticipation of a sudden increase of need-tensions. That sets the pleasure-pain principle into motion, and reactions, such as, e.g., flight, are due to the working of the pleasure principle. The mechanism of the danger

[5] The possibility of such concepts being used, inadvertently, as explana-tory tools is always present. Blum (1951) says of "extra-physical purposive factors, or goals foreseen in advance" that "again and again such factors and goals are proposed as necessary for the understanding of evolution; and not too infrequently teleological implications creep into biological reasoning, and even, perhaps, into the design of experiments."

[6] Epistemologically a superstructure, logically a foundation.

[7] See Bernfelds statement (1932, p. 465): "Freud's long-term goal . . . is to reduce formulations which describe phenomena qualitatively, in terms of function fulfilled, to quantitative formulations." See also E. Kris (1950, p. 26) who calls Freud's previously unpublished and recently discovered, theoretical treatise (ex 1895) "a coherent attempt to describe the function-ing of the psychical apparatus as that of a system of neurones and to con-ceive of all the processes concerned as in the last resort quantitative changes."

signal and the actions which it releases seem clear, but there is still a nonmechanical element left: the *fact of anticipation,* and the question remains how the ego does the anticipating.

THE APPEARANCE OF ADLER'S INDIVIDUAL PSYCHOLOGY

Adler considered teleological thinking in matters of psychology not only as permissible but as required, and he condemned the application of causal concepts to human behavior. We do not act, he said, because of, but in order to. Freud, according to Adler, has erred in applying the causal thinking of the physical sciences to the human mind and human behavior.

In this way, Adler allied his cause with the then dominant German philosophy of knowledge, and won a claim for powerful academic support for his, in itself unimpressive, psychological doctrine of inferiority feeling, overcompensation, and social spirit. German philosophy of knowledge has made a radical distinction between *Naturwissenschaften* and *Geisteswissenschaften,* between *sciences* dealing with repetitive phenomena and trying to organize them in general laws, on the one hand, and *humanities* dealing with unique phenomena and trying to understand them individually, on the other (see p. 23f.).

Freud had erred, according to Adler, by trying to build a *naturwissenschaftliche* psychology, i.e., a psychology after the model of the (natural) sciences, while Adler's was a *geisteswissenschaftliche* psychology, or a psychology after the model of history.[8]

---

[8] It was never quite clear to me to what degree this philosophical underpinning, or superstructure, of Adler's doctrine was the work of Adler himself, and to what degree it was supplied by Adler's philosophically minded

THE DELAYED APPEARANCE OF EGO PSYCHOLOGY
IN PSYCHOANALYSIS

A psychoanalytic ego psychology did not begin to come
into being until the mid-twenties, or until about thirty
years after the first fundamental discoveries about the unconscious and repression, the role of sexuality, and the role
of childhood; and the question has been asked to what
the delay may have been due. Since progress in psychoanalysis in these years was the work of one man, this
amounts to asking a question about Freud's intellectual
development: why it went in one direction at a time
rather than in another. Reflection on such questions can
only yield conjectures. From Freud's writings we may
surmise that it had partly to do with an expansion of what
was considered to be the proper sphere of interest of psychoanalysis, or at least with priorities of subject matters that
psychoanalysis had to study; and partly with changing views
about the actual importance of the "ego." In discussing
Adler's system, Freud points out that parts of it are "useful
contributions to the psychology of the ego" and states that
they "have never been ignored by psycho-analysis, although
they did not deserve any special attention from it; it was
more concerned to show that every ego-trend contains
libidinal components" (1914a, p. 52). Also, these aspects
were not the really important thing in psychic life; Freud
comments on the ample use of the concept of secondary
"gain from illness" by Adler as follows:

---

disciple, Alexander Neuer. The latter, in any case, is responsible for the
name, *Individualpsychologie* ("individual psychology") which did not
mean, in the mind of the inventor, "psychology of the individual," as it is
probably taken to mean by the public, but "psychology of the undivided
(sc. personality)," in antithesis to the supposedly atomistic implications of
the term "psycho*analysis.*"

In the Adlerian doctrine the main emphasis falls on these easily verifiable and clearly intelligible connections, while the fact is altogether overlooked that on countless occasions the ego is merely making a virtue of necessity in submitting, because of its usefulness, to the very disagreeable symptom which is forced upon it—for instance, in accepting anxiety as a means to security. The ego is here playing the ludicrous part of the clown in a circus who by his gestures tries to convince the audience that every change in the circus ring is being carried out under his orders. But only the youngest of the spectators are deceived by him [1914a, p. 53].

Nine years later, Freud sees the development due to logical procedures:

If there are certain things to which hitherto psychoanalysis has not given adequate consideration, that is not because it has overlooked their effects or wished to deny their significance, but because it pursues a particular path which had not yet carried it so far [1923, p. 8].

The "ego" is now a subject receiving full psychoanalytic attention; but emphasis is still on its "dependent relationships" (1923, Chapter VI). Again a few years later, the role of the ego is summed up as follows:

The ego controls the entrance into consciousness as well as the passage into activity directed to the environment; in repression it exerts its power at both places. The instinct representative experiences the one, the instinctual impulse itself the other side of the ego's manifestation of authority [1926a, p. 22].

He confronts this view with "the dependence of the ego upon the id as well as upon the superego" and "its impotence and apprehensiveness towards both" described in the earlier publication and dissociates himself from opinions that have "emphasized the weakness of the ego in relation to the id, of the rational against the demonic in us" (p. 22f.), leaving the matter to further empirical investigations. In a review of the last-quoted work, *The Problem of Anxiety*, I described this situation at the time as follows (1928, p. 103):

. . . . the first fundamental problem of the book is the question of the boundary between ego and id, of ascertaining the part which both systems play in every psychic act. The boundary in question is the boundary between instinctual and purposive processes, between blind propulsion on the one hand and the choice of suitable means for particular purposes on the other hand . . . It is the borderline between 'possession' and control. [In another context (1930, p. 45f.), I summed the matter up in these words]: Psychoanalysis includes in the id everything by which man appears to be impelled to function, all the inner tendencies which influence him, each *vis a tergo*. The ego, on the other hand, represents the considered direction of man, all purposeful activity . . . Psychoanalysis, in so viewing the id and the ego, thus perceives man's being both impulsively driven and his being purposefully directed . . . The scheme of processes in the id would then be, in short: instinct—instinctual expression; those of the ego, however, are: task—task-solving, or attempted solution . . .

What did, probably, most influence the change was the realization that *parts of the ego* (and the superego) could be, and in fact were, *unconscious*. In the original concepts, the ego was identified with the conscious or, more precisely, the potentially conscious, i.e., the preconscious. The ego meant self-preservation, interests, moral and aesthetic concerns—all conscious strivings or considerations. As long as this was taken for granted, psychoanalysis, as the psychology of the unconscious, had indeed little reason to pay attention to it; it could safely assume that it was already known to common-sense psychology, or through the efforts of pre-Freudian, so-called "academic," psychology; or would become progressively known through the efforts of nonanalytic psychology. But then came the experience of patients who seemed to hold on to suffering out of a need for punishment—an observation which suggested that a verdict of conscience could be carried out without having been publicized, i.e., without being conscious; this led to the first assumption of unconscious aspects of the ego, i.e., of unconscious parts of the super-ego (Freud, 1923). Upon closer examination, Freud found that this result was not surprising after all. We cannot forget our deeds, or become unaware of our impulses, as long as we feel guilty about them, for guilty feelings would either keep our awareness alive or, if guilt were felt without being attached to any specific cause, the mind would remain in search for the latter. In order safely to repress an impulse, or a memory connected with it, we must repress the sense of guilt, too. What then remains is a trend toward punishment; one becomes "punishment-prone" as we might say in analogy to accident-proneness.

This concept of an unconscious part of conscience, which is unconscious because of its close connection with the id, was later supplemented by the concept of unconscious parts of the ego proper, i.e., of unconscious resistances, which must be unconscious for precisely the same reason, viz., their close connection with the repressed. If I were aware of the fact that I repressed an urge or an experience, I would also be aware, not necessarily of the repressed urge or experience, but of the fact that such must exist; the success of the repression would be in jeopardy and can only be protected by extending the repression to the very act of repressing itself.

If thus parts of the ego, i.e., particular operations, can be, and as a rule are, unconscious, they become a legitimate concern of psychoanalysis as a pychology of the unconscious and can no longer be left in somebody else's care. The necessity of an analytic ego psychology emerges.

THE DEFENSE MECHANISMS AND
MAN'S RESTRICTED REPERTORY OF DEFENSES

The increased attention paid to the nature of resistance led to an important step. Hitherto, repression had occupied the stage in these matters, and this quite rightfully so as repression was the *conditio sine qua non* for the development of a neurosis. But now Freud advanced the view that repression was not the only technique "of which the ego makes use in the conflicts which potentially lead to neurosis" but only one example of a family or class of defenses, "one which because of the direction that our investigations took was the first with which we became acquainted" (1926a, p. 110). That involved a slight change of terminology. The early term "defense" had been completely replaced by the more plastic term "repression"; Freud now proposed to revive the old name in a new sense, as a generic term for the whole class. Reaction formation, isolation and undoing are immediately suggested as other specimens of the class, with the added hypothesis that while repression seems to be characteristic of hysteria, reaction formation in the form of reactive ego changes, isolation, and undoing seem germane to obsessional neurosis (1926a, p. 111). It was suggestive to add to this list other mechanisms previously described in another frame of reference such as introjection, projection, displacement; or regression when used as a defense. Implicit was the invitation to study the defensive process and to add new defense mechanisms to those already known.

The "defenses" are now the subject of wide interest, not only among psychoanalysts but in a much wider circle. They enjoy a popularity which in earlier days was held by "sublimation," though the defenses have to share their more recent popularity with "aggression." At the present time, the term "defense" is usually used in a broad sense, indicating all responses to physical pain or mental suffering, both present or threatening. It includes, in particular, responses to pain, frustration, sorrow, danger, temptation (instinctual drives), guilt feelings or anxiety.

Any term may, of course, be used in any sense that has been agreed upon, but in order to avoid misunderstandings it seems necessary to point out that the sense in which Freud had reintroduced it was *narrower*: Defense was meant only to "embrace all these processes of similar purpose—namely, *protection of the ego against instinctual demands* . . ." (1926a, p. 111; italics mine).

From this point, the line of thought was continued by Anna Freud (1936). She described some mechanisms of dealing with unpleasant external reality and danger, such as denial and ego restrictions—termed preliminary stages of defense—and some new defense mechanisms proper, dealing with id strivings: asceticism and intellectualization in puberty, and altruistic surrender. In addition to these clinical findings, Anna Freud made a fundamental contribution to psychoanalysis. There was, first, a new perspective on resistances. Resistance had hitherto been seen largely as an obstacle to the progress of psychoanalysis: "whatever interrupts the progress of analytic work is a resistance" (Freud,

1900, p. 517). The way of dealing with it had changed, from hypnosis, a kind of rape of the mind, to the use of positive transference, and finally to the analysis of the motives of resistance, but despite this important development, the basic view was still that resistance, as the word suggests, is an obstacle. Through Anna Freud's study, it became clear that resistances are not only obstacles to the flow of information about the id but are themselves sources of information, viz., about the ego—no less important than the former.

The addition to theory was the proposition that out of the considerable arsenal of possible defense mechanisms, every individual uses but a very few; they are the techniques which he automatically applies in inner danger. We may say that Anna Freud discovered the fact that every man uses only a *restricted repertory* of defense mechanisms. And it is precisely because of this fact that the changed attitude toward resistances is of such significance, because the study of resistance can provide the information about a person's characteristic defense mechanisms.

What the causes for an individual's choice of his characteristic defense mechanisms may be—whether constitution, or selection, by the dominant instinctual drives, of those forms of defense which are congenial to *them,* or early chance application plus fixation by accidental success —is an important question; we cannot yet answer it satisfactorily.

But whatever the causes, one consequence is clear: whenever we see a defense mechanism applied in a particular situation, in dealing with a particular challenge, we have a right to expect that this mechanism is applied by this person in many other situations, too. Once our attention has been called to a person's defense mechanisms, we should be able to spot them in other activities as well, and then to point them out to him, as a *modus operandi* unconsciously and automatically applied by him and characteristic of him. This mechanism, once established, may then be traced back to its beginning in childhood; and, just as happens to an id impulse that had been brought back to consciousness, any operating procedures and their early beginnings, once made conscious, will meet with the patient's judgment of reality and with his reasoning powers, on the level of consciousness, and will become subject to revision.

THE THERAPEUTIC APPLICATION

The application of the new analytic ego psychology to the treatment of patients can be described as a widening of the analyst's outlook; to describe it we have to use also the changed view of psychoneurotic anxiety which had emerged a little earlier.

In the early decades the psychoanalyst had practically only the libido theory to use in his work with his patient. When I joined psychoanalysis in the mid-twenties, I heard a highly respected psychoanalyst of the first generation describe the goal of (therapeutic) analysis in these words: "To search the libido out in all its hiding places and then to guide it toward new uses." The analyst's main, perhaps the only, focus of interest in studying his patients in these days was in their libidinal fixations; the analyst listened to his patients with the question constantly in his mind: *What are the patient's desires?* What does the patient (unconsciously) want?

When, through the revision of the theory of anxiety, it became clear that anxiety in psychoneurosis was not simply a product of intoxication through undischarged libido but a reaction to danger, albeit not a realistic one, it became imperative to think not only of the patient's particular goals but also of his particular dangers. The old question about his desires had to be supplemented by a second question also continuously in the analyst's mind: *And of what is he afraid?*

Finally, the realization that defenses are unconscious, and characteristic for the patient, extended the analyst's alertness to this third question: *And when he is afraid, what does he do?* So far, no further aspects have been added to the analyst's orientation in his study of his analysand.

AN ALPHABET OF DEFENSE MECHANISMS

The various defense mechanisms, described in the literature, appear to be of quite different complexity. Some, e.g., repression or intellectualization, seem to be quite simple, elementary, while others, e.g., altruistic surrender, are highly complicated and may be considered composites of simpler mechanisms. A haphazard collection of known defenses sounds somewhat like this: protein, egg, cake. There seems to be a need for an alphabet of defense mechanisms, i.e., a description of simple forms out of which the more complex mechanisms are composed.

Furthermore, repression seems to hold a unique place among the defense mechanisms in so far as it is present in all other mechanisms; it may occur alone or in conjunction with one of the others. In reaction formation, e.g., what happens is not only that a person becomes oversolicitous and kind to keep his aggression subdued, or becomes meticulously clean to control his anal impulses, but also that the aggressive, or the anal, impulses have become unconscious, i.e., the drive against which reaction has been formed is repressed. So is the original drive in sublimation, etc. Repression, it seems, has not undeservedly held the center of the stage for so long; it is really a universal mechanism to which others may, or may not, be added.

This statement about the ubiquity of repression may need some qualification because repression may only be the most conspicuous, most easily detectable specimen of a subclass of mechanisms which lead toward the more or less complete expulsion from consciousness of a group of mental phenomena centered around an instinctual drive. Isolation may be another representative of this same subgroup, somewhat less effective than repression inasmuch as it succeeds only in blurring out certain connections that would give the story meaning while leaving a few isolated pieces, like the masts of a sunken ship, reaching out into consciousness. I once suggested that denial of a drive may be an even less successful process (1951). If repression is seen as one representative of a subclass, the above statement about the repression accompanying all defensive mechanisms would have to be qualified in this way: that one mechanism of this subclass is present in all defensive mechanisms.

Perhaps one can describe the defensive mechanisms from three points of view, or coordinates, as it were: first, the expulsion from consciousness—more or less completely; then, whether or not, and in which way, provision is made for substitute gratifications; finally, the nature of the countercathexis that watches out lest the warded-off drive regain access to motility, or return to consciousness, or both. Repression, then, is comparable to the outlawing of a revolutionary party, without any provision for integrating the revolutionary forces into the life of the community, such as, e.g., measures that would tie some of the revolutionaries, particularly the leaders, to the existing system, and provision to redress at least some of the grievances of the disaffected; and without any countermeasures against a possible resurgence except police attention. The other mechanisms, on the other hand, would be comparable to the many procedures in which the outlawry of the revolutionary party is accompanied by various inducements for its leaders or the rank and file and with countermeasures other than mere police action, as, e.g., the deliberate strengthening of groups whose interests run counter to those of the revolutionary group, according to the principle: *divide and conquer.*

It seems that these three points of view—withdrawal of consciousness, substitute gratification, and counter-cathexis—are sufficient to describe all defense mechanisms.

POST-FREUDIAN TRENDS

All psychoanalytic ego psychology that stems from Freud's later works, including the innovations made by Anna Freud, still falls within the view of psychoanalysis as a psychology of the unconscious, i.e., it deals with the unconscious aspects only, and leaves other problems, e.g., learning, perception, thinking, to other branches of psychology.

This has changed with the work of Hartmann, who has set out to construct a psychoanalytic theory coextensive with a comprehensive theory of the mind. This expansion has been performed with the help of the concept of a "conflict-free sphere" in the ego or, in later terminology, of an "autonomous ego" which encompasses all phenomena studied by other psychological investigators. Their results can be integrated into a comprehensive theory of the mind under the chapter: autonomous ego.

It amounts to the same whether we say that psychoanalysis is a psychology of the unconscious which, for a
comprehensive theory of the mind, has to be supplemented
by the results from other sources; or say that psychoanalysis
can construct a comprehensive theory of the mind in which
these results from other sources will find their place in a
theory of the autonomous ego—except for the difference
that the job of integrating these various results is, in the
first, older attitude left to unknown hands, while in the latter
there is an implicit claim that psychoanalysts could do
the business of integrating. But whatever may be the case
in this point, it seems that "conflict-free sphere" or
"autonomous ego" are the convenient terms with the help
of which this integration, by whatever hand, will some day
take place.

A different road was pursued by Federn in his papers
on ego psychology which are post-Freudian only in the
sense that they came after Freud's work on this subject;
most of them were published during Freud's lifetime.
Federn's concept of the ego is not that of a problem-solving
agency but rather that of the seat of sensations; it encompasses a person's feelings about himself, in relation to himself (in situations of inner conflict and in self-observation)
as well as in relation to the outside world. Federn cor-
related the various phenomena of "ego feeling" to processes
of libidinal or destructive cathexis. His concept of the ego
is related to, though not identical with, the "self"—a term
widely used in philosophy for reflective activities in which
man takes himself as an object, and introduced into psychoanalysis by Hartmann.

Federn's work may have important implications, particularly for an understanding and treatment of the schizophrenic psychoses. There are some semantic pitfalls to

avoid. It is legitimate to define the "ego" as an integrative, problem-solving agent; and equally legitimate to define it as the seat of sensations about oneself and the outside world. But one cannot do both at the same time without further investigation, i.e., one cannot take it for granted that integrative activities and sensations are always so closely associated that they must be attributed to the same agency. The ego of Federn which experiences the boundary between the self and the outside world, or between different parts of the self, need not be the same as the ego of Freud which signals danger and represses dangerous impulses.

THE SUPEREGO

Moral attitudes have always had their part in the story of inner conflicts as psychoanalysis had described them. But it was only in the "middle years" that Freud suggested to speak of a special agency of the mind which he called ego-ideal—one's ideal of oneself—and to which he attributed self-observation and conscience. The delusion of being observed would then indicate a split, or break, along what is normally a structural relationship. From this point of departure Freud developed his group psychology (1921) in which he proposed to explain behavior in masses by the hypothesis that man had placed a leader in lieu of his ego ideal and that all members of the mass identified themselves with each other on the basis of the common relation to the leader. Through these considerations, mass psychology became an argument in favor of the assumption of a special "level" within the ego, viz., the ego ideal.

Sometime later, Freud's interest was particularly attracted by the experience of the "negative therapeutic reaction," i.e., the behavior of people who seemed to react to every prospect of recovery with an exacerbation of their symptoms. They seemed to consider themselves unworthy of health, Freud concluded; they had accepted neurotic suffering as a deserved punishment, yet they had no consciousness of crime. How was this unconscious need for punishment—or, in looser language, this unconscious sense of guilt—possible?

Freud's answer, as already reported (p. 178), was that part of the conscience—which he now called superego rather than ego ideal, substituting a word of a more solemn ring, of darker or more tragic implications for a word of a more casual sound[9]—was bound to be unconscious because it was so intimately tied up with repressed wishes.

The bulk of the superego was thus described by Freud as an "heir of the oedipus complex." When the oedipus complex is "dissolved" toward the end of the period of the early flowering of sexuality, through frustration of its strivings and through fear, it leaves its imprint upon the ego: the identification with the parents and the acceptance, as part of the ego or, more accurately, as a separate level within the ego which confronts the rest of the ego (superego). This identification is motivated by the need of alleviating fear; it is easier to obey one's own rules than to be subject to someone else's arbitrary power. This identification is the prototype for all "brain-washing," i.e., the acceptance, by adults, of standards held before them by a power at whose mercy they are. The advantage which the child has won through identification with the parent

[9] Some analysts, e.g., Alexander, have actually suggested to keep both terms, ego ideal and superego, but with different meanings—the ego ideal for a person's conscious aspirations, the superego for the unconscious aspects of the matter. I believe Freud himself had no such intentions; the two words were synonymous for him.

and internalization of his commands was won only at a price; the child was subject to parental restrictions or punishment only when the parent was present or knew about his infringements, but the superego always knows and the child is from now on subject to its restrictions all the time.

Whatever the motives for this kind of identification may be, it obviously implies the possibility of a level within the ego, of a reflective attitude; this will be considered later.

With the core of the superego formed, the child enters the latency period. Formal school education with most peoples begins around the age of six, presumably because at that age the child has a bare minimum of inner rules of conduct.

The strongest demands of the superego are those outlawing incest and homicide, reflecting the two aspects of the oedipus complex. It is on this point that, in psychoanalytic view, the superego appears like an iceberg with a large mass spread out below the surface; i.e., that there may be unconscious tendencies to self-punishment which influence conduct and feeling.

But it is only the "core" of the superego that can be said to come into being as late as at the end of the early prime of sexuality. There is sufficient evidence to show that before this stage behavior is restrained not only through the threat of external consequences but also, at times, by internal opposition that has the appearance of a nuclear morality. We then speak of prestages of the superego (W. Reich, 1925; Fenichel, 1926, p. 109ff.). There is no sharp boundary between them and the "superego" or "core of the superego" that comes into being with the "dissolution" of the oedipus complex. But moral attitudes during the early preliminary stages appear as more or less isolated phenomena, while the latter, the heir of the oedipus complex, is more of an interconnected whole. The basis for the early phenomena of conscience is partly identification with adults and inner acceptance, internalization, of their requests, similar to the process through which the later, more massive superego formation will take place; and partly it is the outcome of ambivalent attitudes. Either aggression toward an object, usually a sibling, was prevented from being expressed in action—be it through environmental interference, be it through interference by the child's own, friendly, feelings— and has turned back against oneself in the form of guilt feelings. Or the aggressive act has actually been carried out, the aggressive strivings have become less intense in consequence of the satiation, while the erotic strivings, i.e., the longing for the object, have increased through the damage suffered by the latter; the erotic strivings thus have now temporarily the upper hand and express themselves in repentance and the desire for reparation. Repentance is thus the libidinal, self-punishment the aggressive, aspect of the moral phenomena (Nunberg, 1926; Freud, 1930).

Melanie Klein and her collaborators have gone further than other authors by postulating a much earlier emergence of the superego, not only in the form of preliminary stages, with more or less isolated examples of internalized demands, of repentance, and of self-punishment, but as an integrated whole which has much to do with very early and very deep anxiety. These are very challenging ideas the verification of which has to struggle with the difficulty of entering into the inner life of a preverbal child.

So much about the beginnings of the superego. Its development is by no means closed with the events at the end of the period of childhood sexuality. There is a continuing process of identifications. For quite some time, the internalized parental figures which form the superego do not seem to be stably settled; new figures of authority may appear in the outside world and they may come to evict the former internal parent figures and take their place in the superego, i.e., the conscience is not firmly established and can still be changed through environmental influence. But this accessibility to influence through attachment to new authorities diminishes as one grows older; in the "self-directed" it will eventually disappear. Almost all people, however, remain subject to such influences in a mass situation.

Since the discovery of "unconscious guilt feelings" and the subsequent concentration of interest on the superego in general, the role of guilt feelings in psychopathology has become appreciated. They play a central role above all in depressions and in some types of "fate neuroses" (H. Deutsch). Some authors have been so much impressed by these phenomena that they seemed to them a crucial factor in *all* forms of psychopathology. Alexander, e.g., called it at one time the task of the analysis of neuroses in general to destroy the archaic superego (1925). Such views, I believe, overestimated the role of guilt in the realm of psychopathology. Perhaps we may remember a remark that Freud once made with reference to Kant's declaration "that nothing proved to him the greatness of God more convincingly than the starry heavens and the moral conscience within us. The stars are unquestionably superb, but where conscience is concerned . . . a great many men have only a limited share of it and scarcely enough to be worth mentioning" (1932c, p. 88).

The superego is not only the conscience though this is

its psychopathologically most important manifestation. In conscience, man treats himself critically, like a demanding and punishing parent. But there are also types of behavior in which man treats himself benevolently, like an approving and comforting parent. E.g., Freud described humor, i.e., the higher forms of what is commonly so called, as the manifestation of such a benevolent attitude toward oneself; by joking over one's mistakes, shortcomings or misfortunes, one assumes a superior vantage point, as though one were actually not imprisoned within the same skin, and implies that things are not as important after all—as if a parent comforts a child that cries over a broken toy or a reprimand received in school. Implicit in all this is the ability to step back and to assume such an imaginary vantage point from where to look at oneself, demanding, critical or punishing in the case of conscience, benevolent in the last-described instance.[10] The ability of such self-objectivation may thus be taken as the essential *formal* characteristic of the superego; hence, self-observation should be one of its functions as was originally implied in the introduction of the ego ideal (Freud, 1914b).

But this leads to further vistas if we take the results of other psychological investigations into account. In the last decades, animal psychologists have studied the intellectual performance of animals. Köhler did his pioneering work with chimpanzees during the First World War and showed that chimpanzees did have problem-solving abilities,

[10] Hence, a sense of humor is found only in those who are capable of assuming a tender parental attitude toward themselves; it is not shown by those who cannot step back and take distance from themselves (as, e.g., paranoids) or whose attitude toward themselves is purely punitive (as, e.g., certain ascetic Puritans) or whose loving attitude toward themselves is exclusively on the level of direct indulgence (as, e.g., normal delinquents [see p. 202f.] and related selfish, demanding types, and some depressives).

i.e., that their responses to difficulties could not be explained by mere trial and error but involved insight into the structure of a situation, acquired with a "quantum jump." Intelligence was thus no longer the exclusive prerogative of man.

While this investigation and the many subsequent investigations of the intellectual functions of animals seemed to narrow the gap between man and the subhuman mammals in this point, they showed it to be wide and probably unbridgeable in another point. The intellectual achievement of the animal appears to be bound up with concreteness and vital need, while man's activities are not limited to any such bounds and extend to abstractions without limit; the ability of abstractions has thus crystallized as the specifically human characteristic. Köhler already noticed that the imagination of his apes seemed to fail them when it was a matter of negative rather than positive achievements: if the desired object was placed high above ground and some boxes were lying around within their reach, some animals could grasp that they might be piled one on top of the other to serve as a ladder; their anticipatory imagination could fill the boxes into the empty space, as it were. But if the road to the goal was blocked and it became a matter of removing things that were there, they found the task very difficult; they did not seem to have much ability to anticipate the elimination of objects. This negative achievement may well be the nucleus of abstraction.

The idea that in this area is to be found the dividing line between human and subhuman gained incidental support from the work of Kurt Goldstein who in decades of clinical study of brain-injured individuals could show that damage of certain cerebral areas leads to an "impairment of the abstract attitude," an increased concreteness. The aphasic, e.g., who is not able to name an object when asked in the neurological examination, may have the very same word at his disposal when he needs it in a living situation. Patients of this type have lost, to a greater or lesser degree, the very dimension of the mind that makes man most human.

I proposed on an earlier occasion (1936, Chapter III) to call the ability to take distance from concrete situations and needs, and to assume an imaginary place and take oneself as object of neutral observation or critical or friendly evaluation—to call all this the "formal superego function." It is the underlying characteristic of all activities of the superego and in it we may well see the characteristic dimension through which the mind of man goes beyond that of his relatives in the animal kingdom, and has become able to create symbolic language and that ever-increasing body of knowledge and rules that transcends the immediate biological needs and that we call civilization.

The main stations in the development of the superego thus appear to be these: The *formal* superego function can be proved to exist when the child is capable of understanding a fictitious situation, e.g., a playful pretense. Signs of the so-called *preliminary* stages of the superego can usually be demonstrated in the third year. The *"nucleus"* of the superego, with the bulk of its unconscious parts, appears at the end of the period of early flowering of sexuality and the beginning of latency.

The superego development continues into early adulthood. A kind of re-examination and integration of the superego takes place in adolescence: the various rules that had been internalized in childhood are now compared with each other and allotted different degrees of importance; some are discarded in the process. With most people, the superego remains capable of change in mass situations and, probably, in some other cases of character changes as yet not systematically described.

10

Some Problems in Psychopathology

The following is an attempt to outline some problems in psychopathology which seem to have important implications for a theory of the mind in general.

PSYCHONEUROSES

Among the various psychopathological types, we are most familiar with the neuroses. Yet even here there are some questions of fundamental importance that cannot be considered as "definitely" settled.

As we have seen, the theory holds that the neuroses are due to conflicts over a demand of the libido, unsuccessful repression, and the return of the repressed; and that repression of a libidinal demand occurs for the first time only in childhood. But that suggests a few questions.

First, how does the outcome differ according to the kind of opposition which the instinctual drive encounters—mere fear of external consequences, or fear due to internalized parental prohibitions, or opposition involving another instinctual drive? Anna Freud (1951, p. 130) has made these differentiations and dealt with them in the case of child-

196

hood disturbances; she distinguished between external, internalized and internal interference, requiring for their treatment advice to parents, psychotherapy of the child or full psychoanalysis of the child, respectively. One hopes that there will be further studies along these lines.

Then, is the pathogenic conflict necessarily *always* a conflict over a demand of the id, or can repression of the voice of the superego have similar consequences? Freud (1936) showed that a feeling of unreality can be the consequence of a distorted return of a dismissed guilt feeling. He had once, seizing upon a fortuitous chance, made an unscheduled trip to Athens; it was an unexpected fulfillment of a dream, in those days almost impossible of achievement for all but a tiny few. Standing on the Acropolis, with so little time for inner preparation, he had a sensation of unreality as though all this were not true. Freud analyzed this sensation as an elaboration of a feeling of guilt; this trip, which relative financial ease had made possible and higher education had made enjoyable, had brought it home to him how far he had risen above the modest station of his father. The feeling "it is not right and should not be true" was not admitted to consciousness and instead of it there appeared the feeling "it is not true." In this way, the feeling of unreality is built like a neurotic symptom, with the difference that what was repressed was not the demand of an instinctual drive but a superego interference. I know from my personal analysis that a neurotic symptom can be so structured, and I have found the same to be true in a carefully studied case of my own observation. The question has not, to my knowledge, been treated in the literature. Nor, of course, has the question that will have to be asked next once this possibility is demonstrated, regarding the relation of such superego conflicts to instinctual demands.

Then, after the introduction of the theory of a destructive instinct, the difference between the results of conflicts over a destructive impulse invites further study.

Another aspect of the neuroses that seems to deserve more attention is their relation to perversions. "Neuroses," said Freud (1905b, p. 165) "are, so to say, the negative of perversions"; and he thereby allocated to both neuroses and perversions their respective place in a psychodynamic map of psychopathological phenomena. "The contents of the clearly conscious phantasies of perverts (which in favorable circumstances can be transformed into manifest behaviour) . . . and of the unconscious phantasies of hysterics (which psycho-analysis reveals behind their symptoms) . . . coincide with one another even down to their details" (Freud, 1905b, p. 165f., n.).

But experience has shown that perverse traits are regularly observed in cases of psychoneurosis too, and the question arises whether Freud's above-quoted formula of neurosis as the negative of perversion might apply not only to the relationship between the two groups of cases but also to the relationship between the neurotic and the perverse traits in one and the same case with the clinical diagnosis of psychoneurosis.

One man whom I had the opportunity to study analytically suffered from insomnia; he was very careful not to exert himself too much and when he felt he had, he was worried lest his overexertion may have drained him of all strength so as to make it impossible for him to face the next day. The very worry would keep him awake, thus further increasing his fatigue. He was one of those perpetually concerned about their input and output of energy, a type whom Edward Bibring proposed to call "bookkeepers." This man experienced the height of sexual enjoyment in a form of coitus in which he was lying on his back while his partner sat on him and made the copulatory movements. His fantasy had it that in this position the maximum amount of ejaculate would be extracted from him, or, as he put it, that he would be "sucked dry, with no drop of semen left." Outside of the orgastic situation, to be drained of strength was the object of his fear and he had built up phobic precautions to avoid it; the very same, applying directly to semen, brought him the height of orgastic pleasure in the sexual act. In his neurosis he was afraid of the derivatives of the very thing which he enjoyed in its direct manifestations in moments of passion; his neurotic symptoms were the negative of his own perverse fantasies.

Another man felt most of the time abused and treated with disrespect by other people, in particular by his wife with whom, despite of these neurotic difficulties, he had a basically good relationship. At times in his sexual practices, and even more clearly in his sexual fantasies not carried into action, he delighted in submission and self-degradation. Here again, the very impulses in the struggle against which the neurosis developed, were yet gratified, in action or fantasy, in moments of passion. In both instances the neurotic symptoms are the negative of desires and fantasies which at rare moments, at the height of passion, are admitted to full gratification.

The cases in question show both the conscious expression and satisfaction of one of the component drives and its repression and the struggle against its derivatives — the former in the (regressed) conditions of passion, the latter the rest of the time.

The coexistence, in the same person, of direct gratification of an instinctual drive and of a neurotic symptom due to the unsuccessful repression of the same drive seems similar to what Freud described as the splitting of the ego in the defensive process (1938).

EGO DISTORTIONS, CHARACTER NEUROSES, FATE NEUROSES

Great interest has been devoted by psychoanalysts in recent years to the study of the so-called neurotic ego distortions,[1] and related conditions. In these cases, an impending neurosis was either avoided through suitable personality changes; or a neurosis already developed, or in the process of development, was integrated into the personality. The simplest example of the first possibility is the so-called ego restrictions described by Anna Freud (1936, Chapter VIII). The person withdraws his interest from a certain area in which his aspirations have brought him into danger. He may thereby succeed in avoiding the danger—and the neurosis which may have been one of the possible results of continued exposure—but he is a poorer person from then on.[2]

In the second group, there are many ways of adjusting to a neurosis, or compromising with it. The integration of

[1] See a recent Symposium on this subject with contributions by Gitelson, Gillespie, Glover, Katan, Nacht, Rosenfeld; opening remarks by Waelder (1958).

[2] Against the view that ego restrictions impoverish the personality the argument has been advanced that the ideal of the *homo universalis* is unrealizable, that specialization is necessary and that ego restriction is therefore a normal, beneficial process. There is no doubt about the need for specialization, but it need not, and should not, come about through ego restrictions. It makes a difference whether a person was either never interested in a subject or, though interested, decided not to follow this interest very far because other subjects appealed more to him; or whether he withdrew under fire. In the latter case, one must also consider that self-deception, i.e., the fact that those who apply this mechanism do not admit to themselves the real reason for their withdrawal but embrace a rationalization of the sour-grape variety instead, causes lasting damage to the intellect.

neurotic tendencies into the ego means that the feeling of alienation, so characteristic for the psychoneuroses (p. 35f.), is gone, and that these tendencies assume a function in the service of self-preservative and self-expansive goals; they are now part and parcel both of what one feels to be oneself, i.e., of the sensate ego of Federn, and of the integrative ego of Freud, to which one is now bound by the secondary gain which they provide. A simple example is the integration of an obsessional neurosis into the daily routine of a filing clerk or a low-eschelon bureaucrat in general. We call these types *character neuroses*.

There is another subgroup, however, in which the neurosis has not been assimilated into the ego in the form of character traits which determine a person's day-to-day adjustment, but rather in a form which seems to govern the curve of life in its broadest outlines—the tidal waves of destiny, as it were, rather than its small undulations. For this type Helene Deutsch proposed the term "fate neuroses" (1932).

DELINQUENCY

Delinquent behavior may appear as part of various afflictions, such as, e.g., neurosis, psychosis, mental deficiency, or postencephalitis. There is also deliquency per se, not as part of an otherwise defined psychopathological entity, or normal delinquency, as it may be called.

Delinquency, in this context, should not be understood in a purely legal sense, as persistent unlawful activity—delinquent in this sense are the Amish who refuse to send their adolescent children to school—but in a psychological sense, as repeated offense against the moral law as it is generally understood though not necessarily always articulated.

The moral law implicit in the sentiments of our civilization and implicit already in the rules of conduct expressed
in the ancient Sumerian texts is, in essence, the demand not
to do unto others what we do not want to be done unto
ourselves, or, in Kant's more precise formulation, to treat
everybody else not merely as a means to our own ends but
as an end in himself. If this is the core of our moral senti-
ment, the essence of psychological delinquency may be
seen in an attitude that does treat the other merely as a
means to one's end, with greater or lesser, and in the extreme case, with complete, disregard of his own interests
and aspirations. From the mildest to the severest forms of
delinquency, from the motorist who hit the fender of a
parked car and did not leave his name and address, to
the murderer and kidnapper, there is always the common
element that the action was not restrained by regard for
the rights and interests of others because such considerations either proved too weak in comparison with the motive
to action, or were altogether lacking. Regard for the interests of others rests ultimately on object relationships,
i.e., on the degree of kindness one feels for the other.[3] In
the delinquent, such feeling of kindness for, or of identification with, the victim of the action is either entirely absent,

[3] This statement is in need of qualification, however. Respect for the rights
of others can rest not only on libidinal openness to them but also on the
sternness of a command that had been fully internalized and become part
and parcel of conscience, i.e., in childhood terms, a child may refrain from
aggressive action against a sibling not on account of coexisting libidinal
attachment to the sibling but merely because of the parents' command and
threat. It may be questioned whether this motive of restraint may not
become supplemented, in time, with an attachment to the sibling whom
one has been forced to accept. But it is thinkable that aggression against
oneself, rather than love for the other, can carry the burden of the restraint,
and a person may be a fully socialized member of a community without
much friendly feeling for his fellow citizens. Perhaps some Puritan types
come closest to this description.

or is overcome by the motor force of the delinquent action.

The attitude of considering others only as a means to one's ends or as an obstacle in one's way is, in fact, the earliest condition of all of us. The child at first cares only about the satisfaction of his self-preservative needs; soon, it also wants to be petted and loved (need-fulfilling stage —Anna Freud). The ability to love others, and to love them as they are, not only as givers, develops later; it varies greatly in the width of its embrace and in its depth.

Some individuals commit crimes to rescue themselves from great danger, others for the sake of a love object. They are not necessarily of a criminal type, i.e., they may have lived out their days as law-abiding citizens had they not met with an emergency of this kind.

The point at which inhibitions based on regard for others will give way under frustration or danger is different in different people, but in few is the regard for all others so absolute that no kind and no degree of frustration or danger can overcome it.

If people whose object relations are defective, either in general or outside an ingroup, have strong desires which could be satisfied at the expense of outsiders, if they have an active bend of mind or are favored by opportunity, and not restrained by fear, external or internalized, they will act against the moral law.

Delinquency is only one of the manifestations of a personality lacking in genuine relations. The variety of object relations and their consequences for personality and illness, and for the conduct of life, has recently moved into the center of psychoanalytic interest.

For the detailed treatment of problems of delinquency, see Aichhorn (1925), Friedlander (1947), Eissler (1949), Glover (1959).

THE SCHIZOPHRENIC PSYCHOSES

The problem of the psychological processes involved in the functional psychoses of the schizophrenic group is still basically unsolved, despite many important contributions which psychoanalysis has made possible.

The search for the psychological processes involved in the psychoses in no way implies any assumption of their primarily functional character. There is much to suggest that organic processes play a far greater role in the etiology of the schizophrenic group of psychoses than they seem to play in the etiology of the neuroses. But that does not make the psychological study of the psychoses useless or obsolete, just as a demonstration of the fact that the art of a period is greatly influenced by the cultural trends of the time does not make the study of intrinsic principles of stylistic development useless. Even if the etiology of the psychoses should be proved to be mainly organic, it does not follow that each psychotic manifestation is a *direct* outgrowth of organic destruction or malfunctioning; some psychotic manifestations would be just that, but others could be the *psychological* consequences of the former.

One possible relationship between organic and psychological factors could well be this: schizophrenic psychoses could be the product of understandable psychological processes not unlike those that occur in the formation of the neuroses, with the difference that, through organic destruction or malfunctioning, one factor in the chain of events—as, e.g., the libidinal attachment, or the destructiveness, or the power of self-control, or the anxiety—may be substantially changed in intensity, with completely different outcome.

Just as in the history of religion, philosophy, art,[4] and

---

[4] "Art history should deal both with the internal life of forms and with the relation of these forms to life; and it is not possible to do the second without having mastered the first" (Clark, 1956).

sciences, allowance must be made both for cultural impact and immanent trends, so an intricate web of relationships in brain and mind seems to require the study of both organic conditions and psychic processes in the psychoses.

Several psychological characteristics of the psychoses which set them apart from the psychoneuroses are clearly discernible to the psychoanalytically oriented observer; some pertain to the id, others to the ego. What was noticed first was a difference with regard to the *libido;* the loss of contact with the outside world, an inability for genuine object relations—autistic behavior, in Bleuler's terminology. The first psychoanalytic approach to the schizophrenic psychoses (Abraham, 1908; Freud, 1911b; 1914b) saw these phenomena as consequences of a withdrawal of the libido; the latter was seen as followed by an incomplete, or incompletely successful, restitution of object relations. In the light of this theory, psychotic symptoms are partly due to the withdrawal of the libido from the outside world and its assemblage in the ego, and partly to the incomplete restitution. The basic disturbance of the (schizophrenic) psychoses was thus seen in the distribution of the libido; this was well in accordance with the focus of interest in psychoanalysis at that time.

The theory was unspecific about the causes of the withdrawal, however. For this part of the process, Melanie Klein once suggested that it is due to "the ego's excessive and premature defense against sadism" (1930). More recently, M. Katan (1950) suggested that the break with reality is due to a very intense "bisexual conflict": i.e., the heterosexual position has first been completely abandoned so that the homosexual position provides the only bridge to the outside world; the latter is then given up under the impact of intense anxiety, thus leading to a complete break with reality.

With the introduction of a *destructive* drive, and the new theory postulating two basic drives of the id, Eros and Destruction, it was realized that, in the psychoses, destructiveness appears often pure; in fact, observations on psychotics are among the arguments in favor of postulating a destructive instinctual drive at all. Thus, it was recently suggested that the primary disturbance of schizophrenia might be in the area of aggression (or, more accurately, in the inability of the ego adequately to mitigate—neutralize—aggression) (Hartmann, 1953; Bak, 1954).

The withdrawal of the libido and the appearance of pure destructiveness are id aspects of the psychoses; there are ego aspects, too. First, there is a considerable diminution in the ability of self-control, a *lack of integration* that leads to a flooding of consciousness with id derivatives, often diffusely from various developmental stages at the same time; or an immense fear of that very thing.

Then, the ego has not only been seen as a problem-solving, inhibiting, and integrating agent but also as the place of experience of oneself and of the outside world (or of oneself in the world, as one might say, in a slight allusion to existentialist language) with all the possible variations of experience and interrelation (Federn). Schizophrenics show *unclear boundaries* between the inner and the outer world, or a disturbance of the "ability to differentiate the self from the environment" (Freeman, Cameron, McGhie, 1958, p. 51) and Federn saw in this the basic disturbance of schizophrenia.

Finally, there also seems to exist in psychoses anxiety of an intensity and intolerability not encountered to any comparable degree in normal life or in the neuroses, a *mega-anxiety*, as it were—a factor to which particularly M. Katan has called attention. This factor, too, could constitute the basic disturbance of schizophrenia.

In Melanie Klein's theory all these factors have their place: the intensity of self-destructive forces, the immaturity of the ego that cannot deal with them except by projection, the paroxysmal anxiety aroused by objects who therefore appear as highly threatening, and the break with reality.

But there are objections to seeing in any one of these factors *the* basic disturbance of schizophrenic psychoses. As far as the withdrawal of the libido is concerned, it was always a question why the withdrawal of sexual interest should bring about the profound disturbance in the sense of reality which we find in psychoses and why it is not possible that a person who does not love anybody can yet maintain, not, to be sure, a warm response to people or things, but an adequate perception and evaluation of facts on the basis of self-preservative interest or fear alone, at least as far as they may affect his vital interests. Does one have to love in order to see? This question was answered by Freud in the sense that what happens in the withdrawal of the libido is not merely that such a person does not love anyone else but that his libido is concentrated upon himself, i.e., that he has an excessive love of himself and hence overvalues himself; and that this distortion of perspective leads to the breakdown of the sense of reality. This is undoubtedly a correct description of what happens to many people, but, as was suggested earlier (p. 68), it seems to apply more to the misconceptions and delusions to which, to a greater or lesser degree, we are all prone, and to which Hobbes referred in the famous line that men "see their own wit at hand and other men's at a distance," than to psychotic delusions. It is the essential characteristic of the latter that they are not corrected by experience. It is not explained, it seems to me, why the distortion of perspective, caused by the withdrawal of libido from the objects and its subsequent concentration upon the ego, is not accessible to the slow corrective influence of experience as the emotional distortions of facts usually are.

Furthermore, there are cases of psychoses of the schizophrenic class in which a libidinal retreat from the object world does not seem to have taken place at all; these patients seem capable of genuine object relationships. Their number is small, but a single case suffices to question a theory that would make the withdrawal of libido the necessary first step in the psychotic process.

These question marks apply also to Katan's theory which is an offshoot of the theory by Freud and Abraham, differing from it mainly through a special assumption regarding the *causes* for the withdrawal of the libido from the outside world.

The other hypotheses leave questions, too. Not all psychotics are very destructive. The breakdown, or threatened breakdown, of ego integration appears to be universal, but it is questionable whether this statement is more than a redundant reformulation of the symptoms. Equally, the breakdown or the blurring of ego boundaries has been called merely descriptive and its explanatory value has been questioned. The role of mega-anxiety has not yet been thought through in its consequences. All these aspects are probably relevant for psychoses. But we are not sure how they all hang together: whether they all need be present in every case, whether one of them represents the original disease process from which the others follow, or whether they are all consequences of still another factor, or of a number of factors; or even whether they are not only the psychologically unconnected debris of organic destruction. There are many clues but few secure results.

DISTURBANCES OF IDENTIFICATION

There is another group of people who have trouble with their ego boundaries without being psychotic; their disturbances in the sensate ego compare with those of psychotics approximately as, in Freudian theory, the neuroses compare with the (schizophrenic) psychoses. With these individuals, it is not that ego boundaries are, so to say, in the wrong place so that part of the inner world is experienced as though it belonged to the outer world, and vice versa; they have a proper discrimination between inside and outside. But they are suffering from a feeling of emptiness or nothingness and are trying to fill themselves up, as it were, through appropriating from others without it ever becoming fully their own; or they are struggling against that very state of affairs, trying to maintain their "identity" against the danger of being engulfed by others. Both types would probably clinically qualify as psychopathic personalities, but the correspondence between traditional clinical entities and psychodynamically defined types is never complete.

Among the first group are what Helene Deutsch (1934) has described with the expressive name of "as-if" personalities; such individuals behave "as if" they had feelings or opinions and a personality of their own, while, in fact, they borrow them from other persons with whom they identify themselves and on whom they sponge, as a kind of psychological parasites or satellites, carrying the borrowed features for a while until the next identification takes over.

Some individuals like to merge into others, to be part of the host, as it were, so as to fill their own emptiness with the substance of others. A similar type has been described by Edward Bibring: the person who fills himself up in bodily surface contact with others, skin to skin. In some people, the feeling of emptiness is accompanied by physical sensations of weakness. Some have to fill themselves up with experience, with knowledge, with symbols of strength of various kind, and have to do so unceasingly because their gains are presently lost; their life resembles that of the Danaids who have to fill water into a barrel that leaks at the bottom.

To the second group belong those who cannot, or cannot indefinitely, accept the pseudo existence of the as-if type but struggle against the persons by whom they feel engulfed or owned or by whom they desire, in part of their mind, to be engulfed or owned, and are for ever trying to acquire a feeling of substance of their own. For this type, particularly, the "search for identity," described by Erikson (1956), is a constant effort.

Those who enjoy the existence of ego parasites as well as those who struggle against it have fantasies and symptoms which to the casual view may look like the product of urges for feminine surrender or the struggle against such urges, both so familiar to us from the study of the neuroses. Yet, what these people describe as their feelings goes beyond mere castration fantasies: as though it were not merely sexual submission that is either desired or feared but rather extinction as an individual. One might say that, in these cases, the *castration complex extends into the ego.*

Psychopathological problems like those which we have selected for discussion have obvious implications for a general theory of mental functioning. The questions raised about the neuroses are relevant, e.g., for an understanding of the significance of sexuality, and for the possibility of two or more contradictory solutions of conflicts being applied simultaneously, i.e., of two or more contradictory lines of development branching off from a point of conflict.

The ego distortions illustrate the integrative activities of the ego while delinquency can teach us something about the conditions for the development or disintegration of object relations and the relation between allegiance to the persons of the innermost circle as against allegiance to wider groups. The various hypotheses regarding the psychoses bear on the relationship of ego and instinctual drive, on the possibilities and limits of ego integration, on the special psychopathological significance of pure destructiveness, and on the question of whether great quantitative increase in anxiety can lead to consequences decidedly different in quality; and on the essence and role of the feeling ego and its boundaries from the outer world. The last-mentioned psychopathic types seem to promise insights into other aspects of the ego—world relationship.

11

Principles of Psychoanalytic Therapy

THE RATIONALE OF PSYCHOANALYTIC THERAPY

Psychoanalytic therapy stands and falls with the psycho-analytic theory of the neuroses. If this theory is correct, the psychoanalytic treatment appears as the only causal treatment, so far developed, of the neuroses, which treats the condition by trying to remove its cause; and if the theory should prove to be wholly or partially incorrect, the psychoanalytic treatment would lose its *raison d'être*, and whatever results have been achieved by its application would have to be explained as incidental, due to some other factors.

As formulated earlier, the psychoanalytic theory of the neuroses consists of four propositions, the first three of which deal with the dynamic, and the fourth with the genetic, or historical, aspect of their etiology.

The neurotic process consists of three steps: conflict over a sexual urge, (unsuccessful) repression, and return of the repressed. The psychoanalytic treatment attacks the second of these steps only, i.e., it does not undertake to do away with the existence of inner conflict, however that might be attempted, nor does it try to prevent the return of the

repressed as might, and has, been done by direct therapeutic suggestions. It tries to *undo the repressions* and
thereby to restore to consciousness the full conflict as it
had probably been conscious, if only for a fleeting moment,
and as it would be conscious had the individual not been
unwilling or unable to face up to it, and not tried to escape
from it by repression. One might say that repression has
cut the inner communications, and that undoing the repression and enlarging consciousness restore these communications; the formerly repressed drives are then put in
contact with the tendencies of the rest of the personality—
other drives, self-preservation and ego tendencies in general,
moral considerations, etc.; all tendencies can vie with each
other on the market place of consciousness and a solution
of the conflict may be worked out, not immediately but
with time; a solution not invariably pleasing to others from
a social or moral[1] point of view but one that is not neurotic.
One patient once expressed it well in a remark made during
the working-through period of his analysis: "I should stop
behaving this way and make peace with myself."

Undoing repressions and making conscious the unconscious does therefore establish the situation which would
have prevailed had repression not interfered. It had interfered because one was unable or unwilling to bring those
sacrifices which any solution of an inner conflict unavoid-
ably implies. The establishment of a situation that had
previously been avoided because of the pleasure principle
must bring unpleasure. This is the meaning of Freud's
statement that "analysis transforms neurotic suffering into
everyday misery" (Freud, 1932c). It is precisely in this
point that we can usually find a criterion to decide whether
a therapeutic improvement was a genuine analytic result

[1] For the latter point, see p. 243ff.

or was due to implicit suggestions or reassurances or to satisfactions in the transference, or to similar factors; improvement across the board, so to say, i.e., disappearance of symptoms and increase in general well-being, will probably be due to the latter kind of circumstances, while in the genuine analytic success the improvement and increase in well-being due to the disappearance of symptoms is accompanied by the distress of having to face a dilemma hitherto avoided; patients say that they are both better and worse off.

These three factors, or stages in the neurotic process, that we have so far discussed, form the dynamics of a neurosis; in the case of a childhood neurosis of fairly recent origin, this is identical with the etiology of the neurosis. But if neurosis breaks out in adulthood, there is a further complication; the psychodynamics of the neurosis, its formation out of the current conflict, do not tell us the whole story. Neurosis is not freshly created in adulthood; the current conflict ends in neurosis only if there was a childhood neurosis over the same or a related issue, or if, in any case, the current conflict was fated for repression by its connection with repressed tendencies and experiences of childhood.

From this fact, the fourth principle of our theory of neurosis, it follows that, in adult neurosis, the analysis of the psychodynamics, i.e., of its origin in the current life of the patient, is not enough—though it may practically suffice in very mild cases—but has to be supplemented by a genetic, or historical, analysis which tries to inch backward from the conflicts of the present to the childhood experiences to which they are related, to revive old passions and old battles so that they may be relived consciously, in the perspective of an adult personality, leading to a somewhat different outcome.

But the treatment of a neurosis cannot be limited to a dynamic and genetic analysis of the symptoms; one has to deal with a much wider area. There are many patterns of behavior which are not in themselves pathological but which contribute to neurosis because they restrict acceptable satisfactions and possible responses to frustration and to danger and thereby make the outbreak of conflicts more likely and their solution more difficult. These traits must be analyzed, too. They must not be taken for granted but must be challenged and questioned; repetitive elementary patterns must be sought behind the wealth of manifestations, must be isolated and understood with their unconscious elements and traced back to the emotion-laden situations in which they took shape so that they can to a degree be made liquid and shaped anew.

Theoretically, the whole of the personality falls thus within the scope of analysis. Practically, there are various degrees of closeness to, or remoteness from, the pathological area, and the illness which is being treated remains the point of orientation, or focus, of the analysis and determines the emphasis of the analytic search. Attempts to open the case of personality traits which are not pathological and have no conceivable relation to pathological traits may also have difficult going as the patient may lack motivation for cooperation.

PSYCHOANALYSIS, EDUCATIONAL PSYCHOTHERAPY, PSYCHOANALYTICALLY ORIENTED PSYCHOTHERAPY

Psychoanalytic treatment consists in the exploration of the unconscious and the effort to make it conscious to the patient. It is *exploratory psychotherapy* (Knight, 1949, 1952).

Educational psychotherapy may be the generic term for all forms of influence that try to bring about a better adjustment of a person to the outside world through advice, suggestion, guidance, retraining, occupational therapy, community living, and other means.

There is also the possibility of mixing a fragment of psychoanalysis with a dose of educational psychotherapy—"to alloy the pure gold of analysis freely with the copper of direct suggestion" (Freud, 1919a, p. 168), which Freud thought would have to be done in a mass application of psychoanalytic therapy. It is usually called "psychoanalytically oriented psychotherapy." This mixture is bound to meet with the difficulty that the attitude of neutrality required for analysis (see p. 239) and the attitude of guidance are incompatible; by taking educational measures, the analyst interferes with his possibility of doing analysis. The partnership between psychoanalysis and educational psychotherapy may therefore well end up somewhat like coalitions between democratic and totalitarian parties in which the former are likely to be swallowed up by the latter; in the end, only education remains.

THE INDICATIONS OF PSYCHOANALYTIC THERAPY

It follows from the nature of the psychoanalytic procedure that its indications of therapy depend on the following factors:

(a) that the condition to be treated is either altogether due to the interruption of inner communications through repression or related mechanisms, i.e., is due to inner conflict not faced but evaded—"the dust has been swept under the carpet"—or that repression has at least a major part in its psychodynamics; i.e., that we have to do with a psychoneurosis or at least with a condition involving a significant neurotic component;

(b) that the inner conflicts at stake permit a viable solution without prohibitive cost; and

(c) that the patient is able to understand the psychoanalytic method and willing and able to cooperate with it.

The Type of Illness

Since the psychoneuroses, in the psychoanalytic view, are due to the fact that inner forces are locked in a conflict which is unsoluble because the contending forces do not meet on the same ground, psychoanalysis is the causal treatment of the psychoneuroses.

More recently, however, psychoanalysis has been applied to conditions other than psychoneuroses, viz., to perversions, delinquencies, and behavior disorders, to psychoses and so-called borderline cases; one speaks of the "widening scope" of psychoanalytic therapy.[2] These conditions are not simply constructed like psychoneuroses and it cannot be taken for granted that the task consists in making it possible for the patient to make peace with himself, or even that the unearthing of repressed material will always have beneficial consequences.

Our approach to these other forms of psychopathology has sometimes reminded me of the story of the schoolboy who tried to shorten his preparation for an examination in zoology by taking a gamble and studying the chapter on the insects only. It so happened that he was questioned about the elephant. The elephant, he replied, is a big animal, and it has an enormous trunk. The trunk helps him in many

[2] The expression has been taken from the title of a Symposium chaired by Ernst Kris, with contributions by Stone (1954), Jacobson (1954), and discussion by Anna Freud (1954b).

ways, e.g., against the fleas which molest him a great deal. And from then on he continued about fleas. The story does not report whether he got away with it. We analysts are quite familiar with the neuroses, and when we deal with other conditions we often simply apply what we have learned about neuroses and handle these other conditions as though they were neuroses. I doubt whether we always get away with it.

The intimate relationship of psychoanalytic treatment to the psychoneuroses was pointed out by Anna Freud (1954a, p. 48f.) who stated that "the particular relationship between id and ego . . . on which our analytic technique rests, is valid for neurotic disorders only. In all other instances, whether psychosis, delinquency, addiction, childhood disturbances, etc., there are deviations in quantity or quality from the neurotic patterns to be found in the id or ego respectively, or in their relation to each other. This point of view, I believe, underlies also Dr. Eissler's paper on the introduction of parameters into the technique of psychoanalysis." The following is, to a large extent, an elaboration of this statement, except for the use of the word, technique; the issue at stake, to my mind, is the choice of the treatment appropriate to the cases—whether psychoanalysis, or educational psychotherapy, or a mixture of both—and I would reserve the term, technique, for the way of carrying out a psychoanalytic treatment (see p. 236ff.).

In dealing with pathological conditions other than psychoneuroses, psychoanalysis, as the causal treatment of the neuroses, can do one of two things: it can either search for the neurotic features which may yet be hidden in the picture of other afflictions and single them out for attack, or it can try to stimulate a patient to the production of a neurosis and then treat its own product. The therapeutic chances of psychoanalysis will depend in either case on the degree of *leverage* that the cure of the neurosis dug out, or stimulated, has for the total psychopathology of the case.

The situation may be exemplified with Sachs's paper on perversions (1923). Perversions, according to Sachs, are not simply due to fixation of a component drive of sexuality as the dictum about neurosis being the negative of perversion would let us assume. Rather, they have a more complicated structure. Perverse individuals have reached the genital stage of libido development, i.e., they did advance along the road toward heterosexuality. But, like the neurotics, they ran into conflicts around the oedipus complex, and withdrew to other activities which serve, somewhat in the manner of reaction formations, to protect them against the dangers of heterosexuality.

Whether Sachs's theory covers the perversions exactly is not here at issue; but it should be noted that his theory implies that the etiology of the perversions is similar to that of the neuroses, and that it thereby makes the application of psychoanalytic treatment a rational endeavor. For if it were true that perversions are merely due to a pregenital fixation and the insistence on a particular kind of gratification, it is not immediately clear what the unearthing of unconscious tendencies would change in the situation. But, according to Sachs, the perverse individual had actually moved toward the normal, heterosexual, position and had merely given it up under the influence of anxiety, the causes of which are unconscious. Perversion, then, is the outcome of the process: heterosexual aspirations—anxiety—retreat to a pregenital position. If this is so, the function of psychoanalysis becomes clear. If the sense of danger can be revived in all that it implied, it can now be viewed with the knowledge and the resources of an adult; and in this reappraisal, anxiety may be sufficiently mitigated to allow a resumption of the road toward heterosexuality. The reintegrating therapy of psychoanalysis is clearly applicable if the condition is based on anachronistic anxiety; it would be a different story if the condition were based on something akin to so-called habit formation in addictions, i.e., on a conditioning to a particular type of satisfaction.

The psychoanalyst's search for the neurotic elements of a case is reflected in his alertness for inner contradictions. He is constantly surveying the field to discover inconsistencies in the patient's thoughts or actions. Wherever he discovers any sign of them he will examine the point more closely and present any evidence of inconsistency to the patient. He is thus trying to bring contradictions into the open in order to discover, or to see more clearly, the inner conflicts which they may indicate. In this way, he is trying to open the area of conflict widely and clearly, with a view to discovering possible unconscious elements, ultimately to help the patient to "make peace with himself." This very technique shows the analyst's concentration on unsolved inner conflict, i.e., on the neurotic aspects of a case.

This close relationship between psychoanalysis and psychoneurosis may be further illustrated in the examples of homosexuality and delinquency.

Anna Freud (1951, p. 117ff.; 1954a, p. 50f.) described a type of male homosexuality exemplified by a successfully treated case; the patient had married and was raising a family. Homosexuals of this type had reached the phallic stage of libido development but had abandoned it early under the influence of anxiety. They had found a way out closely similar to a process which Helene Deutsch (1933) described for a certain type of spinster who appropriates another woman's children and raises them, and which Anna Freud (1936, Chapter X) described in general terms as "altruistic surrender." The homosexual individuals in question have given up their own phallic strivings as too dangerous, but they have closely attached and subordinated themselves to other males[3] whose phallic triumphs they enjoy in identification, without the anxiety that has made their own activity impossible; and with a background of hope that through their submission to the master-phallus some of its power will be left in them, i.e., that they will learn in the process and finally become perfected as men themselves. It is understandable that analysis can cure a case so structured. For the perversion is built like a neurotic symptom: the patient's own phallic desires are repressed and his enjoyment of the phallic pursuits of his masculine love objects can be seen as the disguised return of the repressed. If analysis succeeds in unraveling the knots and reviving the earlier stage, it is possible that the castration anxiety which frightened the little boy away from the phallic road may now, viewed by the adult in the cool light of a later day, lose much of its terror; and the abandoned development may be resumed. In Anna Freud's case, this happened over an intermediary stage of exuberant phallic activities.

But what is our situation as therapists if the perverts have acquired a strong taste in their activities? Let us assume that a little boy was intensely stimulated by a father whose unconscious homosexuality was disguised as solici-

---

[3] This *pathological* development of *men*, leading toward passive homosexuality, is therefore closely similar to the *normal* development in *women*, who substitute an attachment to the male owner of a penis for the wish, which they had to give up, of possessing a penis themselves. The main difference between the two processes appears to be that the surrender of phallic wishes is, in one instance, due to impossibility of fulfillment, in the other to anxiety.

tude and kindness. Perhaps the father had amply participated in the handling of the boy in infancy. Later, perhaps,
he had played with him, taken him regularly into his bed
for roughhousing and other sexually loaded games. Or an
older brother had forced the child to play the passive role
in games of sexual content, such as, e.g., horse and rider,
and, by sexualizing the experience, the little boy had
learned to enjoy what he had to endure. Through all this,
the child may have been conditioned to passive homosexual
enjoyment.

All this may not mean anything in terms of later perverse
acts. The storm of puberty may sweep it away; or else,
it may live as an undercurrent in an outwardly normal
heterosexual life, providing, perhaps, some perverse coloring of it, or it may influence social behavior, or be expressed in neurotic symptoms. But let us assume that a boy
so conditioned in his childhood years is in early puberty
subject to homosexual seduction in the manifest sense of
the term and learns to enjoy it. There is no evidence that
such a series of seductions would by themselves *alone* lead
to manifest homosexuality as an *exclusive* sexual expression,
but there is reason to believe that it can substantially re-
inforce the homosexual position, however rooted. The latter
is then no longer only a compromise with repressed masculine drives but has become a source of genuine libidinal
satisfactions for their own sake. At the very least, this might
be compared with the secondary gain in neurosis which
may at times prove an unsurmountable obstacle to psychoanalytic cure.

It therefore seems that male homosexuality offers a good
prognosis to psychoanalytic treatment if, and to the degree
that, it is built like a neurosis. To the degree that it is
due to an acquisition of tastes and a conditioning to certain

pleasures, it does not seem to respond favorably to psychoanalytic treatment. This may be seen also in the case of the
socially accepted pregenital gratifications, e.g., smoking.
It can be given up under "educational" pressure, in the
sense of our definition—e.g., if that appears medically required—but it seems hardly subject to influence through
psychoanalysis—though the latter may work out the use
of smoking as a protection against hidden anxieties.

We find a similar state of affairs in the treatment of
delinquent traits. As is generally known and was mentioned
in these pages, too, there are various types of delinquent
behavior: neurotic delinquency, delinquency of psychotics
(e.g., paranoiacs or maniacs), of mentally deficient individuals, of psychopaths, and what might be called normal
delinquency. *Neurotic* forms of delinquency are built like
neuroses and can be treated by psychoanalysis like neuroses;
a typical example is kleptomania in which a woman is
compelled to steal goods which she is either, in her conscious judgment, not vitally interested in owning or could
well afford to buy. The treatment of the delinquency of
oligophrenics, psychotics, etc., is part of the larger psy-
chiatric problems of the treatment of these conditions. But
what are the chances of psychoanalytic treatment of the
various forms of behavior disorders, i.e., of psychopaths
and of so-called normal delinquents?

Normal delinquency, as was pointed out before (p. 202f.)
is in the last resort the consequence of a defect in object
relations; its accessibility to influence through psychoanalytic treatment depends on the possibility, by psychoanalysis, to establish or to improve object relations. Whether
or not this is possible, depends on the nature of the inadequate development or the disturbance of object relations.
If object relations had been damaged, perhaps through ex-

periences of desertions in childhood which made the child afraid to attach himself again lest it suffer once more, analysis may well revive sufferings and anxieties of old, and unless the old ability to love had meanwhile withered beyond repair, the development may yet be taken up where it had been injured, and lead to the rise of genuine object relations. These are neurotic types of disturbed object relations and, once again, psychoanalysis can deal with them. But what about other cases in which object relations, for whatever reasons, have never developed beyond the need-fulfilling stage? One does not see how psychoanalysis, by making the unconscious conscious, could teach such individuals to feel what they had never felt and never had come near to feeling.

The restriction of psychoanalytic therapy to psycho-neuroses and related conditions was expressed by Freud many years ago in these words: "the field in which analytical therapy can be applied is that of the transference-neuroses, phobias, hysterias, obsessional neuroses, and besides these such abnormalities of character as have been developed instead of these diseases. Everything other than these, such as narcissistic and psychotic conditions, is more or less unsuitable" (Freud, 1932c, p. 212). If our present examination of the conditions, a quarter of a century later, did not lead to a different answer, it is due to the fact that these limits of psychoanalysis are not the consequence of inadequate knowledge and likely to be expanded when knowledge expands, but that the very nature of the psychoanalytic process makes it the key that fits the neuroses but does not fit other disorders.

Accessibility to Solution

It must be said, first of all, that not all conflicts permit of a tolerable solution; there are some neurotics who "would not, under the conditions we have assumed, support the conflict but would rapidly succumb or would cause a mischief greater than their own neurotic illness"; in such instances neurosis was still "the mildest possible outcome of the situation" (Freud, 1910b, p. 150). But such cases are very rare exceptions among applicants for psychoanalysis, rarer than they were half a century ago when Freud wrote the quoted words, presumably because psychoanalysis has meanwhile learned to deal with some of them.

A solution of a conflict between instinctual drives and opposing forces can be either in favor of the instinctual drives or in favor of the opposing forces, or can be a compromise between the two, giving each some, though not all, of their demands; or it could be through a sublimation of the drives (Freud, 1910a, p. 53f.). Any one of these solutions might have occurred in the course of the development, had repression not intervened and, by pushing the drive underground, prevented it from direct expression, on the one hand, and protected it from the influence of experience, on the other.

A solution in favor of the instinctual drive will usually occur if the adult feels his opposition to the drive no longer justified or no longer necessary; perhaps, opposition had been due to fear of dangers which frighten us no longer. Such a solution reflects, for better or worse, increased *courage*.

In a great many instances, the decision will fall against the gratification of the instinctual drive. The drive, no longer repressed, but received into the ego, i.e., recognized as part of oneself, is then, as Freud put it, condemned, i.e., consciously denied gratification. This, of course, causes unpleasure. What usually happens is that over a certain period of time a wish that is persistently denied satisfaction is gradually given up; just as people forced to follow a diet, or to give up smoking, after a time—usually not a very short time—lose their craving. Such people may search for, and find, new gratifications instead.

The situation is comparable to all weaning processes and to the process of mourning. After the loss of a loved person, the longing for the lost one breaks out time and again, and the realization that the beloved no longer lives or is no longer available, and that longing is therefore in vain, renews the pain each time. The persistently returning desire meets an equally persistent answer: "it is impossible"; and under the influence of this often repeated experience the longing is gradually blunted and the survivor eventually turns his interest to new objects. This is so, as a rule, in people not too old; most very old people, and some people not so old, never overcome a loss.

What happens during the working-through process in psychoanalysis with regard to desires that are not accepted for satisfaction may well be compared to the process of mourning. Is it a mere chance or does it have biological significance that the time of normal mourning—one or two years—is of the same order of magnitude as the time of working through in analysis?

Ordinarily, a real solution of a conflict involves the frustration of one or the other of the contending forces, or a partial frustration of both; the gain of one side is the loss of the other. The ability to make this kind of settlement depends either on the degree that anxiety has diminished or that anxiety is borne with more equanimity; or on the ability to bear frustration, at least temporarily. *Tolerance for frustration* and *tolerance for anxiety*—both together make what is often roughly called the strength of the ego —are the conditions of the cure.

But there are also solutions through sublimation, involving the possibility, external and internal, to find substitute gratifications and the willingness to settle for them. It is in view of this type of conflict solution that factors like the *flexibility* of the libido, the extent of a person's *talents*, the *range of his interests,* the *ability to sublimate,* have been mentioned as conditions favorable for a psychoanalytic cure.

While inflexibility—the adhesiveness (*Klebrigkeit*) of the libido—stands in the way of many solutions, the very opposite quality, an easy shift from one object to another, may render any result shallow and not durable. In this latter type, "the results of analysis often prove very evanescent; . . . one feels . . . as if one had been writing on water" (Freud, 1937, p. 344f.). This kind of shallowness may not augur well for lasting results of analysis unless it can itself be analyzed as a disturbance in the development of object relations.

Among the indications of psychoanalytic treatment one must therefore consider what the chances are for the patient to arrive at a workable solution of his conflicts once they have been brought to his consciousness—a prospect to be considered in the light of his life constellation and of the various psychic factors involved. Any one of these factors may itself be of neurotic origin and is in this case, or to this extent, liable to change by analysis. But it should also be borne in mind that the unconscious wisdom of life sometimes puts to shame our calculations.

The following episode may be interesting in this connection. An opinionated young analyst who was convinced that sexual inhibitions—in the conventional sense of the word—were due to the sins of a class society and fully to be remedied only by the abolition of classes once challenged Freud with the question what psychoanalysis could do for a spinster; for even if her inhibitions regarding genital sexuality could be lifted, she was too old and too unattractive to be able still to find happiness as a woman. He could see a satisfactory solution only on the side of complete genitosexual expression and, because of his youth, he took a dim view of the chances of those not so young. In his reply, Freud talked about a case from his own experience, a woman who, liberated from crippling inhibitions, had soon found a suitable partner under quite inauspicious circumstances, and he added: "For this the Lord Almighty has His own miraculous ways and He will never let you into the secret of them . . ."

Freud, apparently, had confidence in the ability of the average person to deal with average difficulties if he was only free from neurotic impediments. It was for this reason that he rejected the idea, advanced in some quarters, that analytic treatment should be followed, or crowned, by a "synthesis," i.e., an educational effort.

The discussion of the various factors on which the solubility of conflicts depends may help us to understand whatever therapeutic results have been achieved through relationship therapy, i.e., through an unspecific form of influence which bypasses symptoms as well as their causes and merely tries to provide the patient with the experience of a human relationship. Whenever this has actually been achieved and true relationship could be developed, some solutions of inner conflicts, which had been out of question as long as a person was exclusively concerned about himself, will become possible.

From all these considerations we cannot infer much about

the role which the age of the patient plays for the prospects of psychoanalytic therapy because the various factors vary with age in different ways, some increasing, some diminishing, some doing first the one and then the other. A change of external reality, virtually impossible for the child and difficult for the adolescent, is relatively easy in the early adulthood years, and becomes quite difficult once the first big decisions—career, marriage, family—have been made; middle and old age, finally, often regain considerable freedom in this respect. Flexibility diminishes with age; frustration tolerance and the ability to wait increase.

Analyzability

The conduct of an analysis depends on the patient's cooperation. He must be willing to appear regularly for his appointments, on time, or reasonably so; nobody can be analyzed *in absentia*. He must be willing and able to follow the analytic rule to permit everything to enter his mind and to say it once it had entered it; it is probably not possible to fulfill this rule exactly all the time, but he must struggle for it with reasonable success. And he must be willing and able, to some degree, to face up to things as they crystallize in analytic work, and not for ever evade them.

To make this possible, the patient must, first of all, be intelligent enough to understand the procedure. We have no exact studies to define precisely the minimum intelligence required, but it is safe to say that a more than average intelligence is needed to undergo analysis successfully.

Then, the patient's willingness and ability to cooperate with the treatment depends on how strongly he is motivated in favor of analysis—or, rather, on the balance of his motives pro and con. Motives in favor of analysis include, above all, his wish to recover; mixed with it are, however, "irrational" factors, i.e., the search, partly unconscious, partly preconscious, for satisfactions or self-punishment in analysis (Nunberg, 1924). On the other side of the scales are the costs of analysis in terms of time, money, and other sacrifices such as self-exposure and, above all, the resistances. An individual in his own right will, as a rule, enter analysis only if the sum total of the motives in favor of analysis — both rational and irrational — outweigh the forces, both rational and irrational, that militate against it.

Once a person has entered analysis, the balance of forces changes. To the side in favor of analysis is now added, as a rule, the relief which comes from unburdening oneself, from the beginning of a relationship to the analyst, and, often, from a reinforcement of the at first vague hopes for cure through simple but effective interpretations which the analyst may already have been able to suggest. On the other side of the scales is the increase in resistance, which is bound to occur once the patient faces the immediate danger of the rising unconscious. But, with very rare exceptions, patients who enter analysis out of their own volition are sufficiently strongly motivated to be able to do their part with the help forthcoming from an experienced analyst.

The situation is different with those, mostly children and youths, who do not seek analysis out of their own initiative but are brought to it by someone else; they lack sufficient motivation. For the analysis of children Anna Freud discussed the need of a preparatory treatment in which the child should find a stake of his own in the analysis (1927). In general, the analysis of individuals who entered analysis not out of their own initiative faces the problem whether the missing motivation can yet be awakened. In many cases it is wiser not to start analysis under inauspicious circumstances but rather to wait until enough disappointments have accumulated in life to bring home the need for therapy.

Such are, roughly, the conditions of analyzability. There are, of course, relations between the requirements of analysis and the *modus operandi* of various psychological types— e.g., hysterical or obsessive types—which make one or the other aspect of analytic work difficult for a specific type, but we consider them as difficulties within, rather than contraindications to, analysis; they are subjects of clinical research. It is possible, however, that a refinement of indications will sometime emerge from these researches which will permit the analyst to recognize some cases as poor analytic prospects on this ground.

THE SCOPE OF EDUCATIONAL PSYCHOTHERAPY

Patients for whom psychoanalytic treatment is not indicated or does not work to its best advantage are often treated by educational psychotherapy or by "psychoanalytically oriented psychotherapy." This does not mean that the latter can deliver the goods which psychoanalytic treatment cannot; with some characteristic exceptions, it merely means that a genuine cure cannot be hoped for but that some relief can be expected from these other forms of treatment.

The exceptions, i.e., the cases in which educational psychotherapy is neither *Ersatz* nor a stopgap, nor a temporary palliative but the *therapy of choice,* are the behavior disorders of nonneurotic character, i.e., individuals who have not made the step from the pleasure principle to the reality principle, or have made it only too inadequately, and individuals whose superego standards fall short of the standards of their milieu. They both need education. Examples of the first type are, e.g., many alcoholics; they often respond favorably to educational treatment at the hand of a therapist who is familiar with their needs.

In cases of neurosis in which frustration tolerance is very low, not on a neurotic basis but due to overprotection in childhood ("I have never been made to do what I did not want to do," said one such person in analysis), educational psychotherapy is necessary with regard to this aspect of the case, i.e., psychoanalysis (of the neurosis) may have to be mixed with education (of the immature ego).[4] The fact that an educational attitude interferes with the analytic attitude has been emphasized before; that sets limits to the amount of education that can safely be applied in analysis.

The psychotherapist—or the psychoanalyst trying to educate—will often find that his modest powers of influence are inadequate to do the job. Adults will often prove to be educable in serious matters only by the parental powers of adult life, i.e., by destiny.

THE TREATMENT OF PSYCHOSES

There is general agreement that real psychotics cannot be analyzed. They usually cannot be made subject to the procedure in the acute stage, and those who might be

[4] See Anna Freud's comment in her *Technique of Child Analysis* (1927) to the effect that an adult neurotic who "should prove to be so impulsive, so undeveloped intellectually, and dependent to such a degree on his environment as are my child patients" would probably be given by psychoanalysts a mixed treatment: "as much pure analysis as his nature could tolerate while the rest would be child analysis, because on account of his quite infantile character he would deserve nothing better" (p. 58).

willing and able to submit to it, to lie down and to follow, by and large, the analytic rule as, e.g., paranoids may, are not cured by the procedure.[5] The treatment of psychotics which psychoanalysts have practiced or advocated has therefore been a form of psychotherapy based on psychoanalytic concepts, but operating not through the undoing of repressions and the enlargement of consciousness, but through other therapeutic agents such as the granting of satisfactions, the assistance in re-repressing, or the development of a personal relationship. The consideration of these methods lies outside the topic of this chapter; moreover, having never applied any of these procedures myself and having only scant information about their results, I do not feel competent to judge them. But an outside observer of these efforts cannot fail to be impressed by the fact that they all seem to require an amount of personal investment on the part of the therapist that far exceeds anything necessary in the psychoanalysis of the neuroses in which personal investment of the analyst is limited to friendly interest, a strong desire to help, and careful attention to the patient's productions.

The imperative necessity of great personal investment in terms of time, availability and effort, in the psychotherapy of the psychoses, is characteristic for these illnesses, and a testimony of their severity; it necessarily limits the social usefulness of the therapies in question.

THE BORDERLINE CASES

It is altogether different with many so-called borderline cases. This term, as used here, should comprise two groups.

[5] I am aware of the fact that analysts of the Kleinian school of thought have made different claims and I regret the fact that I have had no opportunity of first-hand acquaintance with their results. The above statement should be read with this qualification in mind.

On the one hand, there are those highly self-centered persons with a peculiar type of object relationship that might be called long-distance relationship, with hypochondriacal symptoms, or feelings of physical weakness, and many oddities of behavior; some are given to abstract intellectual pursuits. There is another group, partially overlapping with the first, of people who are, on the whole, successfully fighting off a psychosis of a schizophrenic type; they may have paranoid ideas, even at times hallucinations, but they never lose the knowledge of their unreality. In dealing with these cases, psychoanalysis is therapeutically highly promising though the therapeutic result does not simply rest with the reintegration of the repressed as is the case in the analysis of psychoneuroses.

One part of the effectiveness of psychoanalysis in these cases is due to the fact that understanding serves to them as a weapon in their struggle against the inner processes of which they have to keep control. One such person in analysis used to refer to interpretations as "weapons" and if he had received none during an analytic session, or several sessions, he felt apprehensive or weak, naked to his (inner) enemies, to adapt a Shakespearean line. This sort of use of interpretations can, perhaps, be understood as similar to intellectualization as it is described by Anna Freud (1936, Chapter XII). In this process, which occurs in severe puberty conflicts and in the prepsychotic stage of schizophrenia, individuals struggling against powerful drives seem to be helped in their struggle by speculating about this matter, or its derivatives, with great efforts; the struggle against a strong masturbatory urge may thus lead to, and be reflected in, speculations about the freedom of the will. It is, as Anna Freud put it (1936, p. 178), an "attempt to lay hold of the instinctual processes by connecting them with ideas which can be dealt with in consciousness." In the same way in which manipulation of ideas can serve as a defense against the buoyancy of instinctual drives, psychoanalytic interpretations can be used by the persons under discussion in their struggle against a threatening psychosis.

Furthermore, psychoanalysis is therapeutically effective for another reason, too. Whether there will be successful resistance to psychosis or surrender seems to depend on where a person stands in the scales of activity vs. passivity (in men also: masculinity vs. femininity, sexual surrender), contact with others (object relations) vs. isolation, and existing, or possible, sublimations vs. absence of sublimations or inability to sublimate. The more active a person is, the more will he intend to translate his psychotic fantasies into action, which will usually be a bad thing if he is dealing with people but may be a good thing if he is dealing with nonpersonal objects; and the more intelligent and capable of sublimation he is, the more will he be able to find a way of expressing them in reality which is socially possible and which may even be valuable if he has sufficient talent. The more masochistic he is, the more will he be inclined to surrender to psychosis rather than to fight it. And the better his object relations, the stronger is he bound to the common world and the less likely is he to be torn away from it by his delusions into a private, psychotic, world. Analysis is helpful inasmuch as it strengthens activity, masculinity in men, and sublimations; occasionally object relations, too. Psychoanalysis is in these cases therapeutically effective *not by* actually *curing the illness* (as is the case in the successful treatment of psychoneuroses) but *by strengthening* the resistance of the *remainder of the per-*

sonality. But that may well make the difference between adequate functioning and collapse.

PSYCHOANALYTIC TECHNIQUE

If the treatment chosen is psychoanalysis, the question arises how one has to proceed in order to search out the "active" unconscious and how to help the patient to see and to face it. This is the subject of psychoanalytic technique.

In psychoanalytic papers and discussions the term "technique" has often been used in a much wider sense, comprising all procedures that are applied in a treatment conducted by a psychoanalyst; not only the ways of conducting an analysis but also the choice of the psychological treatment to be applied—whether psychoanalysis or educational psychotherapy or a mixture of both; and, in the latter case, what kind of educational psychotherapy should be added to what parts of psychoanalysis, when and how, is commonly treated as "technical." One can, e.g., read that in a particular type of patient the "classical technique" must be altered and the analyst must be "more active." Such recommendations may, or may not, be valid in the particular case, but they are not questions of technique. What is meant is rather that the respective author does not recommend in these cases the application of psychoanalysis pure and unmixed but considers a mixture of psychoanalysis and educational psychotherapy as better suited for the patient. The question of whether surgery is, or is not, indicated in a particular case, or, if indicated, whether or not it should be supplemented with other forms of treatment, is not a question of surgical technique.

Psychoanalytic technique consists of three groups of measures:

1. procedures necessary to establish and to maintain an "analytic situation," i.e., a setup designed for the search into the repressed;

2. the handling of resistance and transference; and

3. ways and means of how to introduce the patient into the insights gained by the analyst or the hypotheses formed by him, so as to assure it as far as possible that the analysand will understand them accurately and completely and face up to them.

Ad 1. An *analytic situation* is a situation of artificial, partial, and controlled regression for the purpose of a study of inner conflicts. In an analytic situation, the balance between the inner forces—between the conscious and the unconscious, between purposive, goal-directed, activities and impulses acting upon us—is altered artificially in favor of the unconscious and the impulsive. Such a change is necessary to make it possible for those aspects of the personality which are ordinarily prevented from direct expression to manifest themselves more clearly, while at the same time being able to see the inhibitory responses which are stimulated into increased activity by the very emergence of otherwise checked impulses. Were it not for the latter consideration, i.e., were it not for the need to see not only the impulses but also the responses which they elicit—were it only a matter of getting manifestations of repressed impulses, it might be proper not merely to change the inner balance but to eliminate, as far as possible, the inhibitory tendencies altogether. That was, in fact, done in the cathartic treatment of Breuer and Freud (1895), the predecessor of psychoanalysis, when hypnosis was used to silence opposition to the emergence of the repressed; and it was used again in more recent times in the pharmacological revival of catharsis, i.e., the pentothal interview.

We can distinguish in the analytic situation between the regression in relation to a person, the analyst, and the shift from the normal goal-directed behavior to a tolerance for impulse-ridden expressions. As far as the repression in relation to a person is concerned: the analysand is asked to lie down on a couch and to relax; this is a position of defenselessness, similar to the position assumed by patients in medical procedures. The analyst sits behind the analysand; he can see him without being seen. The unilateral exposure is further emphasized by the requirement that the analysand reveal everything about himself in complete frankness—which invariably includes confessing embarrassing things; the analyst does not reciprocate in kind. All this contributes to putting the analysand into a position similar to that of a child vis-à-vis an adult.

The shift from ego expression to id expression, on the other hand, is achieved by the so-called basic rule of psychoanalysis, also known as the rule of free associations. The analysand is urged to abandon the ordinary habit of goal-directed thought, and instead to permit everything freely to enter his mind and to verbalize it as soon as it appears, without censorship or editing of any kind. The (relative) elimination of conscious steering tendencies which determine the ordinary course of organized thought leads neither to a psychologically meaningless jumble of ideas nor to a sequence of associations in which each idea stimulates the emergence of others similar to it or connected with it in space or time—as was assumed by the association psychology dominant at the end of the nineteenth century (Wundt)—but rather to a situation in which *unconscious* steering tendencies, ordinarily subdued or obfuscated by

the superimposed conscious steering tendencies, are permitted to prevail. Hence the unconscious begins to express
itself. Its emergence must lead immediately to anxiety—a
fact which threatens to stop the process—but the simultaneous assumption of a more childlike attitude toward
the analyst makes it possible for the latter to serve as a protection against danger.

The maintenance of an analytic situation requires, i.a.,
that the analyst refrain from any action or attitude, consciously adopted or unconsciously assumed, that would
steer the analysand away from the expression of certain
psychic contents, or that would cooperate, consciously or
unconsciously, with such ever-present tendencies in the
analysand; and refrain from actions or attitudes that would
gratify the analysand's desires or alleviate his anxieties
and guilt feelings (beyond a minimum that may be necessary for the very continuation of the analytic treatment)
and thereby lead to a drying up of sources of information.
In the first case, the analyst's steering tendencies would
take the place of the patient's conscious steering tendencies
which had been effectively reduced by the working of the
analytic rule of free associations, and that would defeat the
purpose of this rule, viz., to make it possible for unconscious
steering tendencies in the patient to prevail and thus to
express themselves; and the gratification of desires or
alleviation of anxieties and guilt feelings would work like
the application of an analgesic in medicine, removing pains
which should guide the diagnosis.

Ad 2. Resistances, in analysis, have a double role. On
the one hand, they obstruct the entry of derivatives of the
unconscious into consciousness, and prevent the patient
from recognizing them as what they are once they have
entered it, and from facing up to them once they have been

recognized. In this way they are obstacles to the treatment. On the other hand, they are an important source of information about the working of the patient's mind when under the challenge of an inner danger, and are therefore essential for a complete understanding of the conflict.

Resistances are handled by studying them and making them conscious; this procedure at once distills the necessary information from them and prevents them from thwarting the progress of the analysis.

One can often find it said in analytic literature that resistances have to be analyzed before instinctual drives—ego defenses before id material. Yet, in a literary sense, this is not possible because of the intricate relationship between drive and warding off. One cannot say to an analytic patient: "You are fighting off, by such and such means, a certain desire or a temptation," without implying, at least in general terms, what kind of desire is warded off. Also, the attempt to study and explain the resistances alone will carry for the patient an implicit admonition to give them up and is therefore prejudicial to the attitude of neutrality in the patient's inner conflicts which the analyst must observe if he is to fulfill his role as a mediator of these inner conflicts.

The supposed rule—analysis of resistances before analysis of id material—stems from a time when resistance was still viewed as purely negative, as only an obstacle to the progress of analysis, and when the close relation between resistance and repressed material was not yet appreciated.

The old rule does, however, express a *partial* truth inasmuch as defense and resistance, while unconscious, are still closer to consciousness than the warded-off material, and analysis can therefore investigate them in detail at a time when id strivings are seen, and can be discussed, only in broad outlines.

The "handling of the *transference*" presents a somewhat more complicated problem than the handling of resistances. We mean by it procedures which are appropriate to the double role of transference: on the one hand, a resistance against the progress of analysis which under circumstances may wreck it; and, on the other hand, a source of information about the most potent childhood desires and attitudes. The latter aspect would make it advisable to permit the transference to develop fully, without interference—which in some instances may lead to manifestations which one might call quasi-psychotic—while the former aspect would suggest to interfere with it, through confrontation with reality and through interpretation. Transference is properly "handled" if the analyst can extract a maximum of information from it without permitting it to harm the analysis.

Some papers in the vast psychoanalytic literature on this subject may give the impression that the above definition is too narrow, and that the handling of the transference involves manipulation of a relationship, e.g., providing a so-called corrective experience. But these are features not of psychoanalysis but of educational psychotherapy. It may be therapeutically justified to add a dose of educational psychotherapy to pure analysis, but it should be distinguished from psychoanalytic procedures. As long as what we are doing is pure psychoanalysis, unmixed with educational procedures, the handling of the transference is confined to steps made necessary by the double role of transference as interference with the analysis, on the one hand, and as a source of information, on the other.

Ad 3. The third aspect of psychoanalytic technique, how to help the patient to acquire new insights into himself as they gradually emerge in the analysis, and to face up to them, presents problems quite similar to those of teaching in general: how insights or hypotheses can be presented in a way that it "clicks," "hits home"; how people can be helped to discover things for themselves; how the newly learned can become understood in all its implications, how at the same time the pitfalls of indoctrination and propaganda can be avoided, etc. The ingenuity of the analyst has here a wide open field.

For the theory of psychoanalytic technique, see, among others, in addition to the writings of Freud: Nunberg (1932, Chapter XII), E. Bibring (1937, 1954), E. F. Sharpe (1950), and the monograph by K. A. Menninger (1958).

THE COMPLETION OF ANALYSIS

If one sets as goal of an analysis the complete understanding of a person's psychic life, both normal and pathological, and a complete resconstruction of the development of his personality, then an analysis can never be complete. This is all the more so as life goes on during the analytic treatment and new experience accumulates daily that has not been fully evaluated consciously.

But analysis is interminable only as long as we think of scientific completion. As far as the needs of therapy are concerned, the goals of a complete analysis are much more modest (although still ambitious enough). An analysis is complete from a therapeutic point of view if the pathological structures have been fully understood, both dynamically and genetically, and if this investigation has been extended, beyond the directly pathological traits, to a surrounding area of psychic structure likely to be related with them, or interfering with a viable solution of the underlying conflicts; if all this has been worked through with the patient in many manifestations time and again; and if the psychopathology has thereby disappeared or has been rendered controllable.

These goals are achievable, and are being achieved, in any fully satisfactory analysis, and in this sense a complete analysis is possible and is often the actual goal of analytic work.

It is an altogether different question, however, when an analytic treatment *should* be terminated because this point does not necessarily coincide with completion. Some cases cannot, and others need not, be completed. Regardless of completion, an analysis should be *terminated* when one has reached the *point of diminishing returns*, i.e., when further results which can be reasonably anticipated do not seem to justify the further time and effort which would have to be expended. That is a matter of judgment; it involves many factors.

THE MORAL PROBLEM OF PSYCHOANALYTIC TREATMENT

As we have seen, it is the nature of psychoanalytic treatment to bring wholly or partially unconscious conflicts into consciousness where a real solution rather than a neurotic pseudo solution can be worked out. This process involves the possibility that the patient may arrive at a solution which is not in accordance with the moral standards of his culture or his environment. This fact presents a serious moral problem for the practice of psychoanalysis. Can a profession—any profession—operate outside of the moral climate of the culture?

It would not do for the psychoanalyst to evade this

question by asserting that all he had done was to make unconscious factors conscious, that he has not influenced his patient's decision and that the responsibility for the latter is therefore entirely the patient's; it will not do because the issue is precisely whether, in certain cases of moral significance, people should be encouraged to make their own decision. Nor does it really solve the question if the analyst claims medical indication (although resort to medical necessities usually carries enough prestige to silence criticism), because it can be questioned to what degree it is permissible to put considerations of health ahead of moral values or the interests of the society.

Whether the analyst has to face this problem depends on the patient's superego and its relation to the moral standards prevailing in his society. If the demands of the patient's superego coincide, on the whole, with the valuations of his society, and if the superego is sufficiently well integrated into the ego, i.e., if it does not contain hidden contradictions so that it might change when the unconscious factors of its operation or development have become conscious,[6] then the patient's solution of the inner conflicts which have been raised into consciousness by analysis will be, on the whole, in accordance with the social standards. But if this is not the case, if the patient's superego has standards different from those of his society, or harbors hidden inconsistencies and contradictions so that analysis may bring about changes in the superego, the outcome may well be unacceptable from the viewpoint of social standards.

The problem has little importance in a free Western society because the inner requirements of the people's

[6] For a more detailed discussion of this point, see Waelder (1928) and here (p. 213f.).

consciences are largely identical with the cultural requirements, with the two significant exceptions of normal delinquents and of revolutionaries; for the latter types psychoanalytic treatment is, as a rule, not indicated. But apart from these two groups there are likely to be only marginal differences between the values of the group and the values of the individual.

In totalitarian societies of our time, on the other hand, the problem is constantly alive as long as there are psychoanalysts who try to practice psychoanalysis. Virtually every day will the analyst in such countries find himself confronted with the alternative of either, through his silence, becoming the accomplice of an illegal act—*qui tacet consentire videtur*[7]—or setting himself up as an executive agent of the government, a kind of subsidiary police. Both roles are naturally unpalatable for the analyst; the former may also endanger him personally. But apart from the unenviable position in which the analyst finds himself, the analysis itself will probably be wrecked in either case. If the analyst remains neutral with regard to the patient's illegal actions or plans, a kind of *de facto* conspiracy between analyst and patient against the regime has come into being. Such a situation will give great satisfaction to many patients; perhaps it fulfills an old fantasy which it would be important to know and to analyze. But a fantasy that is fulfilled in reality is unlikely to manifest itself because satisfaction has blunted the driving force. Perhaps the patient has been resentful of parental figures whom he felt to be callous or cruel or to discriminate against him; with the current satisfaction provided by the analyst's tolerance, such feelings of grievance may never appear in the analysis and the whole attitude may remain unknown and hence

---

[7] He who keeps silent gives the impression of agreeing.

unanalyzed as to its causes and consequences. Another group of patients will feel in such situations that since they can implicate their analyst in an illegal act, they are now holding him in their power; they may enjoy this situation and exploit it sadistically or in the service of resistance. Each time they feel negatively disposed to their analyst during the analysis, they will do something that might lead to their being apprehended and their analyst thereby being implicated. The analyst may thus be under pressure from the patient, comparable to the blackmail to which a therapist may be exposed in the treatment of depressives through their threat of committing suicide, or in the treatment of criminals through their threat of committing a crime.

If, on the other hand, the analyst takes the opposite stand and requests that the patient refrain from any illegal activities, the result may be a degree of antagonism—hatred or contempt—so strong as to make treatment impossible; and once again the stand taken by the analyst may interfere with the emergence of feelings of a different type which may be an essential part of the patient's neurosis. Unconscious guilt feelings toward the father, e.g., are unlikely to escape from unconsciousness at the very time when the father substitute in reality behaves like an oppressor.

The practice of psychoanalysis has therefore turned out to be virtually impossible in totalitarian states even if the government had not expressedly outlawed psychoanalysis. It must, however, be borne in mind that the totalitarian states in which experience on this issue has been collected were relatively new creations; in all of them, the majority of the people still carried in their superego the values of the pretotalitarian society and their acceptance of the new values was at best incomplete. Hence a difference between individual superego and social standards existed. But if a totalitarian society has existed for generations, a state of affairs will probably be reached in which the new value system is taken for granted by the people and is fully inculcated; then, perhaps, the social and political values of the system may again be part and parcel of the superego of the individuals, and analysis of inner conflicts may be expected to lead, as a rule, only to solutions which are also socially acceptable.

Hence, we may sum things up this way: the practice of psychoanalysis is possible only in *established societies* in which individual and sociocultural values are largely identical (except for delinquents and for revolutionaries) and in which therefore the neutrality required by analytic technique is not offensive to society. In societies of *transition* from a less restrictive to a more restrictive pattern, analysis will lead to an involvement of the analyst in issues of moral or political significance, an involvement which is not only unpalatable and sometimes unbearable for the analyst but which actually goes a long way toward destroying the analysis.

POSTSCRIPT

The Value of Psychoanalysis

In a recent meeting of psychologists and psychiatrists in which psychoanalysis was discussed, a prominent psychiatrist who took a dim view of the value of psychoanalysis asked the rhetorical question: what has come out of all these vast labors? and answered it in this way: what is emptying our mental institutions today is not psychoanalysis but a revival of humanitarianism and a progress in pharmacology.

It is, of course, true that psychoanalysis has not emptied our institutions, but this fact is not relevant for the evaluation of psychoanalysis. To my knowledge, no responsible analyst has ever promised, explicitly or by implication, that psychoanalysis will provide a cure for the permanent hospital population, the chronic psychotic, the most stubborn part of a group already noted for its poor accessibility to influence.

It is necessary to stop from time to time in order to consider what one's work is all for.[1] It is, of course, too early for any reasonable objective evaluation; the perspective is

[1] Alluding to the saying by Sir Richard Livingstone that an expert is a person who knows everything about a subject except what it is all for.

too short. Sixty-odd years are a short time in the history of man. Things may look one way after 50 years, quite different after 100, and altogether different again after 300 years. At the most, we can give an interim report.

Psychoanalysis is, first of all, a venture in pure science. The gist of what we know today about the central personality problems, to use Hartmann's term—i.e., not about peripheral problems nor about circumscribed mental functions, such as, e.g., learning, but about the whole conduct of a life from the great decisions to the small mannerisms —we owe to psychoanalysis, either directly or indirectly. As we have seen, its results are neither complete nor final, but such is the condition of human knowledge. The value which those who are satisfied of the substantial correctness of psychoanalytic claims will attribute to psychoanalysis as a body of knowledge depends on the esteem which they hold for knowledge as such, in particular for insights of the kind that psychoanalysis has to offer.

Psychoanalysis as a therapy of the neuroses offers to those neuroses that are more than responses to transient challenges but accompany a major part of life, with their roots in childhood, the only therapy so far developed that is not merely symptomatic but tries to remove, or to weaken, their causes. But the value of psychoanalysis as a therapy is limited by the narrow criteria of indication—in fact, only an elite among the neurotics can qualify—and by the fact that analysis takes a long time and needs, for each case, a substantial part of the total lifework of a highly trained practitioner. Beyond these considerations, the fact that every year a few thousand individuals from the higher- and middle-income brackets the world over get full or partial relief from neurotic afflictions may seem to many to be of little importance—the very emphasis has been taken by some as a symptom of a civilization that has grown too soft.

But as Freud and we older psychoanalysts have always insisted, the most important applications of psychoanalysis will, in the long run, not lie in psychiatry, not in the treatment of emotional disease or emotional disequilibrium, but in education—in prevention rather than in cure. Even today, when serious psychoanalytic work with children is hardly more than a generation old, psychoanalytic ideas have had a considerable influence on the whole approach to the phenomenon of childhood; it has been well expressed by the British anthropologist, Geoffrey Gorer (1958):

> Chiefly by diluted influence, Freud has profoundly modified our (and particularly American) attitudes toward children, child-rearing, and education, to the sick, the criminal, the insane. Because Freud lived and worked, the weak and the unhappy are often treated with a gentleness and charity and attempts at understanding which constitute one of the few changes in the climate of opinion in this century of which one need not be ashamed.

And beyond the field of education, psychoanalysis is making people aware of the existence of an unconscious psychic life and of the vast possibilities of self-deception. It has already stimulated in many people a certain self-consciousness, a willingness to question their motives, a readiness to entertain the possibility that their conscious motives might be rationalizations. If the humane civilization which began to grow in the West in the eighteenth century, largely as a reaction against the fanaticism and the cruelty of the Wars of Religion, can survive the new pressures to which it is exposed—secular though no less fanatical for it—the process is likely to continue. It will not lead to the rise of supermen as some enthusiasts seemed to think,[2] nor will it do away with suffering, or with Evil, in the world. Human suffering has many roots in the human situation: in man's mortality and the fragility of his body, the helplessness of his beginnings and the decline in his advanced age, the limited malleability of his environment, the clash of human wills, the contradictions between the aspirations in the same breast. And there are sources of Evil in human nature—at least in the nature of some humans. The enlargement of consciousness will not do away with it all just as it is not an effective therapy for all pathological conditions.

But the enlargement of consciousness and the personality integration which is thereby made possible can, if carried out under the guidance of the humanistic ideals which are at the bottom of our civilization, do away with much suffering and with much evil, and can mitigate some of the rest. In this sense, psychoanalysis may turn out to have been a great civilizing force—the most hopeful, perhaps, in the long run, that entered our world in the last century.

---

[2] Most articulately Otto Rank in his brilliant, if youthful, paper on the artist (1907) with which the eighteen-year-old had introduced himself to Freud.

ANNEX

A List of the Most
Common Misunderstandings
of Psychoanalytic Concepts

Neurosis, in psychoanalytic usage, does not mean a general malaise and diffuse discontent but affects, impulses, thoughts, actions, or bodily expressions which a person experiences as strange and incongruous but which he cannot control; whenever the term is used in psychoanalytic literature in a wider sense (as in character neurosis, fate neurosis, neurotic ego distortions) the wider use is justified through a genetic relationship.

Instinct, in psychoanalysis, is not an unlearned behavior pattern which is not subject to change by experience, but an elementary urge, rooted in bodily tensions, which environmental influences may deflect from its course and modify in many ways but probably cannot eradicate.

Wish, or *wish fulfillment,* in psychoanalysis, does not imply a wish that is felt and adhered to by the undivided personality, to be translated into action as soon as circumstances permit, but merely means one wish among many wishes—some of them, as a rule, contradictory—and which, in the average case, would never congeal into action. This is as different from an unambiguous goal as a popular movement is from a settled government policy.

Sexuality, in psychoanalysis, refers not merely to matters pertaining to copulation or preparatory to it but includes all sensual strivings and satisfactions.

Repression is neither a frustration of sexual urges nor an inhibition against living them out but a flight from awareness of sexual urges as well as of other impulses.

The rise of *ego psychology,* in psychoanalysis, does not mean a retreat from interest in the unconscious id and growing interest in conscious psychology but rather an extension of interest from the unconscious id to the unconscious responses which it elicits.

Defense mechanisms do not mean negative responses to any kind of stimuli but quite specifically automatic responses to inner dangers.

Transference is not simply the attribution to new objects of characteristics of old ones but the attempt to re-establish and relive, with whatever object will permit it, an infantile situation much longed for because it was once either greatly enjoyed or greatly missed.

Psychoanalytic treatment is neither a way of getting rid of one's conscience nor an automatic elimination of undesirable traits through knowledge of their origin nor a re-education trying to correct the "mistakes" of the parents but a school in facing oneself unflinchingly, with a view to working out a viable solution of inner conflicts rather than evading them.

A *psychoanalytic approach to education,* finally, does not mean that children should get what they want when they want it; rather, it means an attempt to find for each situation the proper balance between satisfaction and frustration, in the light of the general principle that we have to search for the optimal mixture between two equally important but partly conflicting ingredients of healthy development, viz., love and discipline: how to love without pampering and how to discipline without traumatizing.

BIBLIOGRAPHY

ABRAHAM, KARL (1908). The Psychosexual Differences between Hysteria and Dementia Praecox. *Collected Papers of Karl Abraham*. London: Hogarth Press, 1942.

————— (1924). A Short Study of the Development of the Libido Viewed in the Light of Mental Disorders. *Collected Papers of Karl Abraham*. London: Hogarth Press, 1942.

AICHHORN, AUGUST (1925). *Wayward Youth*. New York: Viking Press, 1935.

ALEXANDER, F. (1925). A Metapsychological Description of the Process of Cure. *Int. J. Psychoanal.*, 6.

ALPERT, A. (1949). Sublimation and Sexualization. *The Psychoanalytic Study of the Child*, 3/4. New York: International Universities Press.

ANDREAS-SALOMÉ, LOU (1912/13). *In der Schule bei Freud*. Zurich: Max Niehans, 1958.

ARONSON, MARVIN L. (1952). A Study of the Freudian Theory of Paranoia by Means of the Rorschach Test. *J. Proj. Tech.*, 16.

BAK, ROBERT C. (1951). Discussion of Dr. Wexler's paper. In: *Psychotherapy with Schizophrenics*, ed. E. B. Brody and F. C. Redlich. New York: International Universities Press.

————— (1954). The Schizophrenic Defence against Aggression. *Int. J. Psychoanal.*, 34.

BALINT, ALICE (1939). Love for the Mother and Mother-Love. *Int. J. Psychoanal.*, 30, 1949.

BERLIN, ISAIAH (1958). *Two Concepts of Liberty*. Oxford: Clarendon Press.

BERNFELD, SIEGFRIED (1931). Zur Sublimierungstheorie. *Imago*, 17.

————— (1932). Der Begriff der Deutung in der Psychoanalyse. *Z. angew. Psychol.*, 42.

————— (1934). Die Gestalttheorie. *Imago*, 20.

————— (1935). Über die Einteilung der Triebe. *Imago*, 21.

BIBRING, EDWARD (1936). The Development and Problems of the Theory of Instincts. *Int. J. Psychoanal.*, 22, 1941.

————— (1937). Versuch einer allgemeinen Theorie der Heilung, *Int. Z. Psychoanal.*, 23.

————— (1953). The Mechanism of Depression. In: *Affective Disorders*, ed. P. Greenacre. New York: International Universities Press.

————— (1954). Psychoanalysis and the Dynamic Psychotherapies. *J. Amer. Psychoanal. Assn.*, 2.

BINSWANGER, LUDWIG (1956). *Erinnerungen an Sigmund Freud.* Bern: Francke Verlag.

BLAU, A. (1952). In Support of Freud's Syndrome of "Actual" Anxiety Neurosis. *Int. J. Psychoanal.,* 33.

BLEULER, EUGEN (1910), *Die Psychoanalyse Freuds. Verteidigung und kritische Bemerkungen.* Wien: F. Deuticke, 1911.

BLUM, HAROLD F. (1951). *The Arrow of Time.* Princeton: Princeton University Press.

BRENNER, CHARLES (1953). An Addendum to Freud's Theory of Anxiety. *Int. J. Psychoanal.,* 34.

———— (1955) (Reporter) Re-evaluation of the Libido Theory. Panel Report. *J. Amer. Psychoanal. Assn.,* 4, 1956.

BREUER, JOSEF and SIGMUND FREUD (1895). Studies on Hysteria. *Standard Edition. The Complete Psychological Works of Sigmund Freud,* 2. London: Hogarth Press, 1955.

BROSIN, HENRY W. (1955). Report on the panel: Validation of Psychoanalytic Theory. *J. Amer. Psychoanal. Assn.,* 3.

BURLINGHAM, D. and A. GOLDBERGER, A. LUSSIER (1955). Simultaneous Analysis of Mother and Child. *The Psychoanalytic Study of the Child,* 10. New York: International Universities Press.

BUTTERFIELD, HERBERT (1949). *Christianity and History.* New York: Scribner.

CANNON, WALTER B. (1932). *The Wisdom of the Body.* New York: Norton.

CLARK, KENNETH (1956). The Study of Art History. In: *The Historical Association,* 1906-1956.

CRAIG, W. (1909). The Expression of Emotions in the Pigeons. *J. Comp. Psychol.,* 19.

DERI, FRANCES (1939). On Sublimation. *Psychoanal. Quart.,* 8.

DEUTSCH, HELENE (1925). *Psychoanalyse der weiblichen Sexualfunktion.* Vienna: Internationaler Psychoanalytischer Verlag.

———— (1932). *Psychoanalysis of the Neuroses.* London: Hogarth Press.

———— (1933). Motherhood and Sexuality. *Psychoanal. Quart.,* 2.

———— (1934). Some Forms of Emotional Disturbance and Their Relationship to Schizophrenia. *Psychoanal. Quart.,* 11, 1942.

DOLLARD, JOHN and L. W. DOBB, N. E. MILLER, R. R. SEARS. (1939). *Frustration and Aggression.* New Haven: Yale University Press.

EISSLER, K. R. (1949). (Ed.) *Searchlights on Delinquency.* New York: International Universities Press.

———— (1953). The Effect of the Structure of the Ego on Psychoanalytic Technique. *J. Amer. Psychoanal. Assn.,* 1.

ERIKSON, ERIK H. (1956). The Problem of Ego Identity. *J. Amer. Psychoanal. Assn.,* 4.

ERLENMAYER, E. H. (1932). Notiz zur Freudschen Hypothese über die Zähmung des Feuers. *Imago,* 18.

FEDERN, PAUL (1927). Narcissism in the Structure of the Ego. In: *Ego Psychology and the Psychoses.* New York: Basic Books, 1952.

———— (1929). The Ego as Subject and Object in Narcissism. In: *Ego Psychology and the Psychoses.* New York: Basic Books, 1952.

────── (1930). The Reality of the Death Instinct, Especially in Melancholia (Remarks on Freud's book, *Civilisation and Its Discontents*). *Psychoanal. Rev.*, 19, 1932.

────── (1936). On the Distinction between Healthy and Pathological Narcissism. In: *Ego Psychology and the Psychoses*. New York: Basic Books, 1952.

FENICHEL, OTTO (1926). Identification. In: *The Collected Papers of Otto Fenichel*, First Series. New York: Norton, 1953.

FREEMAN, THOMAS and JOHN L. CAMERON, ANDREW McGHIE (1958). *Chronic Schizophrenia*. New York: International Universities Press.

FREUD, ANNA (1927). *Introduction to the Technique of Child Analysis*. New York: Nerv. & Mental Disease Publishing Co., 1929.

────── (1936). *The Ego and the Mechanisms of Defense*. New York: International Universities Press, 1946.

────── (1951). The Anna Freud Lectures in America, 1950. *Bull. Amer. Psychoanal. Assn.*, 7.

────── (1954a). Problems of Technique in Adult Analysis. *Bull. Phila. Assn. Psychoanal.*, 4.

────── (1954b). The Widening Scope of Indications for Psychoanalysis: Discussion. *J. Amer. Psychoanal. Assn.*, 2.

FREUD, SIGMUND (1900). The Interpretation of Dreams. *Standard Edition*, 4, 5.

────── (1901). *The Psychopathology of Everyday Life*. New York: Macmillan, 1914.

────── (1905a). Fragment of an Analysis of a Case of Hysteria. *Standard Edition*, 7.

────── (1905b). Three Essays on the Theory of Sexuality. *Standard Edition*, 7.

────── (1905c). On Psychotherapy. *Standard Edition*, 7.

────── (1905d). My Views on the Part Played by Sexuality in the Aetiology of the Neuroses. *Standard Edition*, 7.

────── (1905e). *Wit and Its Relation to the Unconscious*. New York: Moffat, Yard, 1917.

────── (1909). Notes upon a Case of Obsessional Neurosis. *Collected Papers*, 3.

────── (1910a). Five Lectures on Psychoanalysis. *Standard Edition*, 11.

────── (1910b). The Future Prospects of Psychoanalytic Therapy. *Standard Edition*, 11.

────── (1910c). The Psychoanalytic View of Psychogenic Disturbance of Vision. *Standard Edition*, 11.

────── (1910d) "Wild" Psychoanalysis. *Standard Edition*, 11.

────── (1911a). Formulations Regarding the Two Principles in Mental Functioning. *Collected Papers*, 4.

────── (1911b). Psychoanalytic Notes Upon an Autobiographical Account of a Case of Paranoia (Dementia Paranoides). *Collected Papers*, 3.

────── (1914a). On the History of the Psychoanalytic Movement. *Standard Edition*, 14.

────── (1914b). On Narcissism: An Introduction. *Standard Edition*, 14.

———— (1915a). Instincts and Their Vicissitudes. *Standard Edition*, 14.

———— (1915b). The Unconscious. *Standard Edition*, 14.

———— (1915c). Some Character-Types Met with in Psychoanalytic Work. *Collected Papers*, 4.

———— (1916/17). *A General Introduction to Psychoanalysis*. New York: Liveright, 1935.

———— (1917). Mourning and Melancholia. *Standard Edition*, 14.

———— (1918). From the History of an Infantile Neurosis. *Standard Edition*, 17.

———— (1919a). Lines of Advance in Psychoanalytic Therapy. *Standard Edition*, 17.

———— (1919b). Introduction to *Psychoanalysis and the War Neuroses*. London: Hogarth Press, 1921.

———— (1920). Beyond the Pleasure Principle. *Standard Edition*, 18.

———— (1921). Group Psychology and the Analysis of the Ego. *Standard Edition*, 18.

———— (1923). *The Ego and the Id*. London: Hogarth Press, 1927.

———— (1924). The Economic Problem in Masochism. *Collected Papers*, 2.

———— (1925). *Autobiography*. New York: Norton, 1935.

———— (1926a). *The Problem of Anxiety*. New York: Norton, 1936.

———— (1926b). *The Problem of Lay-Analysis*. New York: Norton, 1950.

———— (1927a). *The Future of an Illusion*. New York: Liveright, 1928.

———— (1927b). Humour. *Collected Papers*, 5.

———— (1928). Dostoevsky and Parricide. *Collected Papers*, 5.

———— (1930). *Civilization and Its Discontents*. London: Hogarth Press.

———— (1931). Female Sexuality. *Collected Papers*, 5.

———— (1932a). Why War? *Collected Papers*, 5.

———— (1932b). The Acquisition of Power over Fire. *Collected Papers*, 5.

———— (1932c). *New Introductory Lectures on Psychoanalysis*. New York: Norton, 1933.

———— (1933). Preface to Marie Bonaparte's *The Life and Works of Edgar Allan Poe*. London: Imago Publishing Co., 1949.

———— (1936). A Disturbance of Memory on the Acropolis. *Collected Papers*, 5.

———— (1937). Analysis Terminable and Interminable. *Collected Papers*, 5.

———— (1938). Splitting of the Ego in the Defensive Process. *Collected Papers*, 5.

———— (1940). *An Outline of Psychoanalysis*. New York: Norton, 1949.

FRIEDLANDER, KATE (1947). *The Psychoanalytical Approach to Juvenile Delinquency*. New York: International Universities Press.

GIBBON, EDWARD (1776-88). *The Decline and Fall of the Roman Empire*. New York: Modern Library, 1932.

GILLESPIE, W. H. (1958). Neurotic Ego Distortions. *Int. J. Psychoanal.*, 39.

GITELSON, MAXWELL (1958). On Ego Distortion. *Int. J. Psychoanal.*, 39.

GLOVER, EDWARD (1958). Ego Distortion. *Int. J. Psychoanal.*, 39.

———— (1959). *The Roots of Crime*. New York: International Universities Press, 1960.

GOLDSTEIN, KURT (1948). *Language and Language Disturbances.* New York: Grune & Stratton.
GOMME, A. W. (1954). *The Greek Attitude to Poetry and History.* Berkeley and Los Angeles: University of California Press.
GORER, GEOFFREY (1958). Freud's Influence. *The Encounter,* November, 1958.
GREENACRE, PHYLLIS (1952a). Pregenital Patterning. *Int. J. Psychoanal.,* 32.
———— (1952b). *Trauma, Growth and Personality.* New York: Norton.
HADAMARD, JACQUES (1945). *The Psychology of Invention in the Mathematical Field.* New York: Dover.
HARRISON, JANE ELLEN (1903). *Prolegomena to the Study of Greek Religion.* New York: Meridian Books, 1957.
HART, H. H. (1948). Sublimation and Aggression. *Psychiat. Quart.,* 22.
HARTMANN, HEINZ (1948). Comments on the Psychoanalytic Theory of Instinctual Drives. *Psychoanal. Quart.,* 17.
———— (1952). The Mutual Influences in the Development of Ego and Id. *The Psychoanalytic Study of the Child,* 7. New York: International Universities Press.
———— (1953). Contributions to the Metapsychology of Schizophrenia. *The Psychoanalytic Study of the Child,* 8. New York: International Universities Press.
———— (1955). Notes on the Theory of Sublimation. *The Psychoanalytic Study of the Child,* 10. New York: International Universities Press.
———— and ERNST KRIS, RUDOLPH M. LOEWENSTEIN (1949). Notes on the Theory of Aggression. *The Psychoanalytic Study of the Child,* 3/4. New York: International Universities Press.
HARTMANN, MAX (1909). Theorie der relativen Sexualität. In: *Allgemeine Biologie.* Stuttgart: Gustav Fischer Verlag, 1956.
HEIDEN, KONRAD (1936). *Adolf Hitler.* Zurich: Europa Verlag.
HILGARD, ERNEST R. (1952). Experimental Approaches to Psychoanalysis. In: *Psychoanalysis as a Science,* ed. E. Pumpian-Mindlin. Stanford, California: Stanford University Press.
HOOK, S., ed. (1959). *Psychoanalysis, Scientific Method and Philosophy.* New York: New York University Press.
HORNEY, KAREN (1923). On the Genesis of the Castration Complex in Women. *Int. J. Psychoanal.,* 5, 1924.
———— (1926). The Flight from Womanhood. *Int. J. Psychoanal.,* 7.
———— (1932). The Dread of Woman. *Int. J. Psychoanal.,* 13.
———— (1933). The Denial of the Vagina. *Int. J. Psychoanal.,* 14.
———— (1939). *New Ways in Psychoanalysis.* New York: Norton.
ISAKOWER, OTTO (1936). A Contribution to the Pathopsychology of Phenomena Associated with Falling Asleep. *Int. J. Psychoanal.,* 19, 1938.
JACOBSON, E. (1954). Transference Problems in the Psychoanalytic Treatment of Severely Depressive Patients. *J. Amer. Psychoanal. Assn.,* 2.
JUNG, C. G. (1956). Vorwort zu: Eleanor Bertine, *Menschliche Beziehungen.* Zurich: Rhein Verlag, 1957.

KATAN, M. (1950). Structural Aspects of a Case of Schizophrenia. *The Psychoanalytic Study of the Child*, 5. New York: International Universities Press.

───── (1958). Contribution to the Panel on Ego Distortion ('As-if' and 'Pseudo As-if'). *Int. J. Psychoanal.*, 39.

KEYNES, J. M. (1936). *The General Theory of Unemployment*. New York: Harcourt.

KINSEY, ALFRED C. and WARDELL B. POMEROY, CLYDE E. MARTIN (1948). *Sexual Behavior in the Human Male*. Philadelphia and London: Saunders.

KLEIN, MELANIE (1930). The Importance of Symbol-Formation in the Development of the Ego. In: *Contributions to Psychoanalysis* 1921-1945. London: Hogarth Press, 1948.

───── (1935). A Contribution to the Psychogenesis of Manic-Depressive States. In: *Contributions to Psychoanalysis* 1921-1945. London: Hogarth Press, 1948.

───── (1940). Mourning and Its Relations to Manic-Depressive States. In: *Contributions to Psychoanalysis* 1921-1945. London: Hogarth Press, 1948.

KNIGHT, R. P. (1949). A Critique of the Present Status of the Psychotherapies. In: *Psychoanalytic Psychiatry and Psychology*. New York: International Universities Press, 1954.

───── (1952). An Evaluation of Psychotherapeutic Techniques. In: *Psychoanalytic Psychiatry and Psychology*. New York: International Universities Press, 1954.

KÖHLER, WOLFGANG (1917). *The Mentality of Apes*. New York: Vintage Books, 1959.

KRIS, ERNST (1936). The Psychology of Caricature. In: *Psychoanalytic Explorations in Art*. New York: International Universities Press, 1952.

───── (1950). Introduction to: *The Origins of Psychoanalysis. Letters to Wilhelm Fliess, Drafts and Notes*, 1897-1902, by Sigmund Freud. New York: Basic Books, 1954.

───── (1951). The Development of Ego Psychology. *Samiksa*, 5.

───── (1955). Neutralization and Sublimation. *The Psychoanalytic Study of the Child*, 10. New York: International Universities Press.

KUBIE, LAWRENCE S. (1952). Problems and Techniques of Psychoanalysis, Validation and Progress. In: *Psychoanalysis as a Science*, ed. E. Pumpian-Mindlin. Stanford, California: Stanford University Press.

───── (1959). Social Forces and the Neurotic Process. *J. Nerv. & Ment. Dis.*, 128.

LAFORGUE, RENÉ (1930). On the Erotisation of Anxiety. *Int. J. Psychoanal.*, 11.

LEVY-SUHL, MAX (1933). The Early Infantile Sexuality of Man as Compared with the Sexual Maturity of Other Mammals. *Int. J. Psychoanal.*, 15, 1934.

LEWIN, BERTRAM D. (1946). Sleep, the Mouth and the Dream Screen. *Psychoanal. Quart.*, 15.

LORENZ, KONRAD Z. (1952). *King Solomon's Ring.* New York: Thomas Y. Crowell.
—— (1954). *Man Meets Dog.* London: Methuen.
MASLOW, A. H. and FRANZBAUM, S. (1936). The Role of Dominance in the Social and Sexual Behavior of Infra-Human Primates: II. An Experimental Determination of the Behavior Syndrome of Dominance. *J. Gen. Psychol.,* 48.
MENNINGER, KARL A. (1958). *Theory of Psychoanalytic Technique.* New York: Basic Books.
NACHT, S. (1958). Causes and Mechanisms of Ego Distortions. *Int. J. Psychoanal.,* 39.
NUNBERG, HERMAN (1924). The Will to Recovery. In: *Practice and Theory of Psychoanalysis.* New York: International Universities Press, 1955.
—— (1926). The Sense of Guilt and the Need for Punishment. In: *Practice and Theory of Psychoanalysis.* New York: International Universities Press, 1955.
—— (1932). *Principles of Psychoanalysis.* New York: International Universities Press, 1955.
—— (1934). The Feeling of Guilt. In: *Practice and Theory of Psychoanalysis.* New York: International Universities Press, 1955.
—— (1949). *Problems of Bisexuality as Reflected in Circumcision.* London: Imago Publishing Co.
—— (1951). Transference and Reality. *Int. J. Psychoanal.,* 32.
ONIANS, R. B. (1951). *The Origin of European Thought on the Body, the Mind, the Soul, the World, Time and Fate.* Cambridge: University Press, 1954.
PEISKER, Y. T. (1911). The Asiatic Background. *Cambridge Medieval History,* Vol. I: The Christian Roman Empire and the Foundation of the Teutonic Kingdoms, Chapter XII, A. New York: Macmillan.
PETO, ANDREW (1937). Infant and Mother. Observations on Object Relations in Early Infancy. *Int. J. Psychoanal.,* 30, 1949.
POLANYI, MICHAEL (1958). *Personal Knowledge.* London: Rutledge Kegan Paul.
PORTMANN, ADOLF (1943). *Grenzen des Lebens.* Basel: Friederich Reinhardt.
—— (1946). *Natur and Kultur im Sozialleben.* Basel: Friederich Reinhardt.
—— (1953. *Das Tier als soziales Wesen.* Zurich: Rhein Verlag.
PUMPIAN-MINDLIN, E. (1952). The Position of Psychoanalysis in Relation to the Biological and Social Sciences. In: *Psychoanalysis as a Science.* Stanford, California: Stanford University Press.
RADO, SANDOR (1933). Fear of Castration in Women. *Psychoanal. Quart.,* 2.
—— (1949). Emergency Behavior; with an Introduction to the Dynamics of Conscience. *Proc. Amer. Psychopath. Assn.,* 39.
RANGELL, LEO (1953). On the Psychoanalytic Theory of Anxiety: A Statement of a Unitary Theory. *J. Amer. Psychoanal. Assn.,* 3, 1955.

RANK, OTTO (1907). *Der Künstler; Ansätze zu einer Sexualpsychologie.* Vienna: Heller.

RAPAPORT, D. (1951a). The Conceptual Model of Psychoanalysis. In: *Psychoanalytic Psychiatry and Psychology,* ed. R. P. Knight and C. R. Friedman. New York: International Universities Press, 1954.

—— (1951b). The Autonomy of the Ego. In: *Psychoanalytic Psychiatry and Psychology,* ed. R. P. Knight and C. R. Friedman. New York: International Universities Press, 1954.

REICH, W. (1925). *Der triebhafte Charakter.* Vienna: Internationaler Psychoanalytischer Verlag.

RITCHIE, ARTHUR DAVID (1958). *Studies in the History and Methods of the Sciences.* Edinburgh: University Press.

ROSENFELD, HERBERT (1958). Discussion of Ego Distortion. *Int. J. Psychoanal.,* 39.

SACHS, HANNS (1923). Zur Genese der Perversion. *Int. Z. Psychoanal.,* 9.

SANTAYANA, GEORGE (1902). The Dissolution of Paganism. In: *Interpretations of Poetry and Religion.* New York: Harper, 1957.

SCHELER, MAX (1926). *Wesen und Formen der Sympathiegefühle.* Bonn: Friedrich Cohen.

SCHJELDERUP-EBBE, T. (1931). Die Despotie im Sozialleben der Vögel. Thurnwald, *Forschungen zur Völkerpsychologie und Soziologie,* 10.

SCHMIDL, FRITZ (1955). The Problem of Scientific Validation of Psychoanalytic Interpretations. *Int. J. Psychoanal.,* 36.

SCHUR, MAX (1953). The Ego in Anxiety. In: *Drives, Affects, Behavior,* ed. R. M. Loewenstein. New York: International Universities Press.

SCOTT, JOHN W. (1942). Mating Behavior of the Sago Grouse. *Auk,* 59.

SHARPE, E. F. (1950). *Collected Papers on Psychoanalysis.* London: Hogarth Press; see Chaps. I-IV.

SMITH, JOHN MAYNARD (1958). *The Theory of Evolution.* London: Penguin Books.

STEINBACHER, G. (1938). Über einige brutbiologische Beobachtungen im Berliner zoologischen Garten im Jahre 1937. *Beitr. Fortpfl. Biol. Vögel,* 14.

STERBA, RICHARD (1930). Zur Problematik der Sublimierungslehre. *Int. Z. Psychoanal.,* 16.

STONE, L. (1954). The Widening Scope of Indications for Psychoanalysis. *J. Amer. Psychoanal. Assn.,* 2.

TINBERGEN, N. (1951). *The Study of Instinct.* Oxford: Clarendon Press.

TREVOR-ROPER, H. R. (1957). *Historical Essays.* London: Macmillan.

VON BERTALANFFY, LUDWIG (1958). Comments on Aggression. *Bull. Menninger Clin.,* 22.

WAELDER, ROBERT (1928). Review of Freud's *Hemmung, Symptom und Angst. Int. J. Psychoanal.,* 10, 1929.

—— (1929). Die Psychoanalyse im Lebensgefühl des modernen Menschen. *Almanach der Psychoanalyse.*

—— (1930). The Principle of Multiple Function. *Psychoanal. Quart.,* 5, 1936.

———— (1936). The Problem of the Genesis of Psychical Conflicts in Earliest Infancy. *Int. J. Psychoanal.*, 18, 1937.

———— (1939). Kriterien der Deutung. *Int. Z. Psychoanal.*, 24.

———— (1941). Introduction to: *The Living Thoughts of Freud*. New York: Longmans, Green.

———— (1949). Notes on Prejudice. *Vassar Alumn. Mag.*, May, 1949.

———— (1951). The Structure of Paranoid Ideas. *Int. J. Psychoanal.*, 32.

———— (1955). The Functions and the Pitfalls of Psychoanalytic Societies. *Bull. Phila. Assn. Psychoanal.*, 5.

———— (1958). Neurotic Ego Distortions. Opening Remarks to the Panel Discussion. *Int. J. Psychoanal.*, 39.

———— (1960). Characteristics of Totalitarianism. *The Psychoanalytic Study of Society*, 1, ed. W. Muensterberger and S. Axelrad. New York: International Universities Press.

WEAVER, WARREN (1955). Science and People. *Science*, 122 (No. 3183).

———— (1957). Science and the Citizen. *Science*, 126 (No. 3285).

WEISSBERG-CYBULSKI, ALEXANDER (1951). *Hexensabbath*. Frankfurt a. M.: Verlag der Frankfurter Hefte.

WIENER, NORBERT (1948). *Cybernetics*. New York: John Wiley.

ZUCKERMAN, S. (1932). *The Social Life of Monkeys and Apes*. London: Kegan Paul, Trench, Trubner.

INDEX

Abraham K., 8, 165, 205, 208, 255
Abstraction, 193f.
Activity and passivity, 235
Actual neurosis, 154f., 156f.
Adjustment, 39f., 45, 64
Adler, Alfred, 70f., 74-81, 174f.
Adlerian doctrine, psychotherapy, 74-77, 80, 175f.
Aeschylus, 129
Aggression, 113; see also *Destructiveness, Destructive drives*
Aichhorn, A., 203, 255
Alexander, F., 180, 191, 255
Alpert, A., 130, 255
Altruistic surrender, 180, 183, 221
American and German attitudes; in philosophy of science, 23f., 174; to Jung and Adler, 78f.
Anal stage, 109, 111, 141
Analysis; see *Psychoanalytic therapy*
Analyst; Freudian, "orthodox," 38, 88, 91ff., 155
 ingenuity of, 242
 neutrality of, 216, 239f., 247
 as protection against danger, 239
 in totalitarian countries, 245f.
Analytic rule, 23, 229, 238
Analytic situation, 237
Analyzability, 229ff.
Andreas-Salomé, Lou, 77, 255
Animal and man, 148, 194
Anxiety, 154-166; see also *Danger, Fear*
 affective component, 165
 anachronistic, 220, 225
 diffuse, 35
 extreme, 142f., 190, 204, 207f., 211
 forms of, 158-162
 and narcissism, 68, 164
 neurotic, in psychoneurosis, 82f., 153, 156ff., 173, 182
 "objective," 153, 156, 165
 and perversion, 219

 sexualization of, 160
 tolerance for, 226f.
Archaic residue, 72
Aristotle, 170
Aristotelianism and Platonism, 24
Aronson, Marvin L., 47, 255
Art, 89
Artistic talent and psychoanalysis, 56, 124
"As if" personality, 209
Asceticism, 180
Association psychology, 238
Autoerotism, 108

Bak, Robert C., 206, 255
Balint, Alice, 21, 255
Becker, Carl, 26
Behavior disorders, 223, 231f.; see also *Delinquency*
Berlin, Isaiah, 39, 65, 255
Bernadotte, Count F., 144
Bernard, Claude, x, 81
Bernfeld, Siegfried, 5f., 69, 130, 133f., 173, 255
Bertine, Eleanor, 259
Bibring, Edward, 8, 131, 140, 198, 210, 242, 255
Bibring, Grete L., 21
Bisexuality, 110, 205
Blau, Abram, 166, 256
Bleuler, Eugen, 5, 205, 256
Blum, Harold F., 169, 173, 256
Bohr, Niels, 89
Boltzmann, Ludwig, 171
Bonaparte, Marie, 56
Borderline cases, 236
Brahé, Tycho, 89
Brain-washing, 10, 188
Brenner, Charles, 99, 166, 256
Breuer, Josef, 49, 70, 85, 167, 237, 256
Brosin, Henry, 6, 256
Burckhardt, Jacob, 148

265